Education the Wasted Years?
1973–1986

Education
the Wasted Years?
1973–1986

Edited by

Max Morris
and
Clive Griggs

 The Falmer Press

(A member of the Taylor & Francis Group)
London · New York · Philadelphia

UK   The Falmer Press, Falmer House, Barcombe, Lewes, East Sussex, BN8 5DL

USA The Falmer Press, Taylor & Francis Inc., 242 Cherry Street, Philadelphia, PA 19106-1906

First published 1988

Library of Congress Cataloging in Publication Data

Education, the wasted years?
  Bibliography: p.
  Includes index.
  1. Education—Great Britain—History—20th century.
  2. Federal aid to education—Great Britain—History—
  20th century. 3. Education and state—Great Britain
  —History—20th century. I. Morris, Max. II. Griggs,
  Clive.
  LA631.82.E38 1988   370′.941   87-37976
  ISBN 1-85000-340-8
  ISBN 1-85000-341-6 (pbk.)

Jacket design by Caroline Archer
Jacket illustration by Bryan Reading

Typeset by Mathematical Composition Setters Ltd.

Printed in Great Britain by Taylor & Francis (Printers) Ltd, Basingstoke

Contents

Contents

List of Tables and Figures

List of Abbreviations

ACAS	Advisory Conciliation and Arbitration Service
ACC	Association of County Councils
ACSET	Advisory Committee on the Supply and Education of Teachers
ACSTT	Advisory Committee on the Supply and Training of Teachers
AEC	Association of Education Committees
ALBSU	Adult Literacy and Basic Skills Unit
AMA	Association of Metropolitan Authorities
AMMA	Assistant Masters' and Mistresses' Association
APS	Assisted Places Scheme
ATC	Adult Training Centres
ATO	Area Training Organization
BEC	Business Education Council
BEEA	British Education Equipment Association
BTEC	Business and Technician Education Council
CATE	Council for the Accreditation of Teachers' Education
CBI	Confederation of British Industries
CEE	Certificate of Extended Education
CEO	Chief Education Officer
CGLI	City and Guilds of London Institute
CLEA/ST	Council of Local Education Authorities/School Teachers
CNAA	Council for National Academic Awards
CPVE	Certificate of Pre-Vocational Education
CSE	Certificate of Secondary Education
DES	Department of Education and Science
ESL	English as a Second Language
FE	Further Education
GBGSA	Governing Bodies of Girls' Schools Association
GCE	General Certificate of Education

GCSE	General Certificate of Secondary Education
GPDST	Girls' Public Day School Trust
GRIDS	Guidelines for Review and Institutional Development in Schools
GRIST	Grant Related In-Service Training
GSA	Girls' Schools Association
HMC	Headmasters' Conference
HMI	Her Majesty's Inspectorate
IAPS	Incorporated Association of Preparatory Schools
INSET	In-Service Training
ISIS	Independent Schools Information Service
LACSAB	Local Authority Conditions of Service Advisory Board
LEA	Local Education Authority
MSC	Manpower Services Commission
NACTST	National Advisory Council on the Supply and Training of Teachers
NAHT	National Association of Headteachers
NAS/UWT	National Association of Schoolmasters/Union of Women Teachers
NATFHE	National Association of Teachers in Further and Higher Education
NCPTA	National Conference of Parent Teacher Associations
NIACE	National Institute of Adult and Continuing Education
NUT	National Union of Teachers
ORT	Organization for Rehabilitation through Training
PGCE	Postgraduate Certificate in Education
PICKUP	Professional Industrial and Commercial Updating
REPLAN	Adult Unemployment Programme
RSG	Rate Support Grant
RTA	Remuneration of Teachers Act
SCDC	School Curriculum Development Committee
SCISP	Schools Council Integrated Science Project
SEC	Secondary Examinations Council
SHA	Secondary Heads' Association
SHIS	Society of Headmasters of Independent Schools
SSEC	Secondary Schools Examination Council

TEC	Technician Education Council
TOPS	Training Opportunities Scheme
TUC	Trades Union Congress
TVEI	Technical and Vocational Education Initiative
UCAC	National Association of Teachers of Wales (translated into English)
UCET	University Council for the Education of Teachers
UDACE	Unit for the Development of Adult Continuing Education
UGC	University Grants Committee
WEA	Workers' Educational Association
VAT	Value Added Tax
YOP	Youth Opportunity Programme
YTS	Youth Training Scheme

Acknowledgements

We are grateful to a number of people who provided information and assistance in the production of this book. In particular we would like to thank Margaret Morris of the City Polytechnic for invaluable editorial help. Caroline Allan and Celia Ellacott for indispensable technical assistance always generously given including in the latter's case help with the subject index, Dr Jan Toporowski of the South Bank Polytechnic for economic advice, Ian Brinkley of the TUC for information concerning unemployment and the staff of the libraries of Brighton Polytechnic the Department of Education and Science and the National Union of Teachers for their courtesy and kindness in checking various references.

Introduction

The great confidence enjoyed by the education system during the 1960s gave way to considerable disenchantment in the 1970s and 1980s. This book is an attempt to describe and analyze what took place in the major areas of education between 1973 and 1986, by when a general consensus in favour of education as it was practised had disappeared.

Although each of our contributors has written independently on his/her own area of expertise there is a common thread throughout their work which may be summed up by the view that the education service deserved greater support than it received from either government or the public.

Inevitably there are overlaps between various chapters: education cannot be satisfactorily treated in sharply separated compartments. Some themes necessarily appear more than once. We trust that differences of emphasis or nuance will illuminate the work as a whole. The absence of an essay on the under 5s, an area shamefully neglected by the powers that be, is deeply regretted; a planned contribution unfortunately did not materialize.

We hope that the chapters written by our distinguished and authoritative contributors will provide an accurate record to help informed discussion at a time when educational issues are the subject of the sharpest controversy in living memory.

**Max Morris and
Clive Griggs**
July 1987

Chapter 1: Thirteen Wasted Years?

Max Morris and Clive Griggs

Max Morris is a former headmaster of a large comprehensive school, who served on the NUT Executive and was President of the Union. He writes regularly in the educational press on a variety of topics. Previous publications include *The People's Schools, From Cobbett to the Chartists, Your Children's Future* and *An A-Z of Trade Unionism and Industrial Relations* (with Jack Jones).

Clive Griggs left school at 15 years of age and worked in a signal box for several years before going on to college to qualify as a teacher. He has taught in a technical school in London, a language school in Sofia and a comprehensive school in Sussex. He was education correspondent for *Tribune* (1975–82), has published articles in a variety of academic journals, contributed chapters to D. Rubinstein's *Education and Equality* (1979), K.D. Brown's *The First Labour Party 1906–14* (1985) and is author of *The Trades Union Congress and the Struggle for Education 1868–1925* (1983) and *Private Education in Britain* (1985). At present he is Senior Lecturer in Education at Brighton Polytechnic.

★   ★   ★

December 1973 was the end of an era. The Barber Special Budget of that month, with its big package of education cuts, shocked the educational world. One of us recalls how, as President of the National Union of Teachers (NUT), he led a deputation to the then Secretary of State for Education and Science, Margaret Thatcher, making the strongest protest about the harmful effects the measures would have on the service. This was not just another example of 'stop-go' by the Tories. The cuts were too severe for that and presented the perspective of a new turn in policy with long-term implications.

Mrs Thatcher was unmoved. She doggedly defended the new policy, even though it was in conflict with her boasted 'Framework for Expansion' of only a year earlier. She even insisted, in spite of the evidence, that books and materials for schools would not be affected. Her Permanent Secretary, mandarin Sir William Pile, treated the teachers' protests with lofty and amused contempt. 'So the children will have to sit on broken chairs for another year!'

Barber's £200m. package of education cuts was not fully implemented, such was their impracticable severity. But neither were they restored, for, to the chagrin of the world of education, they were followed by a continuous policy of restricted expenditure carried out by Labour ministers, Reg Prentice, Fred Mulley and Shirley Williams. We were now living in a different world from the sixties and early seventies, looked back upon with nostalgia, if not with complete historical accuracy, as an era of steady expansion.

The cutback in educational finance was to be the harbinger of new and often negative attitudes to the education system in the years that followed. These are described with authority by our contributors, all experts in their chosen fields. Naturally, each has his/her own approach and interpretation of the events of the period under review and comes to his/her own conclusions. It is for the reader to judge whether the case is made out for our title *The Wasted Years?*. In the end, judgment will depend on the reader's point of view on the gap between what happened and what might have been. One thing we believe is undeniable: the close connection between what happened in education and the social, economic and political events of the period. These we outline below and in their context try to present an overview of the main educational developments, using a broad brush and without going into great detail.

Things had seemed to be going quite well for the Heath government in the early seventies; a counter-inflation policy which had operated fairly successfully by Act of Parliament and an economy growing at 5 per cent in 1973. Yet by the end of the year government policy and credibility were in ruins. As one economist has written:

> The whole strategy suffered a spectacular shipwreck at the end of 1973, partly because of the internal crisis over pay caused by the miners' overtime ban and subsequent strike, partly by the loss of control of monetary policy, but, in the main, because of the abrupt termination of the world boom by the quadrupling of oil prices by OPEC which was the trigger for the commencement of a generalized recession and plunged Britain into a Balance of Payments crisis which dwarfed the previous experience.[1]

With petroleum such a vital ingredient in the cost of many commodities, prices of goods rose rapidly and the necessary exports became more difficult to achieve to balance the higher cost of imports. Barber's December Budget was a desperate attempt to plug the dyke—with the same tired old measures to which the country had become accustomed over the years: cuts in public expenditure alongside a tightening of the screw on incomes.

Labour in Office, 1974-79

Heath failed to vanquish the miners and when he went to the country for a new mandate it was refused, even if only narrowly, and Labour was left to deal with the problems. The three-day week—an extraordinarily unpopular measure—was ended and Michael Foot's immediate settlement of the miners' dispute brought temporary peace in that troubled industry. In education, his sanctioning of a settlement of the long-running London Allowance issue, which had evoked teachers' strikes, not only ended confrontation with the teachers but forestalled its extension to other major London unions.

Being determined to undo Heath's legislative attacks on incomes and act by agreement with the unions, the government loosened the reins and both nurses and teachers, for example, received a substantial upgrading, the latter through the Houghton Committee recommendations in December 1974—which gave them a 29 per cent increase, at a cost of £432m. The unions were also made to feel their power by the passage of important new protective legislation for people at work (the Employment Protection Acts etc.), and in the TU and Labour Relations Acts which repealed Heath's hated Industrial Relations Act of 1971 and restored to the trade unions the legal immunities for their activities which they had previously enjoyed. For the government and trade unions, Harold Wilson's 'In place of strife' of the late sixties was like a bad dream, gone if not forgotten.

Some way still had to be found to enable the economy to cope with the massive balance of payments deficit that Labour inherited, and restrictions continued in public expenditure, despite the Social Contract. This was the agreement by which the TUC influenced the unions to restrict wage and salary increases in return for promised social gains. But not only did Reg Prentice brusquely refuse to restore the Barber cuts, he refused to honour Roy Hattersley's pledge as Shadow Minister to eliminate classes over thirty. Nor was there an easing in school building: Barber had stopped new building and old ones began to deteriorate as money for repair and maintenance dwindled. The 1975 Budget saw a further education cut of £76m. while the DES drew up plans for cuts of £500m. over the next four years. In the universities the crisis saw the ending of inflation-proof quinquennium funding and a switch to annual funding accompanied by severe retrenchment.

These pressures were very much intensified at the end of 1976 as the economic position continued to worsen and the deficits continued to accumulate. This happened despite the success of the Social Contract agreement in reducing inflation, which had shot up dangerously in 1975. Britain was forced to borrow money from the International Monetary Fund (IMF), in return for which certain stringent conditions on public expenditure were imposed.[2] Education expenditure which had actually exceeded that on defence in the early seventies[3] took a hammering. It became clear that Wilson's earlier demand for 'no sacred cows' was being selectively applied; some cows were more sacred that others.

Effects on Education

Parallel to this were controls over local government expenditure exemplified by the imposition of 'cash limits' from 1976—a drastic measure which imposed fixed allowances in advance for estimated inflation and for wage and salary increases. Though these allowances could be well below the actual increases, the ceiling originally fixed could not be exceeded, so creating severe difficulties for local authorities. But, ominously, the recession and the cuts took their toll in unemployment, which by 1979 rose to what seemed then to be the awe-inspiring figure of 1.25 million. Appreciable teacher unemployment began to surface for the first time since the Second World War as the refusal to bring down classes speedily towards thirty hindered LEAs in absorbing the output of the colleges which had taken on students on the understanding that supply would be equalled by future demand. One could describe this as deliberately creating unemployment and it caused considerable bitterness.

Forecasts of falling rolls led to plans to 'rationalize' the colleges of education, reducing their numbers by a process of closures and mergers with polytechnics. This meant drastic cut-backs in the future supply of teachers, in spite of the need to reduce classes in size and to provide large numbers of new specialist teachers if comprehensive education was to fulfil its promise. The Advisory Committee for the Supply and Training of Teachers (ACSTT) (1973-78) was guided by the government to concentrate on the numbers game and paid little attention to training, devoting most of its time to assessing the reduced quota of teachers 'needed'. Over the years that followed there was a huge drop in numbers in training. Government efforts to increase training for shortage subjects and improve access to training for the disadvantaged, especially ethnic minority students, were feeble. So, unsurprisingly, when Labour redeemed its pledge to make comprehensive reorganization a requirement on LEAs, the 1976 Act did not produce the improved system which 'compulsion' should have demanded.

Cash limits were hitting education severely, creating an atmosphere of panic among some LEAs which led to considerable over-cautiousness and unnecessary underspending in education, giving point to the factual criticisms of the policy by the local government unions and the TUC. As White Papers on public expenditure succeeded each other with their quota of education cuts, alarm and despondency prevailed in educational circles. Education expenditure as a percentage of the GDP had risen by 1975-76 to a peak of 6.3 per cent, and then began to move back. By 1979-80 it had dropped to 5.3 per cent.

Something of the new attitude in the Labour government's influential circles was revealed in two remarks which caused considerable distress at the time. Tony Crosland's comment that 'cuts could be a blessing in disguise' was resented. When had education ever been treated luxuriously? And Denis Healey stated that teachers 'had nothing to complain of as their level of unemployment is far lower than that of their colleagues in industry'—as though Labour's policy demanded an even-handed spread of misery.

As for teachers' pay, the gains of Houghton in 1974, were eroded throughout the years of the Social Contract to which the Burnham Committee adjusted its awards. So by 1979 the pressure for an increase to restore Houghton levels was overwhelming and led to the Prime Minister inviting Burnham to use the Clegg comparability mechanism. The Clegg Committee was set up to meet the very justifiable pay grievances of low-paid public service workers and staunch the outbreak of disruption of the public services. This was one of the consequences of the 'winter of discontent' when, following on a TUC refusal to endorse a fourth year of low-pay increases under the Social Contract, the government attempted unilaterally to impose a norm for pay rises that was well below the rate of price inflation. A rash of strikes broke out in the public sector which had disastrous effects on the popularity of the government. Ironically, it was to this 'low pay' body that teachers were invited to submit their pay demands five years after Houghton!

Attacks of the Radical Right on Education

The new turn in Labour policy involved more than continuing cuts. Under Mrs Williams a perhaps more significant move was being attempted, slowly at first but surely: government intervention in the curriculum. Interventionism was fostered and nourished by the Black Papers which began to appear in 1969 and flowed on in a series of right-wing attacks on the schools for neglecting 'basics' and indulging in far too much informality and 'frills' in pursuit of child-centred education.[4] The Black Papers, and later the right-wing National Council for Educational Standards, finding a receptive press and media, influenced public opinion.[5]

The Black Papers were in intention and content political documents in a shell of educational criticism and were directed both against the maintained primary schools and, more determinedly, against the comprehensives and the abolition of selection. The distinguished Professor, Cyril Burt, grand panjandrum of selection, was the star of their firmament, the giant academic theoretician, soon destined to be seen with his feet in a mire of fraudulent research, a totally discredited, indeed crooked, propagandist.[6] Correspondence between Burt and his sister indicated that he had been in touch with the then Secretary of State, Mrs Thatcher, who was 'interested' to hear from him.[7]

Such propaganda seemed to be justified in 1975 by the notorious case of William Tyndale Junior School of Islington which attracted enormous public attention. Here a group of ultra-left teachers had shaped and were operating what could only be described as a daft curriculum which neglected the most obviously necessary elements of the children's education ('Why teach children to write when we have typewriters?'!) and seemed to be producing a bunch of ill-behaved, ignorant pupils whose conduct and standards appalled most of the school's parents and governors. The ILEA in the end took action, but not before great damage was done to the image of the teaching profession as a whole, despite their union, the NUT, sharply distancing itself from the Tyndale extremists. Of course Tyndale was far from typical. It was extraordinary, even unique in its 'beyond the fringe' excesses, a caricature of the maintained primary schools.[8]

Similarly, the media played up the book by Neville Bennett (1976), a reputable educational researcher, which, it was claimed, showed that children did better when taught by formal than by informal methods in the primary schools. Though Bennett himself after considerable academic criticisms of his methodology, disowned, the exaggerated claims that were being made for his limited research, that schools should devote themselves more to traditional teaching of the '3Rs' was the message that the media drew from his book: the primary schools were hotbeds of fancy methods which prevented this from happening.[9]

But the main targets were the comprehensive schools. Statistics showing the superiority of selective schools were regularly produced and made their impact, though their value and validity, especially in not comparing like with like, were more than suspect. Public attention was focused on individual cases of bad discipline and behaviour and indifferent standards. (A later notorious example during March 1977 was the handling of a BBC TV *Panorama* programme on Faraday, a comprehensive school in West London, whose presentation was so unbalanced and biased as to give the picture little credibility as a portrayal of a school at work.) Yet a report by Her Majesty's Inspectorate (HMI) covering the decade 1977-87, entitled *Good Behaviour and Discipline in Schools*, commissioned by Mr Baker, currently Secretary of State, showed most schools to be orderly with high standards of behaviour and discipline. Unsurprisingly, incidents of disgraceful behaviour in the public schools reported from time to time were not generalized into a critique of the independent sector, as happened for the comprehensives.

The universities and polytechnics were also faced with loss of public confidence because of student disorders and attacks on their competence, symbolized by the publication of Malcolm Bradbury's novel, *The History Man* in 1975.[10]

This was the kind of ambience in which the Prime Minister, troubled by major economic problems, called for a report by the DES on the education system. The notorious *Yellow Book* which resulted was intended to be secret (and so unable publicly to be checked for accuracy) but, in October 1976, it was leaked to *The Guardian* and the *Times Educational Supplement*. It gave the Prime Minister a distorted picture of schools and teachers, and of the Schools Council, whose efforts to reform and democratize as well as broaden secondary school examinations it undermined. It cast doubt in the most biased way on the work of the comprehensives and gave an utterly false impression of the impact of informal methods in the primary schools. Central to its thesis was the assumption of poor performance and declining standards. What might be wrong with education, it argued, was overemphasis on preparing young people for their role in society rather than their economic role. This was the nub of the *Yellow Book's* case.

What was needed, it was claimed, was greater intervention by the DES and Inspectorate in the schools. But if things were as bad as pictured, then surely HMI and the DES were substantially responsible by previously remaining silent. To enhance their role, unreformed, as was proposed, was illogical if not bizarre, as Sir Alex Smith, Chairman of the Schools Council, was quick to point out. But logic never bothered the mandarins when they had a game to win.

The *Yellow Book* has to be seen in the context of the country's serious economic problems. Its criticisms of the schools, fitting well into both the Black Paper propaganda and demands for central government intervention into 'the secret garden of the curriculum', assumed a new importance. Education, boosted earlier as a vital investment for economic progress, had, it was being argued, failed; indeed the 'failure' of the schools became a comment increasingly in vogue in the media. It was just a step on from this to argue that education was in some way *responsible* for failure in the economy. And it was only a short further step to demanding state intervention to bring about change in the schools and to address all educational issues in the light of 'economic needs' and the changes necessary to meet them.

In such circumstances a Labour Prime Minister (Callaghan) brought comfort to his Tory enemies in a speech at Ruskin College, hyped to the skies in advance, which took the schools to task for being so unrelated to Britain's wealth-making processes in industry. As a Labour Prime Minister he should have castigated the old selective system with its academic neglect of technology in the independent and grammar schools from which Britain's leaders were drawn, and the under-resourced 'second-tier' modern schools for the mass of children. It was this class-biased system, he could truthfully have argued, which had produced an elite which looked down on 'wealth-making'—but not wealth-enjoying! And he could have added his deep regret that financial stringency prohibited successive Labour governments from fully developing the new comprehensive system, for example, in training the specialist teachers and equipping the schools with up-to-date workshops and labs. He might also have expressed his appreciation of the way in which the new unselective schools were extending technical education in the comprehensive curricula so many of them were providing. Concluding, he could have pledged more resources for helping to develop a system which could end the class bias in education which had held back its full growth, and on this foundation called for reforms in the curriculum.

But no! Schools were convenient scapegoats, education a sacred cow, which had not met the nation's economic needs. The impression conveyed by the Prime Minister was almost entirely negative. Labour was on the defensive, allowing the Right successfully to take the initiative on the issue of school standards, somehow responsible for the country's dire economic plight. That was the message. Yet in March 1977 in Parliament, pressed by the Tories, Mrs Williams produced convincing statistics to show how standards had risen. She was backed on this by the then Permanent Secretary, Sir James Hamilton, though the DES had organized the *Yellow Paper*, giving the emphatically opposite impression!

Mr Callaghan, in his speech, avoided the subject of the Schools Council, a major target of the Yellow Paper, discreetly leaving this issue to Mrs Williams. The Prime Minister was, after all, known as a friend of the unions and one of the major targets of the mandarins was to end teacher union control of the Council. Where he feared to tread his Secretary of State plunged in and, after acrimonious exchanges, the Council embarked on revising its constitution. In its new suit, it included a lay element and the teachers conceded their majority in the effective control of the Council.

Operating from their esoteric and remote eyrie above Waterloo Station, the DES had succeeded in inserting a wedge into the curricular power of the teaching profession and 'school autonomy'; and the role of the Department was strengthened in the Council's work. It was something but not enough for the mandarins who had decided to kill off the Council at a private DES meeting in 1975 chaired by John Hudson, the chief representative of the DES on the Council. In the meantime, Mrs Williams did her part in dithering, delaying and procrastinating over the reform of the 16 + examinations so that by the time the government's time was up, though approval had been given in principle to a new unified examination, nothing had been achieved in practice, a remarkable negative achievement after three years of huffing and puffing by the Secretary of State.

Moves Towards Central Control of the Curriculum

The moves towards central control had, however, begun. To speed it along, the Secretary of State organized, in 1977, the 'Great Debate' (as she modestly named it) a series of eight regional public conferences which were supposed to 'discuss' four fundamental educational issues: the aims and content of the school curriculum; educational standards and their assessment, the perform-ance of the school system as a whole and the reform of the GCE and CSE; teacher training; and the school and working life. Questions such as these, with their vast scope, were to be dealt with by a large audience, each in about forty minutes flat, in such conditions that no speaker from the floor, if able to catch the eye of the chair, would have more than about four minutes. Yet the 200 representatives included the eight school teacher unions, FE, HE, the LEAs, parents, industry, the trade unions ...! This, said Mrs Williams, would produce 'a more balanced view' of education.

The Great Debate was a publicity exercise in showbiz style, a fanfare for the

DES, now publicly entering the 'secret garden'. As a serious contribution to educational debate it was less than null. Yet, when it was over, the Secretary of State announced that it had come to educational conclusions! One conclusion she told the teachers was that there should not be a national curriculum.

There followed the first of a flow of papers from the DES and HMI on curricular matters. The first of these set the tone: it was a 'questionnaire' of some considerable length to LEAs, asking what influence they were exercising on the curriculum locally and what plans they had to do so. This opened up a whole new educational perspective for LEAs who had not been operating in this way, but used such influence as they wished to exert, indirectly through their appointment of heads and their advisory service. Three papers were also produced, by the DES, by the DES and the Department of Employment jointly and by both these departments jointly with the Department of Trade and Industry on the neglected field of the education and training of the 16–18s—a key area if anything was going to be done about linking education and industry. But no initiatives beyond the papers were undertaken. An attempt to introduce a truncated pilot scheme for Education Maintenance Allowances for students over 16 at school took so long to agree that it failed at the starting gate when the government resigned in May 1979. Mrs Williams was definitely an 'under-achiever'.

One exception may be noted to the lack of initiative on the post-16s. The Manpower Services Commission (MSC) was beginning to make some impact on the area, through the recently-launched Youth Opportunities Programme (YOP) for unemployed school-leavers. At the same time, the City and Guilds of London Institute (CGLI) a vocational educational body, was making efforts to penetrate the schools by offering courses as an alternative to the CSE.

The First Thatcher Administration, 1979–83

Mrs Thatcher took over in May 1979. Her government was wedded to a policy of monetarism whose practical consequences soon became clear.[11] There was a sharp rise in inflation, largely due to the doubling of VAT. A sharply rising pound, caused mainly by an abrupt and large rise in interest rates, wreaked havoc on industrial profitability and exports. Unemployment began to rise alarmingly, as our manufacturing base, already eroded under Labour, suffered its most devastating post-war 'shake-out'.

New technology, a necessary development, was unable to replace anything more than a fraction of the jobs lost in the basic industries. The steel industry in particular suffered as investment in industry and the infrastructure collapsed. Elsewhere, cost-effectiveness was the battle cry, and it was judged by the cash register alone. Deindustrialization had been growing steadily.[12] By 1984, the service sector accounted for 65 per cent of the workforce. In the fourteen years to 1985, over four million manufacturing jobs were lost, 1.7 million of them between May 1979 and mid-1985. By the early 1980s Britain had the lowest growth rate of any developed country in the previous twenty years. In April 1985, 1979 levels of output had not yet been reached again, while, in June 1987, manufacturing output was still below its level in 1979. This was despite the balance of payments benefits of North Sea oil.

Attacks on trade union power came in the 1980 and 1982 Employment Acts. In the former, restrictions were imposed on the closed shop; new ones had to have the support of 80 per cent of the workforce involved to be immune from unfair dismissal claims by workers losing their jobs through the operation of the closed shop; and the statutory 'religious conscience' clause was widened to include other objections on grounds of conscience or deeply-held personal belief to joining a union. Further, immunity for secondary picketing was drastically limited as was sympathetic industrial action. The 1982 Act made new restrictions in the law concerning union immunities, trades disputes and the closed shop to the disadvantage of the unions and their funds. The anti-union hunt was on with a vengeance. Though the teachers' unions were not directly affected, their status *vis à vis* government suffered in this ambience.

Serious limitations were placed on the spending powers of local authorities through legislation. For example, raising a supplementary rate was forbidden from 1982-83 in the Local Government Finance Act 1982, which also set up an Audit Commission to 'ensure value for money'. Worse still it legalized the penalty system operated from 1981 whereby an authority spending more on various services than the government had assessed should be spent was penalized. By this mechanism, grant aid was cut at an accelerating rate as the 'authorized' expenditure was exceeded.

Coupled with growing unemployment, local government expenditure cuts led to considerable hardship for many. Greater difficulty was experienced in winning adequate wage and salary increases, and there was encroachment on the welfare functions of local authorities; for example, the duty of LEAs to provide a meals service for payment was removed in the 1980 Education Act and LEAs could limit free meals to children whose parents were in receipt of Supplementary Benefit or Family Income Supplement. Council house rent increases also took their toll.

The Second Thatcher Administration, 1983-87

These 'new directions' were pursued with determination, especially after Mrs Thatcher's repeat success in 1983 with a large Parliamentary majority, though a minority of the popular vote. Further measures to deal with the unions were taken in the 1984 Acts. Elections of all holding a vote on Executive Committees were to be held at least every five years; and pre-strike ballots were necessary if union immunities were to apply. Unions which operated political funds under the 1913 Trade Union Act had in future to ballot their members at least every ten years if they wanted to continue their political funds. (There was no similar measure introduced to allow for consultation among employees in those companies which regularly donated large sums of money to the Conservative Party). This legislation, indeed, seemed so popular that its repeal was no part of Labour's 1987 Election Manifesto. Meanwhile the unions suffered from falling membership due to unemployment—a loss of over two million in TUC strength between 1973 and 1986. (Affiliated membership now stands at just over 9.2 million.)

Unemployment, 1.25 million in 1979, rose to over 3.25 million by 1985 and only began very gradually to drop at the end of 1986 towards just under three million by May 1987. But these figures have been authoritatively questioned as due to no less than nineteen changes in the official methods of computation between May 1979 and October 1986. Real figures, the TUC and other expert sources claimed, were nearer the four million mark, or even higher. And the numbers were also queried as excluding those on various employment and training schemes of the MSC and the Department of Employment which amounted to 526,000 by the end of 1986.

Structural unemployment, given the changes that technology was forcing on industries that needed large investment to allow them to compete in international markets, remorselessly took its toll. The numbers of long-term unemployed increased and some regions fared worse than others with Northern Ireland, Scotland, the North, and South Wales suffering far worse than London and the South East. By the 1980s the once prosperous West Midlands industry had been decimated by factory closures, and long dole queues appeared. The cost to the country in terms of lost production, lost revenue from tax and national insurance contributions and extra social security benefits amounted, according to a 1982 Treasury Report, to £15 billions in increased benefits and lost taxes, leaving out of account the cost to the nation of lost output, special employment schemes, etc.

The numbers of those on Supplementary Benefit increased dramatically from 4.4 million in 1979 to 7.7 million by 1983; while those below the Supplementary Benefit level rose from 2.1 million to 3.3 million. By any reasonable criterion, some nine million, or one-sixth of the population, were living in poverty as Mrs Thatcher set out on her second mission, and the numbers were to increase as unemployment mounted. [13]

This ambience of increasing poverty and unemployment boded ill for the maintenance of a healthy atmosphere in the schools, and internal problems grew as the stresses pressed hard on the teachers. The legislative attacks on the unions also served to increase tensions between the government and the main teachers' organizations, leading to a growing politicization of previously politically neutral teachers' associations.

Equal Opportunities

Against this background, important educational 'tendencies' gathered momentum, especially among teachers and among Labour LEAs: these are frequently subsumed in the term 'equal opportunities', meaning 'anti-sexism' and 'multiculturalism', sometimes confused with, but not necessarily the same as 'anti-racism'. These developments have, as yet, been insufficiently studied and inadequately, even badly researched for firm conclusions to be drawn on their impact on educational theory and practice. Both in the case of equal opportunities for girls and women and for ethnic minorities, legislation recognized the existence of problems, even if solutions were more difficult to achieve.

Equal pay had already been won for women in the teaching profession as far back as 1961, but this did not automatically bring with it equality of opportunity in promotion and status, as a detailed NUT survey revealed in 1986. But there was movement forward which only old ingrained attitudes and institutional inertia could delay. Similarly, equality of access for girls and also for boys to all subjects in the curriculum came up against these obstacles, though here traditional attitudes influenced many parents and the children themselves. This, on top of restricted resources, meant that good intentions did not materialize in major practical change. Change was often 'tokenist', a few boys doing home economics and a few girls in the workshops, and a few more in the physics labs. Clearly, the resistance to what seemed necessary as well as just developments was harder to overcome than many anticipated: 'curriculum equality' was going to be a slow process certainly in the secondary field.[14]

Equal opportunities for ethnic minority pupils was a much more political and sharply-argued issue, as well as being more complex.[15] While, in the earlier days of the wave of immigration from the New Commonwealth in the fifties, sixties and early seventies, attempts to 'deal' with the 'problem' took crude forms, such as bussing children from one part of an area to another to 'spread' them out more evenly (Bradford, Ealing) the prevailing attitude of most of those in education was to encourage and facilitate assimilation into the British culture, a process not seemingly objected to by the 'immigrants', as they were then normally described. But, as numbers of children were massively concentrated in various inner city areas, for example, in Greater London and the Midlands, there was a change of attitude. Greater attention was demanded to the special needs of ethnic minority pupils, including those born in this country, who formed the majority, as well as those born overseas.

Various studies purported to 'prove' that children of Caribbean origin achieved less well than indigenous children on criteria such as examination passes, while this weakness was not apparent, for example among many Asian children. Explanations, such as the home background of Caribbean children in low-paid and socially-deprived families, and of some—by no means all—Asians from middle-class, entrepreneurial backgrounds, could not explain adequately the differential results achieved. Attention was turned to linguistic difficulties, though here the paradox was that while children of Caribbean origin may have been brought up in homes where parents spoke a form of English which had the status of a language in its own right, Asian children often came from homes where one of the parents, if not both, spoke little or no English at all.

Cultural differences had also to be considered, though, here, complexity was added because the Asian culture could be more 'alien' to the indigenous than the Caribbean culture with which it had important religious features in common.

The Rampton Committee, set up officially after a recommendation by a Parliamentary Select Committee, claimed in 1981 that teachers sometimes had low expectations of Caribbean children and this contributed to underachievement—a word much in vogue in educational circles, but of imprecise meaning. Later the Swann Committee criticized some teachers as being 'racist,' pinpointing this as another cause of underachievement. However, the report also stated that such teachers were very much in the minority.[16] No objective observer could accuse the whole teaching profession, or any appreciable portion of it, of behaving in an unprofessional manner, involving discrimination against any section of pupils on racial grounds.

Increasingly, in the seventies, and much more in the eighties, teachers and some LEAs began to introduce 'multicultural elements' into the curriculum, particularly in subjects that lent themselves to such changes. The intention was to give greater recognition to the cultures of children who sometimes were the majority—and often a very substantial part—of the pupils. There were also moves in some areas to teach the 'mother tongues' of many pupils as a modern language, along with the traditionally taught modern languages of the curriculum. Lower down the age range, there was a greater appreciation in practice of the importance of a child's mother tongue in the educational process. Many books and articles appeared giving advice on how to develop a multicultural curriculum, and it was stressed that this was important, not only for ethnic minority children, but for all children who would be living increasingly in a multiethnic society.

Multiculturalism was, however, opposed by a minority on the ultra-left and some Black politicians and sociologists. Multiculturalism, it was argued, was merely a palliative which deceived the ethnic minority community that their travail was being alleviated. It glossed over the real problems of differential treatment that existed in a fundamentally 'racist' education system. They preferred 'anti-racism' which, it was claimed, involved a much more fundamental approach to the whole curriculum in all its aspects, though it was never explained clearly what this meant in actual curricular terms.

This form of 'anti-racism' as an ideology derived from the 'theory of institutional racism', which argued that racism was an inevitable feature of capitalist society; that, in effect, we were all racists, whether we liked it or not. It followed that the schools as institutions within capitalism were racist and had to be transformed. But how? It appeared that only after the revolution when racist capitalism was overthrown would racism disappear. This seemed to be a counsel of defeatism and despair since the revolution did not seem to be imminent. Strident anti-racism led in some cases to persecution and harassment of teachers. It also provoked a counter-reaction among the extreme Right, who were only too ready to fish in troubled racial waters.

Privatization

After 1983 drastic new steps were taken to undermine local authority power with intensification of the harsh penalty system for 'over-spending' in 1985–86 and even severer measures in 1986–87. Rate-capping was introduced in the 1984 Rates Act to apply from 1985–86. This gave the government the power to establish a legal maximum for the rates of selected authorities. Though public attention was focused in the media on the local authorities which rebelled, the general impact was effective throughout local government even though some LEAs continued to spend well above the limits allowed. The government had found, ingeniously, more efficacious methods of cutting local authority expenditure than ever Labour's 'cash limits' had been. A new dimension was added to the aphorism of the sixties 'private affluence and public squalor' as the free enterprise drive created fortunes for the few while local government found its powers to spend on education and welfare for the many restricted, and inner city decay accelerated. Some local authorities tried to circumvent government legislation by 'creative accounting' which allowed high spending to continue, but only at the cost of a catastrophically mounting debt. The government was determined to end this 'circumvention' of the law.

Attacks on local authorities included a drive towards privatization, for example, of school cleaning and school meals. And the government's new Social Security legislation threatened, when operated (from 1988), the free meals of half a million children. The privatization drive was also directed against the NHS through hiving off various operations such as cleaning, laundry, catering, etc. Its clearest and most determined expression, however, was the sell-off in the Stock Market of nationalized industries or enterprises. Over the first eight Thatcher years it included British Telecom, British Gas, Rolls Royce, Jaguar, British Airways and the government now intends to sell off the ten water authorities worth £27 billion, as well as the electricity boards.

There was also a massive programme of Council house sales at below market price which reached a million in 1986[17] and whose popularity led the Labour Party from original outright to muted opposition then to ultimate acceptance, though without great enthusiasm. By 1986, £17.2 billion of public assets (including Council houses) had been privatized and proceeds from privatizing state assets were planned to reach £4.7 billion for each of the three years after 1985–86. Sales of national property for private wealth was, said the old 'one nation' Tory, Macmillan, like 'selling off the family silver'. A nation of shareholders and house owners was the Thatcherite declared aim. At the same time, the government maintained strict controls to prevent local authorities from spending all the proceeds of the sales of their Council house assets on more Council housing or better local services.

But this policy had its negative consequences. So far from uniting the nation (an old Tory slogan Mrs Thatcher's ideology had eschewed) the gap between rich and poor was pushed wider by the government's taxation policies which favoured the rich. 'For the very rich tax cuts were dramatic; between 1978-79 and 1984-85 the estimated 65,000 taxpayers with incomes over £50,000 gained an annual average of £19,400—an amount sixty-one times that received by the poorest'.[18] Another estimate is that the rich gained some £2600 million in tax concessions between 1979-84. In spite of some legislative curbs, an expense account society with company cars and low interest-bearing loans, was an integral part of Mrs Thatcher's 'enterprise society'.[19]

Undermining the Maintained Sector

When Mrs Thatcher took office in June 1970 as Secretary of State for Education, the first action she took was to issue a Circular removing the pressure on LEAs to submit plans for comprehensive re-organization. On becoming Prime Minister in May 1979, she immediately approved action to repeal the 1976 Act requiring LEAs to go comprehensive, though few authorities had maintained their partial or total stance against the prevailing comprehensive trend. This trend was so powerful that, even by 1987, no LEA, however strongly motivated ideologically in favour of selection, had actually succeeded in turning the clock back to reorganize on selective lines, though some tried hard. Comprehensives still held about 90 per cent of the pupils and grammar schools in England only 3 per cent in January 1986. One must not underestimate, however, the impact of the propaganda in favour of selection on public opinion in the new favourable political climate. This gathered momentum in the later Thatcher years and was the background to new initiatives in education policy.

The attack on the comprehensives was, of course, part of the drive to extend the government's 'enterprise' ideas to education. Enterprise meant selection in one form or another. It also, in this respect, meant loosening the bonds of local authority control of schools and their pupils.

Encouragement of the independent schools became a high priority finan-cially and ideologically, fitting neatly also into the privatization policy. It was aided by the Assisted Places Scheme, seen through Parliament by her Secretary of State, Mark Carlisle. It was a serious blow to the comprehensives, aiming as it did to wean away their brightest pupils into the private sector.

Public expenditure was made to appear a dirty word and the education service, after years of deprivation, continued to be inadequately funded. The percentage that the Rate Support Grant (RSG) paid of LEA expenditure was reduced from 60 per cent in 1979 to 52 per cent in 1984-85 and to less than 47 per cent in 1986-87. At the same time, there was a plan, not entirely successful, to move resources from the inner cities to the shire counties. But the bluntness of the instrument used made the move a hit-and-miss affair and later the major problems created for the inner cities such as London caused the government to have second thoughts.

One particularly mean example of the cuts was the arbitrary closure of the Centre for Information and Advice on Educational Disadvantage, the only institution of its kind and costing at the time a mere £300,000. Ostensibly an item in the government's inconsistent attack on quangoes (new ones kept being set up as the need arose!), this was chosen, irrespective of educational need, to fulfil the DES quota of quango closures agreed by the Permanent Secretary, Sir James Hamilton, in the secret cabal of top mandarins. The callous disregard of any educational justification was made clear both in a debate in Parliament and a session of the Select Committee on Education and Science in July 1980. The victims of the top mandarins were the country's most deprived children.

Death of the Schools' Council

When the dry Joseph took over from the wet Carlisle the time was judged ripe by the DES to kill off the obnoxiously semi-independent Schools Council. Contrary to the recommendation of a specially-appointed and carefully chosen don, Mrs Trenaman, whom he asked to investigate the Council in 1981, Sir Keith accepted the malevolent advice of the mandarins who had privately nourished their spite against it since the days of their abortive DES Curriculum Study Group in the early sixties and announced the abolition of the Council in April 1982, at the very point when it was making its greatest impact under John Tomlinson's leadership. It was finally closed in March 1984. Its story reveals the extraordinary duplicity of the DES, taking up one stance publicly and another privately.

The Council was replaced by two bodies, one entirely government appointed, the Secondary Examinations Council (SEC), to take over its examinations functions; the other almost entirely government appointed, the School Curriculum Development Committee (SCDC) (the LEAs who accepted the constitution of the former jibbed at the latter and secured their own representation). Teacher representation ended on both bodies. An era involving democratic teacher participation in control of curriculum and examinations had ended. Abolition of the Council and its replacement in this way was another step in the government's interventionist policy. Throughout the Tory years the paradox persisted of moves to greater central control of education alongside greater emphasis on privatization and individual enterprise.

The Effects of Financial Stringency

Despite higher spending on education its percentage of the GDP declined from 5.7 in 1980–81 to 5.1 by 1986-87 and is planned to be 4.7 in 1989-90.

Although government claims of increased spending per pupil in schools 1979-1987 held up, this is due to sharply falling rolls coincident with relatively stable, continuing 'overheads' including a reduction in staffing, big enough though it is, which has not matched falling pupil numbers. In addition educational costs have far exceeded the inflation measured in the retail price index. Spending therefore fell well short of need. This is seen in the decay of school buildings, the increasing shortage of books and materials, and the lack of resources for the full implementation of the 1981 Education Act. There was also the continued shortages of specialist teachers in science, maths, technical studies, etc., where even the very limited attempts to make good these deficiencies began to take effect only in the late eighties. Spending on 'capitation' declined in real terms by 12 per cent in secondary schools and by 16.6 per cent in primary schools between 1978-79 and 1985-86, according to the Director of the British Education Equipment Association (BEEA). The Educational Publishers Association showed spending on school books as having fallen by 1986 to over 44 per cent in secondary schools since 1978-79 and 32 per cent in primary schools.

Four reports by HMI, following previous ones going back to the last years of Labour, which had shown up the deleterious effects on the schools of the government's financial policies, remain unpublished at the time of writing. The reports dealt with the nitty-gritty of the material resources needed in the schools; school furniture, internal decoration, charges to parents, and the effects of spending policies on the quality of education. Among facts alleged and not denied by the DES to be in the reports, were that repairs needed to furniture would cost more than £100m. The journal, *Education* wrote of a follow-up study on one comprehensive school that 'splintered chairs, tables and cupboards, broken plastic seats and jagged metal tubes are now a common hazard in every classroom and corridor'. Another report quoted members of HMI as saying that 'it is difficult to see how, on present funding, the education service can prevent further decline, let alone reverse the situation'.

The Secretary of State, Mr Baker, denied the existence of a report on internal decoration; but anyone acquainted, even superficially, with the schools would surmise that the rapidly deteriorating situation was so obvious as to render an official report supererogatory. A fourth report covered the charges increasingly being made by LEAs for music, field trips and cookery lessons. Mr Baker admitted that, if the government was re-elected, it was considering a Bill to make the charges legal—the thin edge of a serious wedge into free schooling. A survey by the NUT and the BEEA of spending on books and equipment in 200 primary schools, published in 1987, showed that LEA spending on primary schools of £18.04 per pupil was topped up by £11.89 from parents. In secondary schools parents provided £6.07 to top up the LEA's contribution of £40.27.

In the late seventies the pressures to reduce costs competed with worries about the future decline in the number of school leavers in debates about HE.

The polytechnics had come to the end of their initial period of establishment, although the mergers of colleges of education within polytechnics meant continued growth for some of them. The total provision for teacher training, however, was drastically reduced in this period and the universities continued to experience financial stringency and insecurity. One more hopeful trend was the development of proposals for extending access to higher education to mature people, including those without traditional qualifications, and increasing provision for continuing education, but actual progress was slow and mainly confined to the public sector.

Parental Choice

In the early Thatcher years there had been powerful right-wing influences demanding, as the best way to 'provide' education, the imposition of a voucher system whereby parents would be offered the cost of their children's education in the form of a voucher to be cashed in at the school of their own choice. This won enthusiastic intellectual acceptance from Sir Keith Joseph but an experimental pilot scheme in Tory Kent proved very expensive, and the idea was dropped. It was regretfully declared to be unworkable by the DES. 'Vouchers', said Sir Keith, 'were a noble concept, now dead'. This muted the propaganda of the extreme right-wing of the Tories in favour of vouchers, but it did not kill the intention to put the idea into operation in some form at a more favourable time.

'Parental choice', government spokesmen argued, would lead to a free market in education parallel to the free market which was the Tory economic dream. By oversubscribing the good schools, it would drive out the bad ones or force them to improve. Some steps were taken in the 1980 Education Act to give parents better rights of appeal on school placements but a stronger move was made in the government's second term in the 1986 Act which reorganized governing bodies to give parents and LEAs equal numbers, amounting to about a half of the total—the other approximate half of the total going to teachers and 'the community'. This changed pattern of governing bodies, however, reduced the role of LEAs more than, in practice, it enhanced that of the schools' parents who still remained a minority of the governors. An earlier DES consultative document had suggested a parent majority but the proposal was dropped due to unfavourable public, including parental, reaction.

This betokened a new and frontal attack on the LEAs as controllers of their schools. Ostensibly motivating the Tories were the actions of a number of Labour authorities sometimes under the control of ultra-left politicians, such as emphasis on giving children 'positive images' of gays and lesbians, and strident, maladroit operation of 'anti-racist' policies. Peace studies were another target. In general, the Tories complained of the politicization of education by the Left, blandly begging the question that the status quo equally involved a political stance.

Positive and progressive educational policies of Tory as well as Labour LEAs were ignored, the spotlight being turned on every negative manifestation of untypical extremist Councils that could arouse public antagonism. Also ignored, for example, was the improvement in attainment over the years in the maintained schools as measured in exam results.[20] Turning her back on all this, Mrs Thatcher had declared in 1983 that education was 'a disaster area': for this the LEAs were being held responsible.

The GCSE

This was the backdrop for the long saga of the attempt to merge GCE and CSE. The new lords and masters knew the power examinations have over the curriculum and preferred the divided exam system as they had preferred the divided school system which it reflected. Mrs Williams had dithered and procrastinated, leaving Mark Carlisle to stop further progress for a time. Several more years elapsed before Sir Keith Joseph faced up to the almost unanimous educational view that there should be a single exam at 16 + . To this he finally agreed in June 1984, some fourteen years after the first moves had been made in this direction by the Schools Council. But the new exam bore his imprint, with its emphasis on differentiation rather than on unification. Sir Keith's heart and mind were in the maintenance of an O level type of exam, and in the GCSE, though there was substantial CSE influence, it was 'O level standards' which was one of the two crucial elements; the other was a considerable diminution of teacher control which had been the hallmark of the CSE.

How the GCSE will shape up in affecting school curricula remains to be seen. Typically, however, having decided to establish the new exam, the DES starved it of adequate resources and refused to accept the almost universal advice of the practitioners to postpone its commencement for another year till schools had had time to absorb the required syllabi, secure the books, etc., and teachers had received satisfactory training in the new assessment methods demanded. A National Conference of Parent Teacher Associations (NCPTA) survey of 118 schools showed Heads declaring a shortfall of an average of £15,000 per school.

Vocationalism

Differentiation was also the key to the other new examination development under the Tories and strongly pressed by the Department officials. This was the creation of the CPVE as a 'prevocational' exam for the 16-17 year-old students considered unsuitable for A level courses, and as a replacement for the Certificate of Extended Education (CEE), a single-subject continuation of the CSE which had been the choice of the Schools Council. The CEE was killed in spite of the recommended extension by the Keohane Committee of its general educational character to include a vocational element, in favour of an exam in the tradition of vocational education, which fitted into the government's educational approach: general education on more traditional lines for a minority of young people, vocationally directed education for most.

The CPVE has, however, not 'taken off' as its advocates had hoped. The situation at the post-16 level is still fluid, especially with the development of GCSE (mature) examinations for the 16-17s. Members of HMI have privately admitted the poor quality of the CPVE scheme, and Sir Keith was known to have his doubts about the dilution of general education that was proceeding.

In the name of 'broadening and relevance', the curriculum was, in fact, being sharply differentiated on class lines. Pre-vocationalism, even the introduction of full-blooded vocational elements, though at first advocated only for the post-16s, became keen issues of educational debate for the 14-16s or even lower. The vocational education bodies, the CGLI and BTEC, increasingly tried to penetrate the schools though almost their entire experience was with training vocationally the post-16s and especially adults.

Closer relationships of schools with industry, Mr Callaghan's plea of 1976, was taken up eagerly by Sir Keith Joseph and even more by Kenneth Baker. Industrialists were invited to contribute to curricular development, though the response was sparse and confined more or less to platitudinous generalization. Responsible industrial representatives kept on insisting that what they wanted their recruits to be was broadly educated with good personal qualities and not vocationally or pre-vocationally trained.

Encouraging the vocational trend was the incursion of the MSC into schools through the Technical and Vocational Education Initiative (TVEI). TVEI schemes offered substantial sums to LEAs for selected pupils in selected schools to develop technical studies for the 14-18s. Borough or county-wide schemes for all pupils in all schools were unacceptable. Although there were constructive and progressive curricular changes for the 14-16s the essentially selective nature of the scheme was its cardinal weakness. The comprehensive school objective was always to provide all children with a good technical studies element in the curriculum, but TVEI concentrated the finance on a minority. Unsurprisingly, Labour LEAs deprived of resources responded to the new carrot, in spite of their ideological objections to the MSC control —such was their financial desperation. Even when TVEI 'went national' in September 1987, its selective nature continued.

The MSC also moved into non-advanced further education (NAFE) with a financial takeover of a quarter of their work, a move which aroused considerable LEA opposition. A compromise arrangement was patched up between the MSC and the LEAs and the college teachers' union, NATFHE, which left them more administrative and professional control. The MSC was, however, a cuckoo in the nest.

In its proper sphere, the MSC created the Youth Training Scheme, developed out of the earlier Youth Opportunities Programme under Labour, following upon the *New Training Initiative* document prepared by the Commission. As a scheme for training the young unemployed at 16 and, later, both 16 and 17, it had great merit if applied strictly according to the prescription. Youth unemployment was a fact of life under monetarism and it was better to give young people a chance of training and some education, however flawed, than to leave them hanging about the streets.

Much serious and dedicated effort went into the YTS. But its weaknesses aroused sharp criticism: its main object was to keep young people off the unemployment register; it was being used as cheap substitute labour; the allowances were far too small (the TUC had lost out on this); the educational element was quite inadequate; there was discrimination against ethnic minority youngsters, and girls; concern that it was producing partially trained youngsters without qualifications who did not get the further training they needed—and so on. The government's latest proposal, in 1987, to deny Supplementary Benefit to those refusing a place on the Scheme has aroused considerable opposition as meaning, in effect, compulsion to join.

These criticisms are very serious. But at least the MSC was keeping to its proper function—training—and not trying to colonize areas such as school education where its pedagogical ignorance was only equalled by its ideological arrogance. Looking back over the years the tentative 'education and industry' moves by Labour has become a large-scale and much more penetrating operation under the Tories.

How far was central intervention in the curriculum intended to go? The flood of HMI and DES papers on the curriculum were certainly trying to influence both educational and public opinion in a general direction, pushed on by the publication of HMI reports on individual schools and colleges. By the mid-80s, government interest and concern was firmly established in the public mind. It now became quite normal for ministers to pronounce on detailed questions.

Sir Keith Joseph publicly tackled complex issues such as assessment objectives and methods with the confidence and assurance that he was rightly exercising control in an important educational area, and it was a control to which few now publicly objected, or even criticized. His Sheffield speech on this issue in 1985 had remarkable bipartisan support. Moreover, the tone was quite different from the brash attacks of the Black Paper propagandists; it was more sober, more academic, altogether more serious, and an appreciation was also declared, in words anyway, of the job teachers were doing.

Kenneth Baker at the DES

Whether public opinion was being deliberately and consciously prepared for the next moves historians will be able to assess. These came from Sir Keith's successor, Kenneth Baker, a minister more direct, less subtle, with an air of absolute certainty, a man not beset by any intellectual doubts as was his more thoughtful and philosophically-minded predecessor.

Privatization took a new turn within the general attack on local government and coalesced with both the government's desire to bring schools and industry closer together and its deep-seated belief in selection. All these policies motivated Mr. Baker's proposals for setting up City Technological Colleges in twenty centres, as private schools outside LEA control, largely funded by industry and overseen by a CTC Trust. Business men and women would be the governors responsible for appointment of staff, payment of salaries, and the curriculum. The CTCs proposed were attacked widely and by no means only on party lines, not only because they aimed to weaken the maintained schools and could lead to fee paying. but also because they would be difficult to operate.

These CTCs, if successful, would, it is argued, attract children and staff from the maintained schools and so, along with the Assisted Places Scheme, undermine the comprehensives. There was considerable scepticism, too, that industry on any scale would want to foot the bill or break off their developing relations with schools in the maintained system.

Mr. Baker's pronouncements on the need for a national curriculum seemed to come rather suddenly in the run up to a General Election. The proposals, included in the Queen's Speech in the new June 1987 Parliament, were presented as a natural, progressive extension of previous developments. It all seemed to fit together: the importance of education for the economy, the need to ensure basic educational standards, the desirability of putting curbs on the influence of the teaching profession over the curriculum.

But in spite of seemingly bipartisan political support and a quite favourable public reception, the scheme has been strongly criticized both in detail, as in the proposals for bench mark tests at 7, 11 and 14, which have clearly not been thought through, and in general as holding out the threat of strict regimentation from the centre which would destroy any professional educational initiative. Working parties on the curriculum would be appointed by the Minister and would be overseen by DES officials, and there would be machinery for monitoring and enforcement arrangements to support delivery of perhaps 70 per cent to 90 per cent of the schools' curriculum. A National Curriculum Council would consist of appointees of the Secretary of State. Representativeness seems to have been ruled out.

The Senior Chief Inspector, Mr. Eric Bolton, writing before the scheme was announced, criticized the 'obsession' with evaluation and testing which would result in an 'undue narrowness' of teaching and learning.[21] The tests, critics have said, would control what is taught instead of vice versa, an intensification of the most strongly complained of feature of the old examination system. Professional curricular initiative would be stifled.

Pushed aside was the fact that the original comprehensive idea included a comprehensive curriculum which was unable to be fully operated because of lack of resources and the overwhelming grammar school influence. Mr. Baker's plans show little sign of rectifying these weaknesses and are more likely to accord with the old Black Paper demands for a return to 'basics'. How, also, the national curriculum is imposed in practice remains to be seen. Though the Minister has spoken of its adoption by agreement with the LEAs and teachers, this hardly accords with his other attitudes to the two 'partners'.

Further proposals to give greater powers to school governors and heads show up a basic confusion in government thinking. For this approach to increasing 'school autonomy', the stated government objective, is in glaring contradiction to the centralized control of what matters most in a school—the curriculum. Greater autonomy is to be confined mainly to the distribution of school budgets, although not, to be sure, the global sums that schools need which will be decided elsewhere, higher up. The 'autonomy' will exclude what were previously the head's and staff's greatest powers: the power over what is taught. The head's powers to pay selected teachers 'above the rate' provided he/she can save money in other directions is fraught with problems.

Greater parental choice is to be achieved by schools being allowed to enrol up to their 1979 intake numbers or even more. The assumption is that parents will opt for the 'better' schools and the others will somehow be competitively forced to improve. In practice this could lead to great difficulties and even closures for good inner city schools, already suffering from their unfavourable environment. Popular schools are not, by definition, automatically, better schools. And a proposed increase in the Assisted Places scheme from 25,000 to 35,000 can only further weaken the maintained system.

Plans permitting schools with over 300 pupils on roll to opt out of LEA control on a majority vote of parents, while remaining state financed, are very nebulous at the time of writing. How such a scheme will operate is far from clear; for example, the vesting of the school's ownership in a trust formed by the governors, what costs may fall on parents etc. Is the government's pledge of no school fees to be relied upon? What is clear is that the measure is intended as a further blow at local government. Finally, the legalization of charges for various school services to which parents now contribute, 'bringing the law into line with what exists in practice', creates a new serious threat to free schooling.

Will teachers just meekly comply with this revolutionizing of the whole basis of their work and without any consultation on the major principles involved, only, perhaps, on detailed application? The context of this question is the most troubled period of relations between teachers and government ever.

Sir Keith Joseph's last years and Kenneth Baker's entire period at the DES were scarred by the long-running teachers' dispute. Both in pursuit of a new pay structure and in opposition to the imposition of conditions of service, the teachers suffered a major defeat. Mr. Baker, having failed to get his way by negotiation, removed by legislation in the Teachers' Pay and Conditions Act 1987, their negotiating rights, abolishing the historic Burnham Committee.

His grounds were utterly specious—the continued failure to reach agreement—as though a negotiating machine was expected to be a source of sweetness and light, instead of a battleground over vital issues, in this case, the livelihoods of half a million people. He also imposed conditions of service on a whole profession accustomed to negotiation and consultation.

Teachers have been treated as second-class citizens, denied any real say in determining their standard of living, professional work or status. The LEAs as the teachers' employers felt equally slighted by the government's action. In consequence, Mr. Baker's last days at the DES before the General Election were a period of unexampled bitterness between the three 'partners'. This bitterness has spilled over into the whole educational world. The latest development, the suggested machinery for negotiating pay and conditions in a National Education Council, agreed by a majority of teachers and employers, is a major blow to the government's strategy. It points the way, however, to a solution of the crisis.

It is extremely unlikely that the latest proposed (1987-88) upturn in educational expenditure will succeed in the context of the government's other measures in winning over the hearts and minds of those directly concerned with the education of the mass of the nation's children—teachers and local authorities in particular, but also many parents. Just before the General Election, the Select Committee on Education, in its report on educational expenditure, 1987-90, said, for example, that government spending plans will lead to further deterioration in the state of school building, and reductions in money for books, equipment etc. in 1987-88 in spite of real increases in the previous two years due to LEAs spending 'above the limit'.

Conclusion

In retrospect, the outstanding feature of the thirteen years has been the destruction of the partnership between government, local authorities and teachers which had been the foundation of our education system for many years. It is ironical that the partnership has ended at the same time as the increase in public expectation of education should have greatly strengthened it. Private initiatives, opting out of the democratic system, hardly accords with the need for greater, genuine public accountability. Instead of democratic consensus there will be direction from the centre. The potential for conflict in one of the most sensitive areas of our public affairs will be enormous.

Notes

1 GAMBLE A. (Ed) (1985) *Britain in Decline*, London, Macmillan, p. 124.
2 CONGDON, T. (1982) *Monetary Control in Britain*, London, Macmillan, pp 4-5.
3 In 1972 and 1973 expenditure on education exceeded that on defence:

	Education £m	Defence £m
1971	3023	3164
1972	3559	3493
1973	4068	4004
1974	4864	4889

Source: Social Trends (1975), table 13.4, p 198.

4 As well as the Black Papers a series of pamphlets and books attacking the education system in general and the maintained schools in particular appeared in these years written by those of the radical right. Boyson's *Battle Lines for Education* (1973), *Parental Choie* (1973), both from the Conservative Political Centre, and *The Crisis in Education* (1975) were found to be stronger in rhetoric than fact. Publications from the Institute of Economic Affairs, whatever the subject matter, were written to show 'how far market principles and pricing can be introduced into the disposition of goods and services organized by the government', for example, MAYNARD, A. (1975) *Experiment with Choice in Education.* Such writings were popularized in the mass media.

5 For a critique of the early Black Papers see WRIGHT, N. (1977) *Progress in Education*, pt 2, London, Croom Helm.

6 The authoritative biography of Burt provides full details: HEARNSHAW, L. S. (1979) *Cyril Burt Psychologist*, London, Hodder and Stoughton. See also KAMIN, I. J. 1974) *The Science and Politics of IQ*, New York, Lawrence Erlbaum (published in England in 1977 by Penguin).

7 'The Burt Scandal', BBC Radio 4, 29 April 1982.

8 AULD, R. (1976) *William Tyndale Junior and Infants School Public Inquiry*, a report to the ILEA.

9 Bennett's findings were of course more complex; in fact the best teacher in the sample was considered to be an informal teacher. A reanalysis of the material in *Teaching Styles and Pupil Progress* provided results quite different from those of the original study. For a summary see the chapter in this volume by John Coe on primary schools. Further details are provided by HESKETH, J. (1981) 'When best is not good enough', *Times Educational Supplement*, 17 July. Neither the reworking of Bennett's earlier data nor the larger scale studies published between 1980 and 1983 by a team led by M. Galton and B. Simon, the first volume of which was entitled *Progress and Performance in the Classroom*, received the kind of attention from the media which Bennett's earlier work had done.

10 See also COCKBURN, A. and BLACKBURN, R. (Eds) (1969) *Student Power*, London, Penguin.

11 The dilemma facing the Conservative administration pledged to reduce public expenditure in order to lower taxation was that they already had commitments to increase such expenditure in certain areas such as defence and the police and were obliged to increase it in other areas such as social security and unemployment. This made remaining areas vulnerable such as housing, the health service and education. A commitment to increase defence expenditure by 3 per cent per annum helped to push up a rising defence budget. In 1974/75 defence cost £4.2 billion; by 1978/79 it was £7.4 billion and by 1983/84 £15.5 billion—*Annual Abstract of Statistics* (1986) table 7.2, p 135. Regardless of military or moral arguments Britain's comparative industrial decline (see SHEPHERD, G.,

DUCHENE, G. and SAUNDERS, C. (Eds) (1983) *Europe's Industries*, London, Francis Pinter) meant that no government could spend resources on such a scale without depriving other sectors of the economy of funds.

12 For a detailed study of the rapid changes in British manufacturing and the economy see MARTIN, R. and ROWTHORN, B. (Eds) (1986) *The Geography of Deindustrialisation*, London, Macmillan. Chapter 1 provides an authoritative survey of the post-Second World War period.

13 Post-Second World War 'poverty' was rediscovered in the 1970s and carefully documented in the large-scale study by P. TOWNSEND (1979) *Poverty in the United Kingdom*. This study, together with the work of various pressure groups such as 'Child Poverty Action' and the 'Low Pay Unit' began to focus attention upon the growing number of 'have nots' in Britain. The Labour governments of the 1970s failed to make substantial progress towards greater equality and with the exception of pensioners, most low income groups did not fair well (see Bosanquet, M. and Townsend, P. (Eds) (1980) *Labour and Equality 1974-79*, London, Heinemann). One result of the growing gap between the distribution of incomes could be seen in health. The publication of the *Black Report* (1982) showed that whilst standards had risen for all there had been an 'escalator effect' so that, for example, the infant deaths per thousand legitimate live births for social class 1 had fallen from thirty-two to twelve between 1930-32 and 1970-72; for social class V the fall had been from eighty to thirty-one, hence the gap between the two social groups had remained the same. In his Foreword to the Report, Patrick Jenkins, Secretary of State for Social Services, claimed that the cost suggested to fundamentally improve the health of the nation, £2 billion a year, 'is quite unrealistic in present or any foreseeable economic circumstances ... I cannot therefore endorse the group's recommendations ...'. The persistence of serious health inequalities in the 1980s was documented in a follow-up report, *The Health Divide* (1987). The poor continued to suffer higher infant mortality rates, higher rates of chronic sickness and suffer more from major diseases than the rich. During the 1980s expenditure on private health treatment increased rapidly (see also BROWN, M. and MADGE, M. (1982) *Despite the Welfare State*, London, Heinemann; POND, C. and BURGHES, I. (1986) 'The rising tide of deprivation', *New Society*, 18 April; and PIACHAUD, D. (1987) 'The poor get poorer', *New Society*, 5 June.

14 There was progress on the examination front. 'In 1984/85, 59 per cent of girls leaving school in Great Britain had at least one GCE 'O' level grade A-C or equivalent compared with 53 per cent of boys. In 1976/77 the comparable proportions were 54 per cent and 51 per cent', *Social Trends* (1987), p. 61. There were still differences between subjects passed at 'O' level between girls and boys but over the period 1970/71 to 1984/85 girls began to close the gap in the 'hard sciences' such as physics and mathematics, whilst pulling further ahead of boys in French and English (*ibid*, table 3.14, p 62). Within the professions, including teaching, women made only slow headway in the struggle to obtain senior posts. By 1986 there was only one polytechnic with a woman director. Headships of co-educational secondary schools remained predominantly male, although London made positive and successful efforts to appoint more women in senior posts in secondary schools.

15 For a range of essays with often conflicting points of view in this area see

MODGIL, S. *et al* (Eds) (1986) *Multicultural Education: The Interminable Debate*, Lewes, Falmer Press.

16 DEPARTMENT OF EDUCATION AND SCIENCE (1985) *Education for All: The Report of the Committee of Inquiry into the Education of Children from Ethnic Minority Groups* (The Swann Report), London, HMSO.

17 Council house sales proved to be a mixed blessing as the privatization of such dwellings combined with the collapse of house building in the public sector (the contribution of public sector building to the increase in stock fell from around 140,000 per year in the 1970s to 43,000 in 1985) increased the plight of low income families unable to obtain a mortgage. By 1986 the farcical situation had arisen whereby local authorities were compelled to spend millions of pounds to board homeless families with private landlords yet forbidden by the government to build houses; a policy which would have actually been cheaper as well as more socially desirable.

18 WICKS, M. (1987) 'The decade of inequality', *New Society*, 6 February.

19 'Between April 1979 and April 1986 net earnings for the bottom 10 per cent increased by 2.9 per cent in real terms ... for the highest 25 per cent it was 14.5 per cent. And, among the top 10 per cent of income earners, net pay rose by a massive 21 per cent.' *(ibid)*.

20 The total number of school leavers rose from 790,000 in 1973/74 to 887,000 in 1983/84. During this time the number gaining two GCE 'A' levels/three Scottish higher certificates rose from 103,000 to 131,000; the number gaining five or more GCE 'O' levels/Scottish certificate 'C' grades/CSC grade 1, increased from 68,000 to 92,000, *Annual Abstract of Statistics* (1986) table 5.5, p 93.

21 See BOLTON, E. (1987) 'The debate on a national agreement on the curriculum and its implications for standards', *NUT Education Review*, 1, 1.

Chapter 2: The Funding of Education

Tudor David

Tudor David is a freelance journalist. He was formerly Editor of *Education* (1970-1986) and *The Teacher* (1965-70) and such bizarre titles as the *London Welshman* (monthly) and the *Journal of Oil and Gas Accountancy* (quarterly), as well as being education correspondent of *New Society* and a regular contributor to the *Encyclopedia Brittanica*. He is an honorary member of the Society of Education Officers and the British Educational Equipment Association (BEEA) and a Fellow of the College of Preceptors.

★   ★   ★

Education is very expensive. To send a boy of secondary school age to a school like Hurn Court, Barnstaple, would cost in 1987 £2145 a year; or the independent junior school of Latymer Upper in London would cost £2175. A boy of secondary age at Westminster School in London would drain his parents of £3975 a year. A girl going to a day junior (or preparatory) school, St Mary's in Henley, would cost £1650 a year. These are random but not untypical figures and, of course, all apply to private establishments. The cost of sending children to state, that is to say local education authority, schools is rather different. It is not in fact possible to make direct comparisons but what are called 'unit costs'—a sort of average figure for educating each child in LEA schools—offer the best guide. A child in an Inner London primary school in 1987 costs £1222 a year; in a secondary school £2011. Outside London costs are a good deal less. In Sheffield, £905 per year in primary schools, £1333 in secondary; in Leeds £734 in primary schools and £1253 in secondary; in Bedfordshire £756 in primary and £1143 in secondary. These figures fall far short of what parents with the wherewithal and the willingness to send their children to private education are obliged to pay. Nonetheless, they are large sums and they are larger than they have ever been before. Move on to the really expensive end of schooling—the universities—where rich and poor mix, for there is almost no private university schooling; it cost in 1986 about

£20,000 to put a student through a three-year BA course and £55,000 for a medical course.

We shall take a closer look at these costs later, but it need hardly be said that no government, whether Labour or Tory, is in office long before the Treasury begin to complain that education spending is too high and is getting out of hand. Ironically, the one period since 1970 when there appeared, in retrospect at least, to be some genuine buoyancy was during the Thatcher years at education (June 1970 to March 1974). Mrs Thatcher was not then a Thatcherite, at least so far as education was concerned. Later she appeared to regret bitterly most of what had happened; if only she had brought back some technical schools and not approved all those comprehensives which slipped through. She did some notably unThatcherite things such as seeing in the raising of the school leaving age and she published a much criticized but not unworthy White Paper called *A Framework for Expansion*.

Labour's record (1974-79), in contrast, far from exceeding expectations, fell short of them. After all Labour had sold out on the second raising of the school leaving age (16) and very nearly sold out on the first (to 15). What is more, Labour put a check on public spending. In general, government spending on goods and services went down as a proportion of GDP from 27 per cent in 1974/75 to 23.5 per cent in 1978/79. As far as the Treasury were able, this included a squeeze on education.

There have until now been two big obstacles to the hacking of education spending. No doubt there are also obstacles to cutting big services like defence or health, but they are nothing like as formidable as education. First there is the obstinate fact that education is actually run by local education authorities—104 of them in England and Wales and twelve in Scotland; and LEAs have minds of their own. Secondly comes the fact that the money is largely spent on teachers and there are nearly 700,000 of them in the UK; quite properly they expect a standard of living which at least rises in line with other's, and are going to fight for it. In other words, spending is bound up irretrievably with the way in which the education system is managed on the one hand and the fact that it is monstrously labour-intensive on the other. So that the cost of educational labour is of crucial importance.

Could Teachers Cost Less?

Table 1 shows that there are at least one million adults employed in the education industry, the large majority of them teachers and lecturers. It is hardly surprising that the first concern of most if not all ministers of Education is to reduce their numbers and reduce their cost. Roughly speaking, between 60 to 70 per cent of a local education authority's education budget is on teachers, and some 55 to 60 per cent of an independent day school's budget (see table 2) will be spent directly on teacher labour. Then there are indirect costs; teachers have to be resourced with accommodation and equipment.

You could reduce their numbers in two ways. One by making them more productive. Why should not pupils learn by themselves? For example, by using packages or programmes on a teaching machine or a computer. Why not use 'aides', that is to say full or part-time assistants to whom teachers could delegate the more routine tasks? Ever since the late fifties and especially during Harold Wilson's floruit, when anything with the word 'technology' attached to it was received as though it would release untold benefits, the Department of Education have peddled such wares. Anthony Crosland (Secretary of State for Education from January 1965 to August 1967) was at one time greatly enamoured of what 'educational technology' might do and a

Table 1: Statisitics of Manpower Employed in Education (United Kingdom)

	1970/71 000s	1975/76 000s	1980/81 000s	1984/85 000s Percentage who were graduates
Full-time teachers and lecturers				
Schools:				
Public sector:				
Primary schools	203	240	222	200 23.2
Secondary schools	199	259	281	271 60.9
Non-maintained schools	36	39	43	49 65.4
Special schools	10	17	19	19 30.1
Total	448	555	565	540 46.3
Establishments of further education	69	86	89	93 45.2
Universities	29	32	34	31 98.9
Total educational establishments	546	677	693	667 48.5
Other employees (local authority only)				
Part-time teachers and lecturers	...	21	41	42 ...
Full-time support staff	...	253	235	210 ...
Part-time support staff	...	230	242	227 ...

1. Includes nursery schools.
2. Excludes independent schools in Scotland and Northern Ireland.
3. Includes former colleges of education.
4. Excludes Open University. There were 687 professors and lecturers and 5219 part-time tutorial and counselling staff employed by the Open University at January 1985. Also excludes the Independent University College of Buckingham.
5. Includes miscellaneous teachers in England and Wales (3.6 thousand in 1984/85) not shown elsewhere above.
6. Full-time equivalents.
7. Great Britain only. Figures for 1980/81 onwards include further education and unqualified teachers in Scotland.
8. Great Britain data from the Department of Employment.

Source: Social Trends (1987), CSO/HMSO, Table 3.2.

Table 2: The Cost of Running a Private School

The average cost per pupil for senior independent day schools for 1985-86 together with the percentage that the total of each cost bears to the total general fee income.

	£ per pupil	Average costs Percentage to general fee
Salaries: Teaching	1,007.6	60.9
Other	101.6	6.1
Wages	56.1	3.4
National Insurance	75.1	4.5
Catering: Provisions	36.8	2.2
Wages	39.2	2.4
Books and teaching materials	56.1	3.4
Games and equipment	10.0	0.6
Laundry	1.3	0.1
General expenses	51.8	3.1
Rates, insurance, repairs, fuel, etc.	289.5	17.4.

Source: Independent schools costs survey by MacIntyre Hudson, Chartered Accountants.

Council of Educational Technology (CET) consisting initially of selected whizz kids was set up; needless to say it did not yield the expected results. Teaching machines, now long since abandoned, did not reduce the need for teachers, and still less did computers which if anything, require more teachers.

Aides have had an even more bumpy ride. Despite the protests of would-be innocent politicians the teacher unions never seem to have entertained any doubt that the object of aides was to adulterate the teaching profession. To some extent the arguments about aides were related to teacher shortage. Since the shortage has in general gone, less is heard about them as a cost-cutting device and fortunately the hubbub has not prevented quite a number of LEAs from recruiting teachers' helpers who can offer genuine assistance in the classroom without the threat of usurping the teachers' role. Audio and video cassettes, together with computer programmes have also clearly a big contribution to make. Self-learning packages are in growing use, promoted notably by the MSC's Open College, in industry and commerce, but these are in situations where it is not practical to provide a teacher. For the truth is—and it is quite crucial to any consideration of educational finance—that there is no substitute for the teacher. Ministers of Education have to swallow hard and accept that fact or else look forward to a very short future.

But is there not another way to reduce the number of teachers—simply to make them teach larger classes? The argument was actually much deployed in the fifties and sixties that reducing the size of classes produced poor teaching results and research was quoted from the United States and Britain to prove it. It is sufficient to say here that not a shred of this research has stood the test of further enquiry and it is extraordinary that anyone ever supposed that it would. Otherwise the independent schools would be advertising their larger classes; in fact one of their much vaunted boons is their smaller classes. MacIntyre Hudson, the Chartered Accountants, who analyze costs for the independent schools annually, confirm the figure for non-maintained schools in table 3; for day preparatory schools, the pupil : teacher ratio (PTR) averages thirteen, mostly within the range eleven–fifteen (the figures are for 1985). This does not compare directly with the figure of twenty-two for primary schools in table 3, because the age range is rather different, but it is not far out.

As table 3 shows, PTRs have steadily improved since 1971. It would be nice to think that this was the consequence of deliberate policy, but even the most opportunist of politicians have generally fought shy of claiming this. It is the declining numbers of children in schools that have wrought the improvement and the failure of the Department of Education and Science to close schools and cut down the numbers of teachers in line with the declining school population. They have of course tried. Every year there is a lengthy wrangle between the DES representatives and the LEAs over the number of schools that the LEAs can reasonably be expected to close. The DES figures have always been impossible say the LEAs—and so, in the event, they have proved. The stories are legion of how difficult it is for an LEA to close a school and there is the added irony that the main opposition is almost invariably political. That is to say, the local MP makes representations to the Minister over the heads of the LEA arguing that the local political balance is too threatening to allow a school to be shut down; and so it remains open.

It is a fair argument, though, that there ought to be a bottom limit to PTRs. Large classes seriously impede good teaching, but a class can be too small to act as a satisfactory learning community. This remains at present an academic

Table 3: Pupil/Teacher Ratios (United Kingdom)

	1971	1981	1985	1990 (plan)
Public sector schools				
Nursery	26.6	21.5	21.8	...
Primary	27.1	22.3	22.0	...
Secondary	17.8	16.4	15.9	...
All public sector schools	23.2	19.0	18.5	17.0
Non-maintained schools	14.0	13.2	11.7	...
Special schools	10.5	7.5	6.8	...
All schools	22.0	18.2	17.5	...

Source: Education Statistics for the United Kingdom, Department of Education and Science.

point. Few LEAs have yet faced up to the biggest single classroom issue to emerge from the 1985/87 teacher dispute, namely the adequate provision of cover for teachers' absence. This is made all the more serious by the current emphasis on in-service training for teachers, so the demand for good quality teachers remains.

All political parties would accept this; the question is can the community afford a large army of good quality teachers? Can they, as in Japan or Hungary, be paid less compared with other workers or, alternatively, can the profession be so structured that those at the top get high salaries and those at the bottom very much less, so that the global cost is much reduced. Leaving aside the question of whether such policies are desirable, it is far, far too late to attempt to implement them. Arguably, the biggest single reform of 1944 was not so much the Butler Act, important though that was, but the unification of teachers' salaries which ended the great division between primary school teachers on the one hand and secondary on the other. Burnham scales were unified and over the years though incredibly belatedly, there has been a measure of unification in teacher training as well, so that by the eighties newly-trained teachers are all graduates. Equally arguably, as the NUT have long since contended, there is such a thing as a 'primary-secondary differential'. That is to say the teachers' salary settlements have so operated that the average salary in secondary schools has been higher than in primary, but the differential has been nothing like as great as in other countries, where for the most part primary and secondary schools have remained separated. The other way of creating a primary-secondary differential is to engineer things (as has happened in Italy) so that primary school teachers are almost all women. That has not happened in Britain; the sexes are more or less balanced in the teaching profession and in any case there is equal pay.

But any argument about restructuring teachers' pay begs a bigger question. What is to be done about the erosion of salaries since the Houghton award of May 1974 which added 29 per cent to teachers' salaries in the long-term and the further increase in salaries a year later of some 22 per cent, following an arbitration award. Some measure of how far teachers have lost out relatively has been produced by the research unit of the NUT comparing salary levels in different countries. The source of the NUT's data is the Union Bank of Switzerland's annual review of 'Prices and Earnings around the Globe'. This gives not only earnings but also the costs of a wide range of goods and services in various cities. Table 4 is derived from these data. In the second column are shown gross salaries, that is to say before tax, of primary school teachers in each city, defined as 'a 35-year-old man who has been teaching for about ten years in the primary school system'. The figures in the foreign currencies have been converted directly to pounds sterling. The first column adjusts the salaries in the light of a typical 'basket' of some 126 goods and services. The basket costs nearly three times as much in New York as in Lisbon. London, it turns out, is more expensive than ten of the other cities with prices very close to those in Geneva. Column 1 therefore gives the

Table 4: Primary Teachers' Salaries Compared (£s)

	Gross	Price Adjusted
Geneva	23,682	23,921
Luxembourg	14,656	18,790
Toronto	21,363	16,955
Sydney	16,726	15,930
Dusseldorf	12,089	13,896
Amsterdam	9,936	13,428
Copenhagen	12,503	12,380
New York	24,178	11,681
Dublin	10,019	11,258
Stockholm	10,599	10,391
Brussels	8,860	9,630
Oslo	12,089	9,519
Madrid	7,866	9,365
London	9,274	9,274
Helsinki	9,771	8,142
Paris	7,452	8,100
Tokyo	15,650	7,786
Athens	5,713	6,968
Lisbon	3,312	5,430

Source: National Union of Teachers based on Union Bank of Switzerland figures.

price-adjusted salary. Of nineteen cities, London comes fourteenth. It hardly suggests that British salaries are in any way excessive.

Even with the Baker increases of 1987, teachers will still be a long way from their Houghton prosperity. As a result of the Houghton recommendation, the average pay of teachers at 1 April 1974 was £3080 per annum while the average pay for all non-manual workers was £2259 per annum. Teachers' average pay was, therefore, 136 per cent of non-manual average pay. As a consequence of the Baker award, the teachers' average pay at 1 January 1987 and 1 October 1987 stood at £12,237 and £13,241 respectively. Non-manual average pay as a whole was £11,053 and £11,659 respectively. To restore teachers to the same level set by Houghton relative to non-manual workers generally, would have required the teachers' average pay to be £15,065 and £15,891, that is to say, increases of a further 23 and 20 per cent on the Baker levels. The government would, of course, argue that the proper comparison is to be found by looking at movements in prices and not movement in earnings. Between 1974 and January 1987 prices increased by 267 per cent which makes the Baker figures respectable. Not unreasonably, the NUT point out that earnings for non-manual workers increased in the same period by 356 per cent and that is what the Houghton criteria were all about.

This kind of argument is, of course, anathema to those with Thatcherite convictions. They contend that the market should prevail. Comparisons with other professionals' salaries, with those of teachers abroad, and with what happened in history become irrelevant. What matters is the market now for teachers. The market favours labour which is being sold in London or highly qualified labour such as mathematicians and physicists requiring jobs in secondary schools, but the market is weak for primary school teachers in Wales or in Yorkshire. Why not, then, pay teachers on a regional or an LEA basis or even school by school? Let the market rule and see the cost of teachers come down. This is nothing new, it is a system which applied after a fashion before the Second World War and was one good reason why a unified Burnham scale came into existence. Could it work? It can be said at once that it is most unlikely to work in further education or in Scotland, simply because almost all the teachers in FE are in one union and the large majority of teachers in Scotland are in the Educational Institute of Scotland. But among teachers in England and Wales there must be considerable doubts. Most teachers are divided into three large unions—the NUT, NAS/UWT and AMMA plus two smaller ones (Professional Association of Teachers (PAT) and the Welsh teachers union (UCAC). Even the headteachers are divided into the NAHT and the SHA (see chapter 8). In the history of education, since the beginning of the century, there could be no more open invitation to a government to divide and rule.

Numbers in the Schools

The big cost in education—the number of teachers—depends obviously on the number of pupils and the number of pupils at any one time depends chiefly on the birth rate between five and sixteen years ago. In its essentials the cost of education is summed up in that sentence. When the birthrate began to go down following the post-Second World War baby boom, the anxieties of those politicians and civil servants who were taking a more and more jaundiced view of educational finance began to lighten. Watching the birthrate became almost an obsession. Were there deep-rooted changes going on in attitudes to the family? Would the birthrate plummet down and down? In England and Wales in 1964 the birthrate got to a record high of almost 900,000; by 1977 it had dropped to 568,000. But in 1978 up it went by 4.7 per cent and in 1979 by a further 7.8 per cent. This kind of thing makes life very difficult though a lot more interesting for statisticians and the game began of speculating on 'high variants', that is to say optimistic guesses and 'low variants' or pessimistic ones and inevitably 'principal variants' in between the two. But up to 1991, at least, we can be pretty sure what the outcome will be for the schools; figure 1 spells out the story from 1975 to that date.

It is some consolation in this as in other matters that Britain has not stood alone. In most countries comparable with Britain, births fell throughout the latter years of the 1960s or else at the beginning of the 1970s. In many countries numbers of pupils in primary education have been falling for several years and everywhere there has been at least the opportunity to reduce the average class size and the pupil : teacher ratio in primary schools has improved

Millions

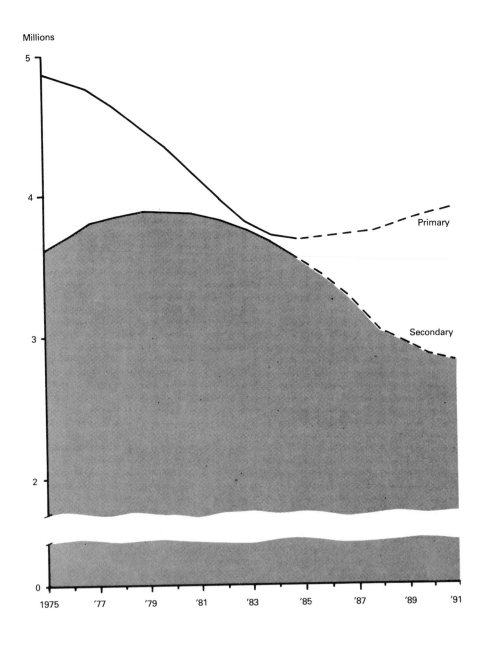

Figure 1: Pupil numbers 1975–1991 (maintained schools in England)
Source: National Audit Office—Falling School Rolls

almost everywhere. Between 1964 and 1978 the number of births practically halved in Germany (a 46 per cent drop)—a good deal more than the UK 34 per cent fall in the same period. In the United States between 1957 and 1973 the fall was 28 per cent. Primary pupil enrolments between 1982 and 1987 fell by some 10 per cent or more in Australia, Denmark, France, Italy, the Netherlands, Norway and Sweden. Student numbers in secondary schools have fallen considerably in the early eighties in Austria, Belgium, Canada, Finland, Germany, Greece, the Netherlands, Norway, Switzerland and the United States as well as the UK and like the UK there will be heavy falls—as much as a fifth to a quarter of 1982 levels by 1990—in Austria, Denmark, Germany, Italy, the Netherlands, Norway and Switzerland.

A Decline in Spending?

If there are fewer children to educate then no government is going to go on spending at the same rate and still less at an increasing one. So it is not surprising that most countries of the Western world, which had been almost generous in their spending on education in the 1960s and early 1970s, began to rein in. Education spending used to be ahead of health and in one or two instances even defence. Now it is generally behind health and especially behind pensions. Canada, Italy, Sweden and New Zealand applied serious cutbacks to educational spending in the early 1970s to be followed by Australia and the Netherlands and, of course, the UK later in the 1970s. In Italy, education's share of the GDP began to recover in the 1980s as it did in Ireland and Belgium and it has to be said that in West Germany, Austria and Sweden, since the middle seventies education has more or less held its own. Not that these international figures can be probed too deeply. Different countries mean different things by 'education'. It is not always clear how far 'non-formal activities' such as the UK's Youth Training Scheme form part of educational expenditure and this after all cost £1000 million in 1982/83 in the UK. Indeed, in the UK spending on work preparation and experience programmes nearly tripled between 1974/75 and 1980/81 rising from the equivalent of 9 per cent of total spending on formal education to 11 per cent. The Canadians, on the other hand, actually cut the share of spending on vocational training in the same period.

It is also not clear how far private education figures in the statistics. The OECD believed in 1985 that in general private spending had probably fallen as public authorities took over more and more responsibilities that had formerly been in private hands, but when household expenditure is examined, it looks as though private spending in many countries may now be quite substantial. In the UK the estimate is that it actually doubled between the 1960s and the 1970s probably representing some 0.5 per cent of the GDP in 1981 (i.e. some £1000 million). The Japanese figure is probably considerably higher and in 1980 was estimated as 3 per cent of the GDP.

Tudor David

Table 5: Education within the gross domestic product and public expenditure (UK)

	Public spending as % of GDP	Education spending as % of GDP	Education spending as % of public spending
1979/80	43.25	5.3	12.2
1980/81	46	5.7	12.3
1981/82	46.25	5.6	12.0
1982/83	46.75	5.5	11.7
1983/84	45.25	5.4	11.7
1984/85	45.5	5.1	11.3
1985/86	44	4.9	11.1
1986/87	43.25	5.1	11.8
1987/88 plans	42.75	5.0	11.6
1988/89 plans	41.75	4.9	11.7
1989/90 plans	41.25	4.7	11.5

Sources: Autumn Statement 1986, Cm 14, table 2.1; the Government's Expenditure Plans, Cmnd 9428 and Cm 56.

So, comparisons of GDP proportions spent on education are not all that useful. Generally speaking, though, you would expect to find a proportion of between 5 and 7 per cent of GDP spent on education in an advanced industrial country and some 10–15 per cent of total public expenditure. Those figures for the UK for the present decade are shown in table 5. It cannot be argued from these figures that a declining proportion means cuts or indeed that an increasing proportion does not mean cuts. The figures have to be read in the light of changes in the school population, as shown in figure 1.

Table 6 moves to a more detailed scrutiny on how spending on education has changed, extending to the plans that at present exist up to 1989/90. It does not go back before 1980/81 chiefly for practical reasons. For one thing in 1976/77 the Treasury changed their ways of accounting from volume to cash terms and without going into the difference that makes, it renders comparisons with previous years unduly complicated. Secondly, there continues to be much confusion between figures for the UK, GB, England and Wales and just plain England, especially since the Welsh Office set up its own statisitical shop. The figures in the table are for England save that in the case of universities and research councils they embrace the UK. It does not matter; the object of the exercise is to look at trends and they are much the same throughout the UK. The figures are also in *real terms*, that is to say they are made comparable by converting them all to 1986/87 prices.

The summary table, table 7, is another exercise in real terms set out more clearly by making the 1981/82 figures equal 100 and comparing the subsequent actual and planned spending up to 1989/90.

Table 6: Education expenditure 1981–82 to 1989–90

	1981–82 outturn	1982–83 outturn	1983–84 outturn	1984–85 outturn	1985–86 outturn[1]	1986–87 estimated outturn[2]	£ million at 1986–87 prices		
							1987–88 plans	1988–89 plans	1989–90 plans
Schools	9,189	9,100	9,123	9,046	8,920	9,923	9,962	10,151	10,139
Higher and further education	4,571	4,707	4,744	4,739	4,523	4,592	4,476	4,470	4,466
Miscellaneous educational services, research and administration	772	789	839	852	867	924	934	922	922
Research Councils and related bodies	575	573	589	596	604	615	632	624	615
Total Department of Education and Science	15,105	15,168	15,294	15,232	14,913	15,954	16,004	16,157	16,130
Central governments— Voted in Estimates									
Schools									
Assisted places scheme	4	10	17	24	30	37	48	51	53
City technology colleges	—	—	—	—	—	—	4	18	30
Music and ballet schools	7	4	3	3	3	3	3	4	4
Building grants to voluntary and special schools	56	46	43	49	56	50	52	51	50
Higher and further education (including teacher training)[4]									
Universities									
Capital	153	144	135	132	138	154	148	143	140
Current	1,331	1,497	1,487	1,463	1,416	1,411	1,456	1,455	1,455
Voluntary and direct grant institutions									
Capital	3	5	5	6	5	6	5	5	5
Current	100	103	100	93	88	90	92	92	91

Table 6: (Continued)

	1981–82 outturn	1982–83 outturn	1983–84 outturn	1984–85 outturn	1985–86 outturn[1]	1986–87 estimated outturn[2]	£ million at 1986–87 prices 1987–88 plans	1988–89 plans	1989–90 plans
Adult education	13	13	15	15	15	15	15	15	15
Postgraduate awards to humanities students and other student awards	8	7	4	5	4	6	6	7	7
Miscellaneous services, research and administration									
Youth service	5	4	4	4	4	4	4	4	4
Research programme and other education services	20	18	22	23	24	23	25	24	23
Administration and inspection costs	40	39	51	53	53	54	56	55	55
Compensation payments	5	4	5	6	6	6	6	6	6
Research Councils, etc.									
Capital	91	91	86	84	93	88	74	74	73
Current (including postgraduate science awards)	485	482	502	512	511	527	558	548	542
Total voted expenditure	2,319	2,468	2,479	2,470	2,445	2,474	2,552	2,550	2,553
Other central government Schools	– 5	– 4	– 4	– 4	– 4	—	—	—	—
Total central government	2,314	2,463	2,475	2,466	2,441	2,474	2,552	2,550	2,553
Of which: Total central government capital expenditure	302	283	265	269	289	299	282	279	271

Local authorities— Relevant current spending

Schools									
Under fives	307	326	337	361	363	402	407	416	424
Primary schools	2,880	2,794	2,751	2,713	2,696	3,031	3,133	3,205	3,272
Secondary schools	4,215	4,216	4,252	4,213	4,143	4,573	4,648	4,762	4,665
Special schools	443	454	469	472	464	503	508	508	514
Meals and milk	505	489	485	467	451	455	434	432	429
Transport	222	219	222	217	213	219	206	200	196
Non-maintained school fees	136	136	134	132	125	125	118	114	109
Teacher centres	27	27	27	31	32	35	40	42	42
Child guidance	33	33	32	34	35	39	39	39	39
Pupil support	31	31	31	35	36	38	36	36	38
Higher and further education[4]									
Advanced further education	642	724	724	730	719	743	707	729	735
Non-advanced further education	1,008	1,045	1,060	1,090	1,017	1,013	985	966	956
Adult education	85	92	98	102	105	110	107	107	108
Discretionary student awards and support	136	144	150	155	165	183	190	196	203
Miscellaneous services, research and administration									
Youth service	110	115	124	128	134	148	152	156	160
Recreational services and research	52	55	61	63	66	73	74	78	80
Administration and inspection costs	517	517	543	549	553	590	602	589	578
Total relevant current spending	11,348	11,418	11,502	11,492	11,317	12,283	12,386	12,576	12,548

Table 6: (Continued)

£ million at 1986–87 prices

	1981–82 outturn	1982–83 outturn	1983–84 outturn	1984–85 outturn	1985–86 outturn[1]	1986–87 estimated outturn[2]	1987–88 plans	1988–89 plans	1989–90 plans
Non-relevant current spending Mandatory student awards[4]	983	796	835	812	732	724	714	706	705
Local authority capital[3]									
Schools	328	317	323	298	277	310	288	271	268
Higher and further education	109	139	132	136	121	135	50	46	46
Miscellaneous education services:									
Youth service	8	14	11	13	11	11	8	7	7
Other education services	17	21	17	14	15	15	6	5	5
Total local authority capital	461	491	483	461	424	471	351	329	326
Total local authorities	12,791	12,706	12,820	12,766	12,472	13,479	13,452	13,611	13,578
Total Department of Education and Science	15,105	15,168	15,294	15,232	14,913	15,954	16,004	16,157	16,130

[1] The 1985–86 figures incorporate a distribution by sector of total current spending by local authorities based on their provisional outturn expenditure on education.
[2] The 1986–87 figures incorporate a provisional distribution by sector of total current spending by local authorities based on their budgets.
[3] From 1981–82 local authority capital expenditure includes provision for the urban programme.
[4] The change in the trend of higher education and student award figures between 1981-82 and 1982-83 reflects the reduction in tuition fees described in Cmnd. 8494.
Source Fourth Report from the House of Commons Education, Science and Arts Select Committee (1987) Cmnd 56, London, HMSO.

Table 7: Education current expenditure, in real terms indexed

	1981–82	1982–83	1983–84	1984–85	1985–86	1986–87 Estimate	1987–88 plan	1988–89 plan	1989–90 plan
Primary	100	97.0	95.5	94.2	93.6	105.2	108.8	111.3	113.6
Secondary	100	100.0	100.9	100.0	98.3	108.5	110.3	113.0	110.7
Special schools	100	102.5	105.9	106.5	104.7	113.5	114.7	114.7	116.0
Non–advanced FE	100	103.7	105.2	108.1	100.9	100.5	97.7	95.8	94.8
Advanced FE	100	112.8	112.8	113.7	112.0	115.7	110.1	113.6	114.5
Universities	100	112.5	111.7	109.9	106.4	106.0	109.4	109.3	109.3
Research councils	100	99.4	103.5	105.6	105.4	108.7	115.1	113.0	111.8

Note: Figures for England only, except for universities (GB) and research councils (UK).
Non–advanced FE figures are affected by the transfer of 25 per cent of the service to the Manpower Services Commission for 1985–86.

Source: Derived from DES Memorandum table 12 House of Commons Education Select Committee's 4th Report (1987), Cmnd 56, London, HMSO.

So Where are the Cuts?

So much for the statistical facts such as they are. On the face of it, it would be hard to draw the conclusion that they point to a continual squeeze on educational spending. Indeed, all the pundits would agree that in real terms spending has actually increased. In a period when there are falling rolls it would be hard for it to be otherwise because even if there were cuts, if pupil numbers fall faster than the decline in the budget then there will still be improvements in unit costs. In other words more is being spent on fewer pupils. So it cannot be argued that government policy has necessarily sustained spending, rather that it has proved impossible for a number of reasons to reduce spending faster than the decline in the number of pupils. However, it is fair to say that during Mrs Thatcher's floruit at the DES, as has already been noted, more resources were released and it looks as though Mr Kenneth Baker may well achieve the same supposing the figures in tables 6 and 7 are held to.

Nevertheless, the belief that there have been cuts and that there should be a great increase if not a surge of spending on the schools and higher education has prevailed for years and shows every sign of growing. It is not simply that people's expectations have been raised by all the growth in the sixties; the evidence is thrown up in articles in the press, public speeches and campaigns, that the cuts are real. Deputations from parents' groups (which grow more articulate at national level), the representations of teacher unions and local authorities, the unprecedented denial of an honorary degree to the Prime Minister, Mrs Thatcher, by the University of Oxford on the straight grounds of the educational cutbacks, are among the many manifestations of this. Most telling of all is the evidence of Her Majesty's Inspectors of Schools. They produce an annual report on the state of the schools and how well or badly the LEAs are running the system. The reports have not been reassuring. The condition of schools in some LEAs has been nothing short of a scandal. So why blameless statistics on the one hand and angry protests on the other?

There is a complete answer to this question, although it is lengthy and not without its complexities. It has to be recognized firstly that the educational system in the UK as in most other countries was not planned on the basis of some grand blueprint and fully resourced in its application. Its various parts, schools, vocational training, further education and universities are only loosely related to each other and in many respects not related at all. Each constituent fights its own corner. In particular, the teachers—the biggest single resource—fight their own battles and are usually rewarded not because of the needs of the system but for quite different reasons such as how they compare with other professions in salary. No-one, least of all the Secretary of State, sits down to manage still less to plan, the whole system in a coherent way and almost certainly no-one ever will. Of course there are bursts of spending—such as followed the *Sputnik* on technical education and such as happened to school building when the school leaving age was raised.

But when public spending has to be reined in—such as followed the visitation from the International Monetary Fund in 1976—anything that can be cut easily such as the maintenance of school building or spending on books is cut with alacrity. So it is not surprising when a major attempt was made in 1977 at a conspectus of the physical condition of the schools of England and Wales—*A Study of School Building*—it was shown that on a conservative estimate £1.5 billion needed to be spent to bring the schools up to a satisfactory condition. The prevailing politicians instantly agreed that this was impossible and the truth is that very little money has been found to put matters right. The first point to be made then is that there is a massive backlog in the provision of resources on the ground and it would take a massive injection of capital to cope with it. The same kind of basic inadequacy applies to books and educational equipment as John Davies chronicles elsewhere in this book.

Some LEAs are, of course, better providers than others and therein lies the second point. Given over 100 LEAs it is not surprising that there are differences between them and it has never been difficult to find LEAs with a shocking record of under-provision. Some indeed have been openly stig-matized by HMI, among them Somerset, Wiltshire and Norfolk. Others, such as Sheffield, have been singled out for praise even by that super watchdog of LEA spending, the Audit Commission. Since there are over 100 LEAs there must be over 100 stories to relate about educational spending, since they have some measure of independence to go their own way within limits. But those limits have been getting tighter and tighter. Indeed the history of local government finance is largely an account of how central government has become more and more strict, if not downright oppressive, towards the LEAs. Even so the differences between LEAs are quite marked. In the period between 1979/80 and 1984/85 for example, Hounslow managed to increase its spending on primary schooling by 12.14 per cent, while South Tyneside reduced its spending by 19.63 per cent. In these comparisons falling rolls have to be taken into account but much the same variation applies to a comparison of unit costs in primary schools; though in nearly all authorities the unit costs went up (in fact in only seven LEAs did they fall). In several there was an increase of between 20-25 per cent. For example, again between 1979/80 and 1984/85, Walsall's unit costs went up by 25.6 per cent and Nottinghamshire's by 24.2 per cent, but Bedfordshire's actually reduced by 2.5 per cent and Durham's by 2.4 per cent.

Much the same story can be told of the secondary schools but the spread of the figures is a good deal more than in primary schools. Over the same period Haringey increased its unit costs in secondary schools by 30.2 per cent, the ILEA by 22.3 per cent. Cheshire on the other hand reduced unit costs by 7.7 per cent and Cambridgeshire by 2 per cent. Rapidly falling rolls in the inner city must have had a good deal to do with this contrast. But it isn't all falling rolls; some councils have been compliant, others have been rebellious and pushed central government almost to the point of frenzy, the consequences of which have ironically been heaped on the just almost as much as on the unjust.

The third point to be made about spending is that those figures in the tables are not as inoffensive as they may seem. When it is said that the comparisons are made 'real' it means that account is taken of the effects of inflation. When inflation is properly considered, then, it should be possible to compare directly the spending of 1986/87 with say 1980/81. But this begs the question—what is meant by inflation? Inflation in wages—to take an obvious example—is often if not usually proceeding at a different rate from the inflation of prices. And among the millions of price changes, some prices are going up faster than others. This happens to be especially true of prices of educational goods and services. What might be called educational prices are regularly measured by the local authority associations and published in *Rate Support Grant (England)* as a table, and there are startling differences between one set of 'deflators' and another. These differences are crucial in the effects they have. Suppose an education authority spent £100 million in 1979/80 and had raised this to £156 million in 1984/85. This, using the government's deflator would represent a 2.5 per cent *increase*. Using the local authority's measure of *education* costs, it shows a *decrease* of 3.2 per cent.

There is further pressure on these increasing costs (and this is the fourth point) deriving from the government's own educational initiatives. As it happens there have been a number of significant ones in recent years, the microcomputer in schools being perhaps the most obvious one. But there is also the emphasis on craft, design and technology in schools, the focus on English as a second language and mother tongue teaching and the introduction of the new GCSE examination—with some additional resources it is true but on all sides claimed to be not enough. Add to this the rising proportion of children qualifying under 'additional educational needs', in part the consequence of the Warnock Report. Any LEA trying seriously to apply these national policies as well as its own local ones is bound to strain the purse strings.

Finally, education, like other social services, once into an expansionist phase as it was in the 1960s generates a kind of in-built expansion. This is no argument for allowing it to continue but there are circumstances in which curtailment becomes severely damaging. The best example is on the science side of the DES. The claim of research scientists that science has been cut is even more strident than that of people in education, yet the government again claims (and table 6 supports them) that real spending has been sustained. Yet it was estimated in 1986 that Britain has been losing a thousand or so highly trained scientists and engineers a year (though not all of them in academic research). This may be in some measure desirable, but there is equally no doubt that too many promising research lines have had to be abandoned or remained unexplored and this in a country whose science is one of its most notable national assets. It is doubtful if any country can sustain its place in science unless it accepts that a measure of growth is necessary.

The Conservative government's reaction to this has been predictable.

Enough public money is being spent and it is high time industry devoted more resources to research and development, the United States being cited as the great exemplar. The difficulty is that changing the structure of research funding is not going to happen overnight; it could take decades. Meanwhile the brain-drain goes on.

Funding the LEAs

Much the same thinking has been applied in prevailing Conservative circles to education in schools, further education and the universities. Industry financed trade schools in the nineteenth century, why not now? In 1980s guise they are the city technology colleges (CTCs) and 'industry and commerce' are asked to be the paymasters. A network of CTCs could, perhaps, lead to the privatization of all the schools at least at a secondary level. The CTCs are not, of course, presented as fiscal in purpose but as concrete examples of what technology-oriented schools can do. An experiment of that kind, if it is needed, could equally well be carried through within selected LEAs.

The effect of the CTCs will be wholly disruptive within the present system and could well become a costly failure, with LEAs left to pick up the pieces as the new local authorities founded after the 1902 Education Act had to do for many of the trade schools. (Not that the CTCs were the first intervention by central government into the LEA domain. The direct grant schools and their successor, the Assisted Places Scheme, were other devices by Conservative administrations to protect and enlarge privilege which the LEAs were generally unwilling to do, though there have always been some local authorities which have directly subsidized independent schools. Somehow the resources have always been available to meet this purpose.)

The desire to prevent the main engines of the system—the LEAs—getting into high gear has afflicted all governments whatever their political complexion. The anxieties over LEA spending took serious shape with the abolition of the percentage grant system in the 1950s despite the hostility of the then powerful Association of Education Committees (AEC) (representing the LEAs) and the main teachers' union, the National Union of Teachers. This method of grant-aiding local authorities—that is, providing them with most of their income—directly benefited the high spenders though it cannot be said that the low spenders seemed to be much discomfited by this. The Treasury never liked it and in the end Whitehall saddled the local authorities with what became known as a Rate Support Grant system (RSG). Most of the RSG is in the form of a 'block grant', that is to say it is not specified for particular services. In theory it can be spent by a local authority in any way it chooses. Since education occupies such a large part of local authority spending (in most counties at least 60 per cent and in most metropolitan districts 70 per cent or more) there were fears that education's share would be diminished, especially when after 1974 education became more 'corporate' in character. It was, in fact, the declared aim of some of the more articulate councillors who emerged in that post-1974 period to cut education down to size. There were LEAs where the education interest was rendered subservient and people in education offices were in effect humiliated. By and large though, education survived. It was after all far and away the most important and universal service within any local authority and unless education were given its head, the Shire counties and metropolitan districts would turn into very small fry. When in the early eighties the DES floated the idea of an education block grant, the corporatists within local government were at once up in arms. They could see the writing on the wall, for an education block grant might lead to education becoming a quite separate local service as it is in a number of countries, notably the United States where the schools are run by local school boards. It is a solution to education finance that has a number of influential advocates and it is not likely to go away, especially as in 1986, the Inner London Education Authority became the first exclusively education authority in England.

The RSG failed to curb education expenditure because in the sixties and early seventies education in this country, as in others, entered into its great period of expansion. Even so, politically, the RSG was not without its uses. The most telling example of this occurs in the Crossman diaries. Richard Crossman revealed in his diaries that in October 1968, Edward Short (then Secretary of State for Education) presented his resignation to the Prime Minister (until the *Diaries* were published, no-one knew this). How Mr Short was persuaded not to resign offers an instructive lesson in the use of fiscal devices:

> This evening the phone rang and the Prime Minister said, 'This is really urgent. Would you come over straightaway?' I trotted round to find him sitting in his study with Roy Jenkins. Mr Short had resigned. He had sent a letter saying that the Prime Minister must make some sense of the education cuts that he had been asked to accept. If the Chancellor insisted on the £10 million increase in further education fees Mr Short would go. The PM said, 'This is really serious. It could be disastrous for the Government.' It was true. Ted Short, an ex-Chief Whip from the centre-right of the Party—if he resigned and spilt the beans on the educational cuts it could create a kind of Bevanite revolt. I saw this immediately. The Chancellor on the other hand wasn't willing to give an inch, so I said to the PM, 'Look, it's quite simple. The first thing to do is play it off. Thank your lucky stars for what we did about the rate support grant. We needn't have all these announcements of cuts and we can postpone the issue. Play it out, Roy. You can still get your cuts but at least let us stop him resigning this week. The reason he has given for resigning now is that he is compelled to make a statement announcing the £10 million increase on Thursday evening, the day before he goes off for two days

in the North. You defuse this by merely saying, "You needn't make a statement".' 'Is that really true?' asked the Prime Minister and Roy was very dubious. Finally we agreed to meet at 10 p.m. and that I should bring Matthew Stevenson with me for a proper discussion. Roy couldn't possibly be there so we would have Fred Peart instead. I went back again with Matthew Stevenson. Ted Short was there and we spent till 12.30 a.m. convincing him, not with drink because he is a teetotaller. What did I give him in exchange? I first got Steve to say, as head of the negotiators for the rate support grant, that they didn't need the announcement and indeed it would be slightly convenient for them not to have it. Steve loyally supported everything I said because I had had a long discussion with him beforehand, cleared it up and got it in writing. He couldn't have been better on this occasion. He was in on high politics and excited that he was doing it well. We gave this to Ted Short, who swallowed it hook, line and sinker.

It was in 1976, however, that the squeeze on the block grant really began. It followed the visitation by the International Monetary Fund representatives, which had such a profound effect on Peter Shore and other members of the Labour Cabinet. When the Conservatives were elected in 1979 the process continued. One simple way of turning the screw was ready to hand by reducing the percentage of rate support grant paid to local authorities. Table 8 shows just how this was done. But the Department of the Environment wanted more, for some LEAs managed to 'overspend' despite the RSG cut. They were 'profligate', said Michael Heseltine, then at the Department of the Environment, and he began a crusade against the overspenders. A system of tapering off the grant was devised, followed in 1981 by a system of targets and penalties. In 1984 rate-capping was proposed and thus began the saga of the rebel local authorities. One kind of ingenious mechanism was piled upon another to make sure that no local authority got away with anything, so much so that by the early months of 1987, legislation had to be introduced to sort out all the mistakes that the Department of the Environment had made in actually operating Rate Support Grant and the rest of its paraphernalia. Still the high spenders seemed to be spending more than they ought and then came the ultimate in proposed draconian measures, the introduction of a so-called community charge or poll tax. At last the profligates would be well and truly clobbered. In Camden (within the ILEA), for example, it was estimated that in 1986/87 the average rates per household were £745. The community charge per adult over 18 would be £652 per person, in other words if there were two adults in the household, the total cost would be £1304. Similarly, in Sheffield the average rate bill for a household was £444 in 1986/87 but the community charge for two adults in a house would amount to £650. LEAs with charges of this magnitude would soon be made to bite the dust by their electorates.

Tudor David

This will pose the biggest single challenge to the present system of administering education. For running education by way of a local system is bound up irretrievably with the method of financing it. If the system of finance collapses then it is hard to see local education authorities in their present form surviving. That would clearly suit some of the Tory radicals who would like to see the system handed over to the schools which could be

Table 8: Relevant expenditure, total exchequer assistance and grant percentage at settlement 1967/68 to 1986/87 (England and Wales)

Local education authorities get their income from various sources: rates, rent, borrowing through the market, interest payments and other minor sources of income, but above all from the Exchequer by way of a 'rate support grant'. This grant gives the government a powerful lever; LEA spending can be forced down by reducing the RSG and it will be seen from the table that ever since 1976/77 this is what has happened.

		Relevant expenditure at settlement	Total Exchequer assistance at settlement	Grant percentage at settlement
1967–68		2,557	1,381	54
1968–69		2,726	1,499	55
1969–70		2,976	1,667	56
1970–71		3,128	1,783	57
1971–72		3,795	2,182	57.5
1972–73		3,970	2,303	58
1973–74		5,216	3,130	60
1974–75		5,671	3,431	60.5 (65.3)
1975–76		8,171	5,434	66.5
1976–77		10,461	6,852	65.5
1977–78		11,717	7,147	61
1978–79		12,531	7,644	61
1979–80		14,109	8,607	61
1980–81		15,737	9,600	61
1981–82	England	18,423	10,895	59.1
	Wales	1,187	871	73.4
	England and Wales	19,610	11,766	60.0
1982–83	England	20,463	11,484	56.1
	Wales	1,301	943	72.5
	England and Wales	21,764	12,427	57.1
1983–84	England	22,307	11,782	52.8
	Wales	1,385	975	70.4
	England and Wales	23,692	12,757	53.8
1984–85	England	22,883	11,872	51.9
	Wales	1,440	996	69.2
	England and Wales	24,323	12,868	52.9
1985–86	England	24,161	11,764	48.7
	Wales	1,574	1,014	67.0
	England and Wales	25,675	12,778	49.8
1986–87	England	25,328	11,764	46.4
	Wales	1,598	1,067	66.8
	England and Wales	26,926	12,831	47.7

Source: Travers, A. (1986) *The Politics of Local Government Finance*

privatized with support given direct to parents by way of education vouchers. It is hard to see such a system leading anywhere except to chaos. Even Sir Keith Joseph though 'intellectually drawn to the idea', in the end wholly rejected it.

There is a curious contradiction in Conservative attitudes. On the one hand Conservative politicians who know the LEAs recognize that at their best they are both innovative and efficient. They respond to local needs and they above all supply the bedrock of local political support that any serious national party must have. At their worst they are viewed by Tories as spendthrift and politically provocative, just as to Labour many are seen as reactionary, parsimonious and preventing working class children from getting a reasonable deal. Yet the mechanism is at hand to ensure that LEAs apply government policy and have the wherewithal to do it, namely by 'specific

Table 9: Specific grants for education and training

Department of Education and Science

	1984–85	1985–86 (Estimate)	1986–87 (Plan)	(£ m. cash) 1987–88 (Plan)
In-service teacher training grant/LEA training grant	5	10	21	114
Education suypport grant		10	45	64

Department of Employment

	1984–85	1985–86	1986–87 (Estimate)	1987–83 (Plan)	1988–89 (Plan)	(£ m. cash) 1989–90 (Plan)
Technical and voca-tional[1] education initiative	25.6	31.4	45.6	58.4	80.7	106.0
TVEI related in-service[1] training scheme	0	5.0	20.0	0	0	0
Work related non-advanced FE[1]	0	65.0	110.0	112.8	115.6	118.5
Industrial language training service[2]	2.1	2.1	2.3	2.4	2.4	2.5
Capital grants for YTS accommod-ation[3]	3.4	2.3	1.7	0	0	0
Scientific and tech-nological equipment for schools—GCSE[1]			5.0			

Notes:
1. Grant paid to authorities in England and Wales.
2. Grant paid to authorities in England.
3. Grant paid to authorities in Great Britain.

Source: Fourth Report of the House of Commons Select Committee on Education, Finance and Arts (1987) Cmnd 56, London, HMSO.

grants'. The corporatists within local government have long been hostile to grants of this kind on the grounds that they are anti-democratic and, of course, anti-corporatist, but certainly on the education side more rational views have come to prevail, if only because the money will not be forthcoming unless there are specific grants. If the purpose of the grant is not specified there is a grave danger, especially when funds generally are constrained, that an LEA will spend its resources on what it most perceives is needed. Certainly the only way to get in-service training for teachers, perhaps the single most important need within the profession, is through a specific grant, just as there had to be specific grants so that LEAs would be forced to make mandatory awards to would-be students who had at least two 'A' levels and a university place. Without such grants being provided, the big expansion in higher education in the 1960s would simply never have got off the ground. Just how significant specific grants are is shown in table 9 and a list of those current in 1987 is set out in table 10.

Table 10: Education Support Grants
Specific grants from the DES current in 1987-88, indicating the expenditure to be supported by the DES, some 30 per cent of which is to come from LEAs.

Activity	Number of LEAs being supported	£000 (at 1987/88 prices)
The provision of books and equipment for GCSE examination courses	97 (i.e., all)	10,000
Pilot projects to develop use of the spoken word by pupils aged 5–16	7	308.5
Pilot projects to promote social responsibility among young people	20	1,112.4
Information systems for the (to be announced) management of FE establishments	(to be announced)	1,395.0
Provision of computerized learning aids in further education for students with special educational needs	32	471.1
The strengthening of college-employer links to improve the quality and relevance of non-advanced further education	12	259.3
The teaching of mathematics in schools	93	6,629.7
The teaching of science and technology as part of primary education	52	8,423.1
Pilot projects to develop records of achievement for young people in secondary schools and colleges	11	2,358.2
Pilot projects to improve the quality of education provided in primary schools in urban areas	11	920.9
Pilot projects to improve the quality of range of the curriculum provided in the primary schools in rural areas	7	1,546.5
Pilot projects to meet the educational needs of those from ethnic minorities	24	2,139.7

Table 10: (Continued)

Activity	Number of LEAs being supported	£000 (at 1987/88 prices)
The development, provision and appraisal of courses of initial training for school governors	10	104.1
Action within the education service to combat the misuse of drugs	95	2,420.0
The management and appraisal of school teachers. LEAs: Croydon, Cumbria, Newcastle, Salford, Somerset, Suffolk	6	1,100.0
The provision of retraining and updating courses directed towards the needs of industry and commerce (PICKUP)	75	1,920.2
The development of information technology at further education establishments	84	7,338.6
The planning, development and coordination of provision to meet the educational needs of the unemployed	95	3,540.7
The provision of support for parents in the teaching of children under 5 with special educational needs	59	1,836.3
The provision of midday supervision for school pupils	All	about 38,000.0
Developing the knowledge and appreciation, among the pupils in schools of Wales, of the heritage and culture of Wales	All Welsh LEAs	302.8 (Welsh Office)

Source: DES Press Notice 9/87, 21 January 1987, pp. 2–4.

The Primacy of Educational Policy

'The search for a perfect or ideal system of school finance is likely to be not only unnecessary but futile', said the OECD report (1979) on *Educational Financing and Policy Goals for Primary Schools*. The OECD should know. No agency has expended more time in excavating the endless documents and statistics which countries produce on the funding of schools and universities. Yet governments go on being unnecessary and futile, supreme among them the British Government. The whole rickety edifice of central grant-aid has become more and more oppressive, until it threatens to crush the very service it is meant to provide for. It is rather like a manufacturing company which has allowed policy to be wholly determined by accountants with no knowledge of or interest in what is being manufactured and wonder after the event why the firm went bankrupt.

For all its faults the system of local management of education by elected bodies which has prevailed for the whole of this century in England, Wales and Scotland has a good record—especially since the Second World War. Take the way in which local authorities have met challenges such as the raising of the school leaving age on two occasions, the expansion of technical education following the *Sputnik* and the move, flawed though it is in some LEAs, to comprehensives, as well as tackling such pedagogic problems as are set by ethnic communities, adult illiteracy and in Wales, bilingualism, and perhaps above all the resolving of the curriculum and examinations tangle in the secondary schools, notably in Scotland. The contrast with a state-run system like the Manpower Services Commission is painful. Ironically, the MSC's biggest single show piece, the Technical and Vocational Education Initiative (TVEI) has been almost entirely the handiwork of the LEAs.

But admittedly the MSC is financially very much less difficult to control, as one national organization compared with a 112 local ones must be. But what evidence is there that central control actually gets better results? What precise improvement, for example, will a system of funding universities and polytechnics through 'contracts' have over what has previously prevailed? Will the separation of the polytechnics from LEAs and the diminution of university independence serve any educational purpose? What educational relevance has the removal of teachers' salaries and their negotiations from LEAs? The purpose of such measures is purely fiscal. They owe their origin not to educational aims but to the stubborn belief that financial subordination is what it is all about. But it is demonstrably possible to apply national policy without the mechanism of stop-go, or the simple strangulation of resources. To give fiscal control primacy over educational purposes is not the way to run the system.

Acknowledgements

Grateful acknowledgement is made to Tony Travers for his help with this chapter notably with regard to the statistical information. He is not, however, to be held responsible for the views expressed.

References

CAULCOTT, T. (Chief Executive, Birmingham) speech to the annual meeting of the Metropolitan LEAs (1984) *Education*, 16 November.
CENTRAL STATISTICS OFFICE (1987) *Social Trends* 17, London, HMSO
CROSSMAN, R. (1979) *The Crossman Diaries* (condensed version), London, McKuen Paperbacks.
DEPARTMENT OF EDUCATION AND SCIENCE (1986) *Falling School Rolls*, report by the Comptroller and Auditor General, London, HMSO.
DEPARTMENT OF EDUCATION AND SCIENCE (1977) *Study of School-Building*, London, HMSO.
HOUSE OF COMMONS SELECT COMMITTEE ON EDUCATION, SCIENCE AND THE ARTS (1987) *Third Report*. London, HMSO.
Independent School Cost Survey (1987), MacIntyre Hudson, Chartered Accountants.
OECD (1985) *Education in Modern Society*, Paris, OECD.
TRAVERS, T. (1986) *The Politics of Local Government Finance*, London, George Allen and Unwin.

Chapter 3: Primary Schools

John Coe

John Coe is an experienced primary specialist. After working as a teacher and headteacher in both rural and urban schools he joined the former West Riding Authority as an inspector. Then he moved to Oxfordshire where for sixteen years he led the primary advisory team. In 1980 he helped to establish the National Association for Primary Education. After serving as National Chairman for three years he has accepted responsibility for the Association's research and development work. Currently he directs postgraduate primary training at the University of London Institute of Education.

$\star \quad \star \quad \star$

A Puddle

I liked the reflections of the trees in the water,
And the clouds, too, floated in the puddle.
I dared not put my foot in the water
In case I disturbed it.
But I kept on looking at it.
I saw the dark brown of the willow trees
And the orangey pink on the clouds,
The greys that the water made
And the blue from the sky.
I thought about all the colours in the sky.
I loved the blues and greys and pinks
All the time reflected in the puddle.

These words were written in the mid-seventies by Susan barely 8 years old, a pupil at Eynsham school. She had been out for a walk in the school grounds following a drenching storm and then back in the classroom had put pen to paper. Her writing and her personal growth as she achieved it epitomize the flowering of primary education in what can be called the Plowden years.

It is fifty-five years since the Hadow Report[1] affirmed in marvellous and timeless words that 'The curriculum is to be thought of in terms of activity and experience rather than of knowledge to be acquired and facts to be stored'. This was at the very birth of the modern primary school and long before even infants' classes had come near a realization of the child-centredness which is so much a part of the primary tradition.

By the mid-sixties steady and evolutionary development mainly affecting the youngest children and then, all too slowly the juniors also, had given rise to a strong minority of schools, even a majority in some communities such as Leicestershire, Bristol, the West Riding of Yorkshire and Oxfordshire, which demonstrated the effectiveness of the liberalization of curriculum and method so firmly endorsed by the Plowden Report[2] in 1967. The prevailing climate of opinion in the country as a whole, both lay and professional, was encouraging to the process of change and public opinion was strongly of the view that the changes were for the better. The spirit of the time was benevolent and this enabled the changes to be carried through in the face of large classes (often nearly fifty children together in a room) and a deplorably low level of financial provision for books and learning materials.

The next decade saw a rapid expansion in the number of schools where both the principles and the practice of primary education were focused on the nature and needs of the children. From the initial groups of pioneering schools came a flow of committed and increasingly expert young teachers who went on to lead their own schools and in their turn to prepare talented members of staff for promotion. It is important to note that, in sharp contrast to the eighties, innovation was firmly rooted in the developing practice of the schools. Fundamentally the role of LEAs and their administrators and advisers and similarly the role of HMI was to be encouraging, at times through the exercise of charismatic personality even inspirational, and above all to help identify excellence in the quality of learning and to disseminate it to others. So it was that the teachers felt well regarded. Their spirits and their expectations of themselves were high and so they grew in the confidence that is essential to the creation alongside children of a curriculum matched to personal needs. A flowering indeed. The powers of even the youngest children were realized to an extent never before thought possible.

It is helpful in identifying the strengths of primary education at the beginning of what were to be for too many parents and teachers the wasted years to examine in greater detail the experience of Susan at Eynham and the learning and growth which grew out of it.

The storm had come suddenly one summer morning as the children walked to school. Down came the rain and within a few minutes the school was full of soaking wet boys and girls chattering excitedly about their experience. Parents and teachers wielded towels, clothes were changed and eventually after a great deal of enjoyable fuss it at last seemed possible to begin the school day. Judith, the teacher, sat with her class grouped around her in the quiet room, a comfortable homely place that served as their base from which they ventured out to other parts of the school. She found them bubbling over, enormously stimulated as are all children by the elements that had so assaulted them on the way to school. It was all too clear that they were far from ready to take up the work she had planned for them or the activities they had left with such reluctance at the end of the previous day. By now the storm had passed away and the sun was coming through so Judith decided that rather than struggle against the children's interests and concerns she would build upon them; she took the class for a walk in the school grounds.

Out they went, the teacher, her aide, two mothers volunteering their help and the thirty-three children ranging from the youngest beginners in school, around 5-years-old, to the oldest in their ninth year. As they walked together in the wet world the children exclaimed to see the pools of water beginning to steam under the sun and they marvelled at the trees so laden that a shower came down at the merest touch. They walked and talked. They used their senses, always present in the young, but too often neglected by the sophisticated apparatus of education. They saw with eyes seeing new things for the first time, they touched with perceptive hands, they heard the soft sounds of the birds, they smelled the damp earth and they learned how to learn. On the walk they grew in a way so helpful to the teachers who would work with them in other classes and schools in the future. This was the vital learning of the early years.

At one point they stopped by a puddle and one of the boys saw his reflection looking back at him from the water. He laughed to see this and the other children clustered round. Judith joined them. She talked about the phenomenon seen, really seen, by some of the children for the first time. They played games with their reflections and Judith provoked the precise and fluent talk which is the essential precursor of later reading and writing.

It was the puddle that the 8-year-old Susan chose as the subject of the writing she began after the class had returned from the walk. Only a few of the children embarked on writing because Judith had learned as a young teacher that nothing so quickly destroys the will to learn as the inevitability that writing must occur after every shared and pleasurable experience. But Susan, a pad of paper on her lap and pencil in her hand, tried for most of the morning to find words to describe the thoughts and feelings that had come to her as she looked with wondering eyes at the surface of the puddle. There are few teachers of 8-year-olds, indeed few teachers of 12-year-olds, who would not have been delighted with Susan's response. Not only were her words charged with meaning but there was careful precision in the punctuation, the spelling and the penmanship. She had tried hard and had succeeded. It was learning of the high quality which many primary teachers had come to demand of their pupils.

Direct experience was the basis of the writing. The black marks, still and silent on the page, were formed out of the images gained through actuality and the observation of actuality. Susan had indeed liked the reflections shimmering in the water, she had exclaimed over the floating clouds, she had with Judith at her side sought to name the colours before her very eyes. So when she wrote it was a recapitulation of her experience and all her effort went into the communication of that experience, not as a mere recorder but as a person with something to say and the saying of it transmuted by her own nature. No other child, no adult, could have so conjured with the names of the colours in precisely the same way. It was right for Susan, the writing she achieved became part of her and she was changed because of it. Most certainly such writing would never have come from a set lesson if the only reason for the search for words had been a chalked subject written by the teacher on a blackboard or the next exercise in an anonymous programme of learning printed in a book for all children but without meaning for Susan, since meaning, true meaning, is gained by the 8-year-old only from direct and personal experience.

A degree of freedom was essential to the writing. Consider the action of the teacher in deciding on the spur of the moment to take her class out for a walk after the storm. It was essential that Judith could make a decision to follow the interests of her pupils without concern for a set timetable or for bureaucratic regulations which so frequently inhibit the movement of children outside the classroom. Children learn best when their activities are related to how they think and feel at the time, this demands great flexibility on the part of the teacher and the implication for all those concerned with the administration of schools is that the teacher must to a large extent be free to seize the unplanned and unanticipated initiatives presented by the children. Not only must the arrangements of schools embody such freedom for the teacher, there must be a feeling of freedom and a trust in the teacher's judgment built up over many years. Freedom cannot be created by regulation, it grows out of the pattern of experience. Without the walk through the wet world the writing would never have occurred. When Judith said 'Come on, we're going out' she knew that all the authority vested in the school would be behind her.

The child, Susan, also needed freedom. For her freedom is best defined in terms of how much choice she has in her life and work. This is how freedom is made real to children. That morning she was able to choose to write. There were other choices open to her; to make a tape recording, to draw, to make a print, to paint, even to turn completely away from the experience of the storm and the walk, to take up once again her work of yesterday, or to begin something entirely new, but she chose to write and once the choice was made she was that much more committed and the commitment sustained her through the long and demanding struggle for words and precision in using them.

The words too were chosen by the child. They were her own and not predetermined by the teacher or the writer of a text book, as would have been the case had she been answering a question in a language programme which almost always is more of a test of memory than a challenge to the emotions and intellect which alone can provoke a significant act of learning.

It was important also that Susan could take two uninterrupted hours to shape, revise and present her writing. Her work began when she was ready to begin, it ended when she had finished. No timetable pre-planned to meet the needs of a curriculum to be followed willy nilly by all children would have met so adequately the particular rhythm and involvement of this child. Indeed the arbitrary clanging of bells, the imposition of a period of play so absurdly differentiated from work, would have been positively harmful to her response. Learning of quality can never be encapsuled in a previously allotted span of time. Children must be free to take as long as it takes to do the work well. The self-containment of the thirty-five minute lesson leads to an inevitable superficiality, an encouragement to trivial careless responses and work left almost in mid-sentence when the children hear the bell which signals the end of the lesson and the beginning of another. Learning which reaches the heart of children often takes a long time, as does any other worthwhile human activity.

An appropriate environment was necessary to the writing. Susan was able to tuck herself away with only a few companions in a place designed to be helpful to quiet personal learning. She wrote in a room very like her own living room back home, furnished with a carpet, comfortable seating, drapes, some bookshelves, and a place for the display of attractive and interesting things. The room did not have the traditional institutionalized feel of school, it was a warm and friendly place and the scale of it fitted the child. Of course there was easy access through a wide curtained opening to other areas furnished and equipped for learning of different kinds where many other children were working. In these larger areas there was more noise and bustle which came from many practical activities. In the quiet room Susan and the others could more easily become absorbed in writing and books undistracted by the hammering of making models, the chatter of creating a play or the attempted tunes of a child using the chime bars for the first time. Susan could work steadily on undisturbed and for quite long intervals unsupervised, although the adults were never far away and always easily on call. At such times she and the others in the quiet room showed that they could rise to the level of trust placed in them, not just in this present class, but ever since their first entry into school.

The teacher played a decisive role in helping Susan to achieve success. Not only through her initiative in providing the initial experience and her creation of a suitable environment for learning but also, and very importantly, through the instruction and guidance given alongside the child as she worked. This newer teaching role differed in a fundamental way from that traditionally followed by a teacher acting purely as an instructor giving class lessons. Such teaching rested upon a deep knowledge of the child gained through the sharing of experience over a long period of time. If all went well the children in Judith's class spent four years with her and this close and continuing contact had provided her with sensitive insights into Susan's nature, needs and pattern of development. So when Judith at Susan's side, reading and discussing her work with her, offered a word new to her growing vocabulary and how to spell it, there was every likelihood that the girl's need for the word would help her to understand it and that it thus would be assimilated. This contrasts with the arbitrary offering of a list of words to the whole class. The words to be learned or at least parroted by some, but not all, the children only to be forgotten at the end of the day or at best at the end of the week.

Judith encouraged Susan as she worked. She praised success whenever it could be found. The praise spurred Susan on to greater effort since the praise had power which was based upon a rapport, even an affection, between the two of them. Feeling was a vital element in the process of education.

The decisions taken and the choices made by Susan as the work progressed during the morning were shared by Judith. Such was the empathy between them that it would be difficult to say which of them was leading at any one moment. Yet the teacher's control, her provocation of the child's action, her evaluation of success and failure, her opening of some routes forward and the closing of others, everything was done within the limits set by the child's nature. This was teaching centred upon the child. Judith was not only an instructor giving direct help at the right time and in the right way, she was a catalyst releasing learning gained spontaneously by Susan through her own thought and actions.

At the end of the day after the last story had been read, Judith asked Susan if she would make a copy of her writing about the puddle and put it in the large class book. The child was pleased and readily agreed to stay behind after the others had gone home. Her mother came for her and stood chatting to the teacher while Susan, alone now in the quiet room, completed the last task. The adults could see the care with which she wrote, her absorption and the proud set to her shoulders as she celebrated her success. They knew they were seeing more than the outcome of a lesson, they were seeing part of Susan's growth. It was happening as they watched her.

For Susan to achieve such excellence so many things had to be right in her school. But by the mid-seventies the evolutionary development of primary education had gone far towards making them right. The design of the building, the furnishing and equipment, the range and availability of materials, the use of direct experience as a powerful way of learning, freedom of choice and pace and time for both children and adults, the changed role of the teacher, the matching of curriculum with the nature of the child, the acknowledgement that feeling is important to learning and the acceptance that the exercise of creativity is indivisible from the acquisition of skill; all had to be right. Needless to say it was not right in every primary school, perhaps not even in a majority of schools except in some communities where the child centred tradition was most firmly established. But an acceptance that developments were on the right lines was widespread among trainers of teachers, advisers and the teachers themselves. A gap between conviction and practice often remained but the passage of time had shown that the gap could close and there was every reason to anticipate that the evolution of the modern primary school would continue in the future. The example provided by the work of the pioneering infants school was like a pebble tossed in a pool and the ripples of influence were continuing to spread outwards affecting more and more schools.

It was a great shock to teachers of young children when the national climate began to change. The reactionary views of the Black Papers [3] seemed to have no place in the optimistic atmosphere of successful schools by now enjoying widespread support in their communities. There is no doubt though that when the tragic front page story of the William Tyndale school [4] broke in 1974 there was an impact on both teachers and parents. Almost for the first time confidence was questioned and at PTA meetings people asked 'Could it happen here?'. The media criticism of modern education gained in strength. Almost all the newspapers and many TV programmes took a line which too few people appreciated was more concerned with political campaigning than a contribution to genuine debate. In October 1976 a leading article in no less a newspaper than *The Times* [5] went so far as to equate the 'wild men of the classroom' with trade union disrupters and argued that 'they must be brought to heel'. For the great majority of those working in primary schools at that time such language was laughable. The practitioners continued to work on quietly and steadily. Change occurred in an evolutionary way with any decisive advances tending to take place following the appointment of a new headteacher. However the national pressure continued to mount. Conservative Party policy looked nostalgically back to a time when society was more hierarchical and the workforce more disciplined. Control over what was seen as anarchy was demanded and there were clear implications for education that were articulated by Rhodes Boyson, prominent in his party and a future Minister of State for Education. It was at this time that the Conservatives began to describe themselves as the party of educational 'standards'. A political riposte was required and this came from the Prime Minister James Callaghan, in his 1976 speech at Ruskin College. The Conservatives suit of 'standards' clothes was promptly donned by the Labour government and in the speech Callaghan warned against the way in which some teachers were using new methods in primary schools. In calling for a great debate he gave a clear intimation that government intervention was intended. He said:

> Public interest is strong and legitimate and will be satisfied. We spend £600m a year on education so there will be discussion.

Alongside the politicians powerful forces with the Department of Education and Science were marshalling the first moves directed towards the centralizing and strengthening of control in education. James Hamilton, the Permanent Under-Secretary of State, in speaking to the annual conference of the Association of Education Committees (AEC) on the 25 June 1976, said:

> I believe that the so-called secret garden of the curriculum cannot be allowed to remain so secret after all and that the key to the door must be found and turned.

At the same time there appeared to be a significant shift of view among members of HMI. Although previously they had been in support of child centred methods in primary schools the *Yellow Paper* drawn up in 1976 to brief the Prime Minister stressed society's fears about education and inferred a criticism of current teaching, in particular the use of new primary methods. The impact of the William Tyndale episode upon the national thinking that surrounded primary education was profound and yet only a minority of practitioners were affected by it to the extent that they felt the need to return to formal methods and the rote learning of basic skills. It was at this time that a wide gap began to open up between the over-hyped political and media treatment of education and the reality of steady evolutionary change at times all too slow, in primary schools. Teachers of young children were puzzled about the national brouhaha but not touched by it to any degree. However other developments were to have a greater effect.

There is no doubt that the schools were worried by the publication of the NFER Study *The Trend of Reading Standards.*[6] It was a shock to read an authoritative statement that the apparently inevitable growth of reading ability indicated by successive national testing programmes had come to an end and that standards had, at best, reached a plateau. Of course the media treatment of the report went even further and many teachers were lead to believe that a decline in national literacy had been revealed. Later the Bullock Report[7] re-examined the data and came to a different conclusion – standards among the least able children were continuing to rise.

> We therefore cannot accept the suggestion made to us in evidence that 'at the bottom of the scale a group approximating to a sixth of the school population has been showing a slight but steady decline in attainment for the last twenty-three years'. Inspection of table 3.6 and figure 3.4 of *The Trend of Reading Standards* shows that the lowest standards have clearly risen during this period. (para 2.19)

Needless to say the correction did not receive as much publicity as the original assertion.

Of some impact also was the research undertaken by Neville Bennett[8] into the merits and demerits of different teaching styles. Publication of the work in an attractive paperback found on the shelves of high street bookshops helped the conclusions severely critical of informal teaching to hit the headlines. The BBC devoted an entire *Horizon* programme to them. Bennett claimed that a survey carried out a year after publication showed that two out of every three primary teachers knew of his results.[9] This was an unprecedently high awareness of research on the part of classroom practitioners. More than a few parents and teachers believed that there was now proof that their schools were working on the wrong lines. However, Bennett's statistical methods came under heavy attack not least from researchers working with the NFER and as a result he reworked his data. In the June 1981 issue of the *British Journal of*

Table 1: A comparison of Bennett's findings in 1976 with those in 1981
Teachers were placed in three categories; formal, informal and mixed.

Curriculum area	1976 quoted from *Teaching Styles and Pupil Progress*	1981 quoted from the *British Journal of Educational Psychology*
Reading	Pupils of formal and mixed teachers progress more than those of informal teachers, the difference being equivalent to some three to five months difference in performance.	Informal teachers get the highest mean scores, mixed the lowest and formal is in the middle.
Mathematics	Formal pupils are superior to both mixed and informal pupils.	The formal and informal styles are close and substantially above the mixed style.
English	Formal pupils have the highest mean. Mixed is the middle and informal lowest.	Formal style has the highest mean, mixed the lowest, and informal is in the middle.

Educational Psychology[10] he withdrew the original findings and offered others much more favourable to child centred methods.

As with the Bullock revision of the NFER reading survey the corrected findings, so much more favourable to informal teaching, were given little publicity, scarcely finding a mention in the popular and usually biased press.

The so-called 'Great Debate' initiated by the Callaghan speech consisted largely of a number of set piece invited conferences. In the main there was little genuine exchange of view. Firm almost unyielding positions were taken up by the participants and rhetoric dominated any attempt to explore the realities of contemporary education. The verdict of most teachers was that the 'Great Debate' was neither great nor a debate. However, the strongly utilitarian line implicit in the guidelines[11] issued by the DES for the conference is worthy of note for it was an intimation of the policy which was to be made explicit in the *Green Paper* almost a year later.

> Whether or not it is found that standards have remained constant, risen or fallen over some past period is less important than whether the standards which are being achieved today correspond as nearly as possible to society's needs.

Now it was emerging that the major political parties, the DES and the Treasury were in agreement. Education should be centred not so much upon the personal needs of children and their development but upon the needs of society in the competitive world of industry and commerce. The greatest strength of primary education was under threat from the state. The *Green Paper*[12] was issued in July 1977. It contained much that could be considered indirect criticism of current teaching and a teacher derived policy of child centred education. An assertion of public disquiet was firmly aligned with the efficient use of public resources to serve the nation's economic needs.

> The speech (by the Prime Minister at Ruskin College, October 1976) was made against a background of strongly critical comment in the press and elsewhere on education and educational standards. Children's standards of performance in their school work were said to have declined. The curriculum it was argued, paid too little attention to the basic skills of reading, writing and arithmetic and was overloaded with fringe subjects. Teachers lacked adequate professional skills, and did not know how to discipline children or instil in them concern for hard work or good manners. Underlying all this was the feeling that the educational system was out of touch with the fundamental need of Britain to survive economically in a highly competitive world through the efficiency of its industry and commerce. (*Education in Schools*, para. 1.2).

The writers of the *Green Paper* were astute in distancing the critics they reported although remaining happy enough to use the criticism unsupported by evidence as a foundation for the making of policy. It was all far removed from the daily work of primary schools. The basic skills of reading, writing and arithmetic were accorded a high priority and this was typical of the national scene as reported by HMI in the 1978 survey.[13]

> High priority is given to teaching children to read, write and learn mathematics. (para. 8.16)

The great majority of children worked hard and were well mannered. This too was the national picture as reported by HMI.

> The children behave responsibly and cooperate with their teacher and with other children. A quiet working atmosphere is established when necessary. (para. 8.6)

> Teachers clearly attach great importance to children learning to live together amicably and gaining a sense of social responsibility. (para. 8.7).

With regard to the level of support for modern primary education, the advisers and administrators closely in touch with schools could affirm with confidence that invariably the level of support by parents was high and that complaints and criticisms were relatively few. In fact this was the situation nationally as shown by SSRC surveys of public opinion reported in *Social Trends* (1976).[14] In 1971 83 per cent of a representative sample expressed themselves as satisfied or very satisfied with their child's primary schooling.

By 1975 this had *risen* to 87 per cent expressing varying degrees of satisfaction. A Gallup poll undertaken for the National Consumer Council in 1976 found a similarly high level of public support for schools. So much for the *Green Paper's* allegation of 'a background of strongly critical comment'. Such comment was rooted more in the policies of political parties and a prejudiced press than in the reality of the children's lives. Even at the end of the thirteen-year period under review and after further years of hostile campaigning by reactionary politicians and their press there has been only a marginal fall in the level of public support for primary schools. It is also significant that approval for primaries indicated by recent polls is higher among parents closely associated with children's day-to-day work than is characteristic of the public in general. Further confirmation of a high level of approval and support can be seen in the policies and activities of organizations of parents such as NCPTA, CASE and NAPE through which the parent-teacher partnership has developed so strongly since 1980. This is all the more impressive when it is remembered that in recent years as a result of the dispute between the teaching profession and the government many schools have been affected by militant action. Nonetheless, at both local and national levels parental support which includes the voluntary fund raising upon which the schools increasingly depend has remained very strong. This is in sharp contrast to the view put forward by the government.

A consideration of the development of primary education over the most recent decade would not be complete without reference to the quite rapid decline in the number of pupils in schools which began in 1973. In only a decade the primary population of almost five million was to decline to three-and-a-half million. Neither administrators nor practitioners were experienced in dealing with contraction on such a scale. The reduction in numbers of teachers and ancillaries, the redeployment of teachers often achieved in the face of threatened redundancy, the proposed, sometimes actual, amalgamation even closure of schools; these and other distasteful measures further alienated the practitioners from the elected members and the officials. Usually it was quite impossible for those in the schools to distinguish between the effects of monetarist policies based upon an antipathy towards the maintained school system and the effects of contraction in the number of pupils. For a primary school the loss of a member of the teaching staff was considered to be a cut and therefore to be opposed, at times through the use of sanctions involving a withdrawal of goodwill. Attempts, to argue that fewer pupils warranted fewer teachers even when the pupil/teacher ratio was unaltered were dismissed as a cover-up by a hostile administration. The effects of ten years of contraction were largely upon the spirit and the morale of primary teachers. They have begun to feel embattled and this surfaced only too clearly during the recent dispute between the government and the teaching profession. The dispute, ostensibly about pay and conditions, has been rooted more fundamentally in a widespread conviction that the government does not trust those who teach the children and does not respect their work. Such attitudes are not at one with the high level of support experienced at local level from the communities surrounding and served by the schools.

Nowhere is the contrast between the needs of children and the demands of the state seen more clearly than in the following two statements separated by fifteen years.

> At the heart of the educational process lies the child. (*Plowden Report* (1966) 2.9)

> The school curriculum is at the heart of education. (DES (1981) *School Curriculum* 15)

Increasingly the government has tightened its grip upon the work of the schools and this has culminated in an all party demand for a nationally imposed curriculum. Those on the extreme right of the political spectrum go even further and seek to introduce benchmarks related to chronological age indicating levels of attainment to be met by all pupils. In this the politicians have had support from some senior members of HM Inspectorate though seldom from the inspectors who have trained and are experienced as primary specialists. Statements made in recent years by the Secretary of State and the Senior Chief Inspector are remarkably similar in content and style. They are at one in stressing the central importance of curriculum and the need to define objectives for the primary phase of education.

> The curriculum needs to accord more than it does now with four principles: breadth, relevance, differentiation, and balance. First it should be broad for all pupils both in the development of personal qualities and in the range of knowledge and skills to which pupils are introduced ... the real world and to the pupils experience of it ... Third, there should be differentiation within the curriculum for variations in the abilities and aptitudes of pupils ... Fourth, the various elements of the curriculum need to be balanced in such a way as to optimise the contribution that each can make to the total education of the pupil. [16]

> It is difficult to find any other way to discuss and plan the curriculum without doing so in terms of subjects in order to determine what the overall curriculum should consist of and to decide the unique contribution each component part will make to the whole, it is necessary to talk in terms of subjects such as mathematics, science, history, geography and art. [17]

It is in respect of the desire of the Secretary of State for balance that there is a serious difference in comparison with the best of contemporary primary practice. Here is the sharpest revelation of the view that young children's learning can be divided into separate disciplines called subjects and that there is a consequent need to match one with another. This is strongly reinforced by Eric Bolton's statement. In contrast an increasing number of primary teachers hold that the child's experience, an undivided whole, is the beginning to learning. Particular skills which might fall beneath the umbrella of a single subject are taught and learned in relation to that experience not in pursuance of the subject itself. In essence the teacher first considers the child who is to be educated and not the subject matter to be transmitted. Then follows a reconciliation or matching between child and curriculum content.

> These principles apply to the curriculum of every type of school —primary, secondary and special. But they will not be so applied unless they are applied deliberately and by agreement, both when it is planned and when it is delivered. That requires an explicit definition of the objectives of each phase and of each subject area of the curriculum, of what in each needs to be learnt by all pupils, and of what should additionally be attempted by some. (Sir Keith Joseph)

> I believe that the primary curriculum will be discussed largely in terms of subjects and that there will be broad agreement about which subjects should make up the curriculum and what the objectives of each should be. It is on the basis of those objectives that agreement could then be reached about the standards that can be expected to be achieved by the broad mass of pupils at age 11. (Eric Bolton)

In practice objectives are not the simple and utilitarian matter implied by these two statements. The true overriding objective is that each child should grow. Skills and knowledge are only part of the growth which embraces a complex web of attributes. In addition many teachers are acknowledging through their practice that there is a very wide variation in human development and need at any one chronological age (a three-year range in language development at the age of $3\frac{1}{2}$ according to the Bristol Language Study[18] and a seven-year range in development mathematically at the age of 11 according to the Cockcroft Report[19]). Interestingly enough the wide variation was mentioned by Eric Bolton in his address to the annual meeting of the National Association for Primary Education from which the above quotations are taken. However he did not go on to discuss the serious doubt that is thus cast on the wisdom of attempting to define objectives and standards for the broad mass of 11-year-olds. Such objectives and standards would be far too limiting for many children and frustratingly incapable of achievement by many others.

Of course objectives should be expressed with as much precision as is appropriate to young children but expressed in terms of a pattern of growth over a number of years rather than as a set of attainments to be achieved at a particular age. It is wrong moreover to dismiss objectives as somehow suspect simply because they cannot always be stated precisely.

It must be remembered also that much of the primary curriculum consists of helping children learn how to learn and the fruits of such personal growth cannot always be seen by the age of 11. Successful learning in the secondary school and beyond depends upon good development in the early years. Thus some objectives for young children are reasonably short-term but many others are realized only in later life.

Beyond question the advocacy, even prescription, and threatened legislation emanating from the government and the Inspectorate presents a serious challenge to the principles and practice of primary education.

The indictment then is that the years from 1973 were wasted years not so much, if at all, in terms of the work of primary schools but in terms of the nation's refusal to acknowledge the strengths achieved through evolutionary development. Even worse has been the nation's determination through its elected government and through a small minority of extremist local authorities to intervene in education in ways intended to weaken and even destroy the quality of learning so powerfully revealed in many schools by the mid-seventies. Only the commitment of primary teachers, so well supported by parents, and their insistence on putting the children first has protected primary education from too much harm. The years though have seen little or no advance. It has been a time of holding on and a time of stern defence against crude attacks made by those whose views and advocacy owe more to political conviction than to a knowledge of young children and how they learn and how much evidence we have of their happiness and achievement in the schools.

It must be hoped that it is not too late and that public attitudes as reflected in the actions of government at both local and national levels will change. If a new partnership with the teacher can be forged. If primary teachers are trusted and can *feel* trusted again. If the achievements of the past are recognized and made the foundation of our tackling of the problems and challenges of a rapidly changing society then the future can be bright once more.

Now in looking ahead from 1986 it is possible to identify some of the contemporary strengths in primary education from which might come the next forward steps in evolutionary development. Indeed some strengths have been drawn from the considerable pressures and unhappiness of most recent times.

1 Parents are involved in pre-primary and primary education as never before. Visiting schools twenty years ago it was unusual to find anyone other than the teachers spending time alongside the children. By the mid-seventies the National Primary Survey[20] found parents helping teachers in nearly a third of the 7-year-old classes and in just under a fifth of 9 and 11-year-old classes. The last decade has seen parental involvement spread into almost all primary classes. In the autumn of

1986 every member of a large PGCE course reported that they had found parents at work in the primary schools visited as part of the preparation for training.

More and more parents are taking part in the management of schools through their membership of governing bodies. The 1986 Education Act is an overdue recognition of the growing desire of parents to enter into direct partnership with teachers. Understandably enough those who teach the youngest children have been cautious in welcoming adults not qualified in the conventional sense. However, professional confidence has grown over the years and the reality of the new partnership is shown by the increasing strength and influence of national bodies representative of parents and teachers. ALPAG, the All London Parents Action Group, sprang spontaneously to life to support the teachers in their recent dispute with the government.

2   The evidence that the provision of educational opportunities for the under-5s has long-term beneficial effects is now conclusive. The Headstart programmes in America [21] have been shown to lead to higher attainments, better employability, less delinquency and better attitudes to learning in later life. More recently the University of Bristol study [22] of 16,000 children born in one week in 1970 has confirmed that early education leads to success in learning as children grow older. Parents and teachers have long been convinced of the need to widen the availability of pre-schooling and the growth of the pre-school play-group movement and the earlier admission of children into school have indicated the way ahead. Needless to say the very young child is not considered in isolation but within the context of the family. So is the essential partnership established: child, parent and teacher.

3   There is an undoubted change in the role of the primary teacher in response to the widening range of demands on the curriculum. Steadily rising standards of achievement among the population have led to calls for even higher attainments. Success in educating children leads over the years, as those children themselves become parents, to greater pressure upon the schools to deliver even more measurable success. Traditionally the teacher of young children has taught almost the entire range of the curriculum to a class for virtually all the time. The National Primary Survey of 1978 found that children were rarely taught by another teacher for a period exceeding five hours per week. A quarter of 7-year-old classes were taught entirely by their own class teacher. This strong identity between one teacher and a class and the resultant unity of learning and close relationships which promote a more exact match between curriculum and individual need has been staunchly and successfully defended by primary specialists. However an appreciable number of schools have developed ways of cooperative teaching which retain the class teacher as the integrator of learning and lynchpin of the personal relationships which facilitate sound progress while opening up

contact with another teacher so that skills and enthusiasms can be shared. This is an almost uniquely primary development which is far removed from the specialist teaching characteristic of many secondary schools.

4   The primary profession has come of age. Qualifications on entry to teaching have been raised quite dramatically in recent years. Teachers of young children are now members of an all graduate profession that sees initial training as only the first step along a path of career professional development through inservice education. It is natural enough that this enhanced professionalism is leading to a stronger advocacy of a teacher-led general teaching council controlling standards of entry, a code of conduct and the disciplinary procedures necessary to ensure high standards of education.

So what might be achieved in the next ten years given a community which is prepared to trust the teachers and to build upon the strengths and successes of the past? A new kind of school could emerge. A school which offers educational opportunities to the families of under-5s by drawing upon the best of pre-school playgroup practice and the best of family centred nursery teaching. A school which throughout the primary years considers the children in the context of their families and which draws upon the contribution of parents and the community both near and far. A school in which the teachers work as a cooperative team, retaining the link between one teacher and a class but at the same time sharing skills through continuing contact through the working day. A school which is expressive of a higher order of professionalism stemming from a general teaching council which through self-regulation will ensure higher standards of education. And of course, a school where the fifty-year primary tradition of a fusion between learning and concern for individual needs is carried further towards the creation of a community which is not so much like an institution insulated from life but a family in the midst of life.

All this and more can be achieved but first we must recover from the wasted years.

Notes

1   BOARD OF EDUCATION (1931) *Primary Children* (The Hadow Report), London, HMSO.
2   DEPARTMENT OF EDUCATION AND SCIENCE, 1966) *Children and Their Primary Schools* (The Plowden Report) London, HMSO.
3   COX, C.B. and DYSON, A.E. (Eds) (1969) *Fight for Education: A Black Paper*, London, Critical Quarterly Society, also *Black Paper Two: The Crisis in Education*, London, Critical Quarterly Society.

4 AULD, R. (1976) *William Tyndale Junior and Infants Schools Public Inquiry: A Report to the ILEA*, London, Inner London Education Authority.

5 *The Times* newspaper quoted in SIMON, B. and WILLCOCKS, J. A. (Eds) (1981) *Research and Practice in the Primary Classroom*, London, Routledge and Kegan Paul.

6 START, K. B. and WELLS, B. K. (1972) *The Trend of Reading Standards*, London, National Foundation for Educational Research.

7 DEPARTMENT OF EDUCATION AND SCIENCE, (1975) *A Language for Life*, (The Bullock Report), London, HMSO.

8 BENNETT, N. (1976) *Teaching Styles and Pupil Progress*, London, Open Books.

9 Interview reported in *The Sunday Times*, 26 April 1981.

10 AITKIN, M., BENNETT, S. N. and HESKETH, J. (1981) Teaching styles and pupil progress: A reanalysis, *British Journal of Educational Psychology*, June, pp. 170–86.

11 DEPARTMENT OF EDUCATION AND SCIENCE (1977a) *Guidelines for the Regional Conferences of the Great Debate*, quoted in The *Times Educational Supplement*, 11 February.

12 DEPARTMENT OF EDUCATION AND SCIENCE, (1977b) *Education in Schools: A Consultative Document*, Cmnd 6869, London, HMSO.

13 DEPARTMENT OF EDUCATION AND SCIENCE, (1978) *Primary Education in England: A survey by HM Inspectors of Schools*, London, HMSO.

14 DEPARTMENT OF EDUCATION AND SCIENCE (1976) *Social Trends*, London, HMSO.

15 DEPARTMENT OF EDUCATION AND SCIENCE (1981) The School Curriculum, London, HMSO.

16 Transcript of a speech by the Rt Hon Sir Keith Joseph at the North of England conference, January 1984.

17 Transcript of a talk by Mr Eric Bolton, HMI Senior Chief Inspector, at the annual meeting of the National Association for Primary Education, 12 May 1984.

18 WELLS, G. (1982) *Language Learning and Education*, Bristol Centre for the Study of Language and Communication, University of Bristol.

19 DEPARTMENT OF EDUCATION AND SCIENCE (1982) *Mathematics Counts* (The Cockcroft Report) London, HMSO.

20 Department of Education and Science (1978) *op. cit.*

21 WEIKART, D. (1984) *High Scope*, quoted in the *Times Educational Supplement*, 5 October 1984.

22 OSBORNE, A. S. and MILBANK, J. E. (1987) *The Effects of Early Education*, Oxford, Oxford University Press.

Chapter 4: Secondary Schools

Robert Spooner

Bob Spooner has taught in grammar, technical high, secondary modern and comprehensive schools. At 62 he has taken on a new headship and is anxious to avoid retirement but fears he will be a victim of ageism. He did a five-year stint as Chair of an Education Committee and served on the National Executive of the Association of Education Committees. He writes regularly for *Education* and occasionally for other journals. He has chaired the teachers' side of the Joint Consultative Committee in Leeds for the last thirteen years.

$$\star \quad \star \quad \star$$

In 1973 the argument over comprehensive education appeared to have been settled. Crosland's forceful injunction[1] had been accepted by all but a few recalcitrant authorities and the secondary sector was soon to become overwhelmingly comprehensive. This resulted in different patterns emerging in different areas. Sometimes the pattern was a hybrid one, but generally authorities opted either for 11-18 comprehensive schools, a three-tier system of first, middle and high schools, or an 11-16 pattern, with sixth form or tertiary colleges for the post-16 age range.

The common feature in most areas was a period of uncertainty, accompanied by inertia, followed by a major administrative reorganization, that if it did nothing else, subjected teachers to the need to readjust to new conditions, often accompanied by considerable stress and sometimes loss of job satisfaction. It destroyed the old tradition of loyalty to an institution and exaggerated the apparent need for ambitious teachers to flit from job to job as they climbed the by now complex promotion ladder.

The tumult in schools during this period was enhanced by the 1972 raising of the school leaving age and the large-scale reorganization of local government that occurred in 1974. However, it was then reasonable to hope that we were coming to the end of administrative change and that schools could settle down to reap the benefits of both comprehensive reorganization and the raising of the school leaving age.

Not all the omens were favourable. Changing the school leaving age twice since the Second World War, coupled with the rising birth rate, had resulted in an enormous increase in the teacher force. Between 1945 and 1976 the number of teachers almost trebled.[2] In the ten years after 1966 there was a 50 per cent increase. As little was done during these years to make teaching a more attractive profession, and as the basic qualification for acceptance by a college of education was a mere five 'O' levels, which could be scraped together one at a time, there had been a very real dilution in quality of the teacher force, which was only partially countered by a longer period of training.[3]

There was to develop a severe shortage of specialist teachers in some key subject areas, particularly in mathematics, science and what was to become known as craft, design and technology.

One should not suppose that the teaching profession as a whole embraced the philosophic implications of comprehensive education.[4] Our education system had been always one of the most divisive elements in society. It was built round the tradition that 'to him who has shall be given, and to him who has not, whatsoever little he has shall be taken away'.

There were two main factors causing this. First of all, in the state sector, the ablest children, provided they came from supportive and well-to-do homes, attracted the best paid teachers.[5] Secondly, education was conceived as a sort of obstacle race, from which one became eliminated not by fulfilment but by failure. Over 75 per cent fell at the first fence, the 11 + , 'O' level accounted for more than half the remainder and 'A' level reduced the field to a mere 5 per cent. However hard teachers struggled to build confidence and self-respect, most pupils left the stage with a sense of failure, with their attention ruthlessly drawn to their apparent intellectual limitations.

The majority of teachers overvalued intelligence and saw a child's success in terms of examination triumph. They had been proud to get jobs in grammar schools and shame-faced if they worked in downtown secondary schools, even though work there demanded greater professional skill and devotion. This is strange, because most people relish difficult assignments. Mountaineers prefer to climb Everest to the Clent Hills. It can be attributed only to the intellectual snobbery that pervaded the educational system.

Those educationists who pioneered the comprehensive system sought not only to make equal opportunity a reality, they hoped to develop an ethos in schools in which the importance of every individual was recognized, and all sorts of diverse talents, even good nature, were appreciated and as well esteemed as intellectual prowess. No-one supposed that this could be achieved by administrative changes alone. They made such aims more practicable, but had no evident virtue in themselves. Unhappily, in the event, comprehensive education was sold on a false prospectus with the emphasis placed on getting rid of the 11 + , and the real issues were so smudged that it was possible for Harold Wilson to talk about 'grammar school education for all'.

Poor Harold has been much mocked for this remark, but already by 1973 there were comprehensive schools up and down the country which judged their own success by grammar school standards. They set out to beat the grammar schools at their own game (sometimes rugby union!). They adopted a uniform, they streamed their pupils into at least a tripartite pattern, and often more divisively, they established prefect systems, they retained corporal punishment and they glorified academic success by publishing their examination results in the local press and by holding speech days at which the graduates on the staff wore gowns.[6]

By these methods they sought to gain parental support, 'improve' their intake, so making greater 'successes' possible, and in the end contrive to avoid a truly comprehensive intake by attracting a higher percentage than their share of pupils who were above average ability. Few local authorities, when they 'went comprehensive', made any real attempt to give their schools a balanced intake. In this respect the ILEA and Hull were notable exceptions, and a few other authorities, by redrawing catchment areas, sought to encourage what was called a 'social mix'. Generally speaking there was a polarization of talent around former grammar schools, and this phenomenon helped to preserve grammar school traditions.

However clearly some teachers saw and subscribed to a 'comprehensive' philosophy, two other factors militated against its fulfilment. The first was the examination system. GCE 'O' level was there, deeply entrenched, with success in at least five subjects the sine qua non of the fifth year. Indeed most schools encouraged pupils to collect as many 'O' levels as they could to decorate their speech day programmes. Less than a fifth of each generation were to taste this sort of success. CSE[7] firmly established by 1973 as a second grade examination, was still supposed to serve only the next 40 per cent of the ability range. Below this level there was an equal number who were supposed to be scratched before the great examination race got under starter's orders.

The other factor was the long-standing tradition that state education existed to help pupils get good jobs and serve the needs of industry and commerce. In this respect the teaching profession as a whole was culpable, as the most common carrot dangled before a reluctant pupil was 'work hard if you want a good job'. From the time of the Forster Education Act, which had as its objective to teach the work force the skills they needed for their employers to exploit their labour efficiently, there have always been those in government who saw state education as social engineering designed to produce appropriately skilled labour.

It was never the public school objective. These schools were always more concerned about the enrichment of living, the building of self-confidence and 'the ability to lead'.[8] With hindsight one can see that, looming over the educational scene in 1973, was the shadow of the independent sector. Crosland had set up in 1965 the Public Schools Commission to recommend a national plan to integrate their work with the state sector, but their first report, presented by Sir John Newsom, was ignored. The subsequent Donnison Report concentrated on eliminating direct grant schools, and any thought of challenging the independent sector seriously, died with it.

Already, in most parts of the country, the state education service was underfinanced. An inadequate sum had been found to prepare for the raising of the school leaving age, and what there was had sometimes been diverted into secondary reorganization.[9] For decades education expenditure had been devoted to 'keeping roofs over heads' and, although there were some pleasant new schools, many had been planned for a selective system, and some were amalgamated on split sites to form comprehensive schools. Many old, lamentably equipped schools remained in service.

It is true that lip-service was still paid on all sides to the importance of education, and there was public confidence in the broad success of our schools. The authors of the Black Papers[10] were held to be amiable or malign eccentrics, according to one's political stance. But in government circles education was far from a top priority. In 1969, the Labour government had, with the connivance of the Minister, P C Gordon Walker,[11] postponed the raising of the school leaving age, and the 1974 reorganization of local government demonstrated a callous indifference to the importance of education, for the West Riding of Yorkshire, one of the most advanced education authorities in the country, was wantonly destroyed.

So the cards, in 1973, were not stacked propitiously, yet the outlook was not entirely bleak. The Houghton Report was to raise teachers' morale, and for a brief time they felt in receipt of a reasonable salary,[12] and that the importance of their job was recognized. There were many teachers in comprehensive schools determined to make them work, who were committed to the needs of pupils across the ability range. More and more schools were introducing mixed ability teaching, and if the country was doing little about 'positive discrimination' in favour of those with special needs, in many, that most valuable resource, teacher time, was being lavished on pupils of apparently poor ability. Many teachers considered this an exciting as well as a challenging time. They felt appreciated and important. Some very able men and women were attracted to teaching because they thought that only through education could society be changed for the better.

The evidence for the gradual conversion of the teaching profession to comprehensive principles lies in the general disregard for the professed intention of CSE to cater for only the most able 60 per cent. School after school declined to brand any of its pupils as non-examinable, and by the end of the seventies over 90 per cent of pupils in England were being entered for either GCE or CSE with at least some limited success. The pupils themselves may not have seen this success as very significant, for the sad effect of an élitist examination system is to motivate only to disappoint the bulk of its entrants, but at least these pupils were kept 'within the pale', and this serves as a shining proof of teacher determination to beat the system.

What is more, there were very positive attempts to cater for the perceived needs of all pupils in curriculum terms. Courses in car maintenance, household management, child care, community studies, engineering science and business studies burgeoned, in spite of a DES determination to keep schools free from the taint of 'vocational studies'.

Let it be acknowledged that some of these courses, particularly in community studies (or social education), engineering science and business studies, were designed to meet the needs of pupils across the ability range, and they were not sops to the supposedly unendowed. Furthermore, valiant attempts were made to reform the curriculum and develop teaching techniques more in tune with the modern world. It was the era of language laboratories, field trips, the video, modern mathematics, Nuffield science, Schools Council Integrated Science Project (SCISP), the technology movement based on Loughborough that foreshadowed everything that has occurred through TVEI, and there was also a growth of work experience to replace works visits, coupled with community involvement. Let no-one suppose that it was a period of stagnation in secondary schools.

The early seventies saw a plethora of mode 3 CSE courses designed to serve the needs of average pupils and then assess their success. Some of them were ill-judged, but all of them were well-intentioned. The same period saw the growth of complex choice patterns which enabled students in their last two years of compulsory education to devote their time to activities in which they could hope to gain some success. More important, these systems were often well designed, and when they offered genuine choices, helped students feel that they were autonomous individuals. They also enabled them to opt out of areas of failure.

This development may not have been an unalloyed gain. It resulted at times in pupils opting out of areas of skill or knowledge to their ultimate disadvantage, and sometimes, by choosing too many similar activities, they tired of the things they were good at. In extreme cases one might see such systems as offering a charter for the workshy.

> See what the boys in the back room will have
> And give them the poison they name

is perhaps not a good substitute for a sound educational policy carefully sold to our clients, but it certainly did not spring from a lack of concern, a determination to stick to hidebound educational attitudes or unawareness of the modern world. Nor did the large expansion of practical, vocationally orientated activities in most schools come from a disregard for the needs of industry or commerce.

It is true that a substantial number of comprehensive schools confined the more adventurous aspects of their curriculum development to the needs of the average and below average pupil, and that in most schools the brightest pupils limited themselves to the orthodox subjects, but this was due to parental pressure and, ironically, the value employers placed on 'O' level success in academic subjects rather than on anything based on art, design or technology. Some attempts were made to attract able students to technology and a number of schools sought to establish 'A' level courses in engineering science, but there was no ready demand. Whether prompted by teachers or not, most ambitious and able sixth formers continued to scorn careers in industry. [13]

Another positive factor in the years after 1973 was the slow but steady growth in the size of sixth forms. It is sometimes argued that the 11 + was the salvation of the working-class child but this is an illusion. Higher education remained a middle-class and upper-class preserve, with those few working class children who beat the system rapidly becoming declassed.

But the development of comprehensive education saw the emergence of the 'open sixth form', to which all comers were welcomed. Once working class children started to stay on in any number it was discovered that the low pupil teacher ratios, which had once been common place in grammar schools, were so uneconomic that the country couldn't afford them, and a new doctrine was propounded that sixth forms should have at least 150 pupils to be viable.

Establishing the open sixth form owed much to teacher ingenuity in devising courses to cater for pupils for whom 'A' level was initially too ambitious, but which left open a route to higher education for those who matured late. The Certificate of Extended Education (CEE) catered admirably for this need and schools that developed it rarely gave it up, although it was always under threat as successive governments failed to give it national recognition on a permanent basis.

There was still reluctance to allow schools to develop courses with long-term vocational significance. The seventies saw the emergence of BEC and TEC general, and some attempts by progressive comprehensive schools to be allowed to provide off the job education for YOP schemes. TEC was often frustrated by the FE colleges who set out the conditions but BEC flourished until it was subsumed by the Certificate of Pre-Vocational Education (CPVE) and made firmly pre-vocational. The fact that some schools tried out Basis for Choice and the dubious City and Guilds 365 [14] is evidence of some determination to expand into vocational education but there was little encouragement for schools to give their sixth forms a tertiary flavour and the trend is all in favour of removing all post-16 education from state schools.

So, although the seventies was a period of bright hopes and fierce endeavour, it all came to very little, and few educationists can be found who look back on the period without a sense of acute frustration. It is reasonable to ask what went wrong with the comprehensive dream.

Six factors cast a blight on all our hopeful initiatives. These may be summarized as the dramatic fall in pupil rolls, with a consequent end to expansion, the loss of public confidence sparked by Callaghan's Ruskin speech and Shirley Williams' disastrous tenure of office, the dramatic rise in unemployment of the school leaver and the failure to use the education service to cope with it, the deliberate undermining of the comprehensive system by the Conservative government and its alienation of the overwhelming majority of the teaching force, and fifthly, the failure to match resources in schools to the enormous technological developments that occurred. Finally there was a retreat from the belief that education is about helping people live happy and rewarding lives and the narrowing of educational objectives into a form of social engineering.

What was needed from government in the period before Mrs. Thatcher's success at the polls was some resolution, some resource and more resources. Already the decline in the birth-rate was known, and with it would obviously come some risks and some opportunities. It would have been possible, for the first time, dramatically to reduce the size of classes, thereby stimulating an expansion of experimental work in science, more emphasis on oral work in English and modern languages, a greater development of field studies in geography, research techniques in history, and more ambitious three-dimensional art. We could have got more rapidly into the new technological world with all that means in terms of training techniques and sensible vocational training. Had Mrs. Williams chosen to commit the country to a period of educational expansion it would have been a hardy succeeding government that would have gone back on her pledges.

Instead she lost the opportunity and we have seen falling rolls used as an excuse for retrenchment, and central government altering the balance of national spending adversely against the education service. Falling rolls resulted in stagnation in the teaching profession, with reduced career opportunities and a sense of neglect. Curriculum development gave place to curriculum preservation as minority subjects came increasingly under threat.

With his infamous speech at Ruskin College, Mr Callaghan, having held all the major offices of state without distinction, now contrived to cast his blight on the education service. Mouthing the platitudes of his industrialist friends, he demanded to know what was wrong with the education service, and why it was failing the country. He called for a 'Great Debate'. Pandora's carelessness with her box was a slip of small consequence compared with the clouds of gloom generated by this speech. Mrs Williams proved an able lieutenant, handing to the enemies of education round after round of ammunition. Had a Minister of Defence travelled about the country gaily proclaiming that all our tanks were obsolete, a shocked press would have demanded a prompt resignation. When Shirley, with her erudite insousiance, wondered in a bemused way why so many teachers hadn't even got 'O' level in mathematics, she was congratulated on her candour and encouraged to go on denigrating the service for which she was responsible.

The 'Great Debate' turned out to be a great flop, but it served as an excuse for Mrs. Williams to postpone all the decisions that were then necessary to gather the fruits from the developing comprehensive system. Instead of underwriting CEE, and encouraging its expansion, thereby giving it more vocational value and promoting some vocational as well as purely educational content, she put it on ice. Instead of taking the then plentiful advice to establish a 16 + examination that catered for the whole ability range, she shied away from decision. Instead of giving a boost to the developing open sixth forms by ensuring that it was financially as beneficial to stay on at school as be unemployed, and by making it easier for schools to offer vocational courses geared to technical qualifications, she closed her eyes to the problem and left it to her successors to finish off working class sixth form education. Nor did she encourage the only sensible alternative, the tertiary college. She had the reform of 'A' level on her agenda with the 'N' and 'F' proposals,[15] and she left it there. Even when it came to defending the school meals service which was under threat, she took water and washed her hands, with the result that instead of remaining a socializing and health-giving adjunct to the education service it has become the purveyor of junk food.

As a smoke-screen to cover her masterly inactivity, she published the confused and confusing 1977 *Green Paper*,[16] which may be considered a watershed in the years under discussion. It warrants close examination, for, within its covers, one may discover the eddying cross-currents that swamped the DES at that time. Its eight aims for schools are worth listing. These were:

1 To help children develop lively, enquiring minds; giving them the ability to question and argue rationally, and to apply themselves to tasks.
2 To instil respect for moral values, for other people and for oneself, and tolerance of other races, religions, and ways of life.
3 To help children understand the world in which we live, and the interdependence of nations.
4 To help children to use language effectively and imaginatively in reading writing and speaking.
5 To help children to appreciate how the nation earns and maintains its standard of living and properly to esteem the role of industry and commerce in this process.
6 To provide a basis of mathematical, scientific and technical knowledge, enabling boys and girls to learn the essential skills needed in a fast-changing world of work.
7 To teach children about human achievement and aspirations in the arts and sciences, in religion, and in the search for a more just social order.
8 To encourage and foster the development of the children whose social or environmental disadvantages cripple their capacity to learn, if necessary by making additional resources available to them.

From none of these aims could one readily dissent and in general they supported the views of those 'progressive' teachers against whose influence the Ruskin speech had railed. Most schools had already responded to them, time-consuming though many of them were. The fourth one, for example, emphasized in the use of the word 'imaginatively' and in the absence of the word 'accurately', together with the reference to 'speaking', the difference between the teacher who devoted his time to spelling, grammar and punctuation, and the vast majority who, while having some regard for these skills, did not allow them to inhibit the development of imagination, or limit the confidence of those who needed encouragement and support if they were to learn to speak confidently in public. The sixth illustrated how modern maths teaching had been developed and foresaw the emphasis that Cockcroft was to put on the limited skills necessary to survive in the modern world, and the fifth has a curiosity value, for while obviously inserted as a sop to the Prime Minister's vanity, it actually referred to those developments that had already taken place on a large scale in the growth in community study teaching, economics, social and economic history, commerce (and sometimes accounts), statistics and business studies.

But it was the pursuit of the first two objectives that had obliged the best secondary schools to abandon authoritarian methods, basing their techniques increasingly on mutual respect between teacher and pupil and a code of self-discipline. Ironically, it was against this very development, this so-called child-centred permissiveness, that the Ruskin speech was aimed.

However, although the *Green Paper's* statement of aims was firmly based on our liberal traditions, the tone of the rest of the Paper foreshadowed what was to come. It emphasized the need for 'accountability' and outlined a series of abrasive techniques designed to keep teachers up to scratch. It lambasted inefficient teachers and suggested ways of removing them from schools, preferably by transfer to other posts in the service! So it set the scene for the next nine years in which public discussions were to dwell on the ills that beset the service, the need for constant appraisal, and the advantage of pinning teachers down to a contract. Added to the financial neglect of teachers they produced an atmosphere of gloom and precipitated the prolonged 'teachers' action' which in 1985-86 affected the schools seriously. It was Mrs Williams' irresolute behaviour and the tone set by this *Green Paper* that cast a blight on all the growth that was then in process.

In essence one must see education either as training in preparation for a job, or as providing an opportunity to live a full life. If the latter choice is one's prime goal, then schools are heavily dependent on teacher commitment outside the classroom. Furthermore, if schools were to sustain an adventurous curriculum during a time of contraction they would need teachers willing to operate outside their own narrow specialisms, willing to welcome innovation and integration of subject material and willing to risk failure. This could happen only if teachers felt secure and appreciated. The price the country was to pay for this advocacy of abrasive management techniques was the destruction of teacher confidence and morale.

The impact of unemployment on schools is difficult to assess. Education is closely associated in the public mind with getting a good job, and educational institutions conspire to confirm this view. Even graduates complain that they have been let down if their degree does not automatically provide them with higher pay than the non-graduate. This widespread belief must be seen as a substantial proof of education failure!

Boys and girls in secondary schools were slow to realize how the decline in job opportunities would affect them. There is still an uneasy belief that unemployment is the result of personal failure,[17] and that if, like Boxer, one worked harder, or stayed at school longer, one would get a job in the end. So the first impact of unemployment was to increase, in areas where there was only limited adult unemployment, the number of pupils staying on in the sixth form. There was for some time little erosion of the will to work, and schools reacted to the growth in juvenile unemployment by increasing their emphasis on careers advice as if there were still jobs to choose from. But once there were 'hard-working' brothers and sisters in the dole queues, some demoralization was bound to set in.

Faced with the problem of mass juvenile unemployment, the government had three options. The classical response would have been to extend the compulsory span of education, first to 17 and then to 18, thus taking all our youth off the unemployment lists. The cost could have been met out of the money saved by falling rolls and a reduced social security budget. Given a redistribution of the teacher force it was a viable option, but few schools were ready to cope with such a challenge, and had the school-leaving age been raised without linking it with massive schemes of work-experience and more skill-based vocational training in schools, such a policy might well have proved a substantial disaster. That it was barely considered was a direct result of the adverse publicity schools had received after the Ruskin speech.

A different choice would have been to seek rapidly to extend the range of post-16 educational opportunities both in sixth forms and further education colleges, and ally them imaginatively with work experience. One could have mounted the Youth Training Scheme within the educational framework that existed. It would have been demanding and difficult, but ultimately beneficial all round, for it would have revolutionized our schools and produced a more cost-effective tertiary system than can now be achieved.

This was never considered as a serious option because the DES had fallen into disrepute. Central government mandarins derided the dependence of the DES on local government and when there was a sense of urgency, Her Majesty's government, whatever its political complexion, saw the DES as a broken reed. The Manpower Services Commission (MSC) appeared to be a much more effective agency. So the government turned its face away from the education service and in doing so laid to waste the most beneficial long-term gains that were already flowing from the comprehensive system.

Indeed, in setting up the MSC in direct competition with the education service the government has effectively killed off sixth form development in many areas. One has to look only at post-16 financial arrangements to see why this happened. Sixteen-year-olds were left with three options. They could stay at school or go to an FE college with a meagre children's allowance (paid to their parents), supplemented, where there was dire need, by a tiny maintenance grant, or they could get up to three times this income be registering as unemployed, or about five times as much by going on a YTS scheme. Historically, this will be seen as the most incredible folly in educational terms that any government has ever perpetrated. Admittedly, our elitist examination system was already driving many away from education, nursing a sense of failure, but this was more accident than design. One must conclude from the financial lure that prevented our comprehensive sixth forms burgeoning, that the government did not wish to see an expanding educational service. It did little for teacher morale to see the fruits of their labour filched away from their care, and still be reproached for failing to attract students in sufficient numbers into our sixth forms.

In reality, the advent of a Tory government spelt the end of comprehensive education in any real sense of the word. In fashioning this end the government, lacking any overt electoral mandate, proceeded by stealth. The policy was in fact set in motion by Sir Keith Joseph's predecessor, [18] but it was master-minded by him and came to fruition under his care.

Of course, one can take the view that there was no coherent policy, and that the decline of a comprehensive system was fortuitous and a by-product of falling rolls and local mismanagement, but although this is a tenable theory it is not intellectually an appealing one, and when the result of policy coincides with the philosophical aims of government it is churlish not to give credit for intention.

From its inception the development of a truly comprehensive policy was made difficult by two factors. One was that the 'natural' catchment areas each school served, rarely, in our larger conurbations, produced anything resembling a balanced intake, [18] either in terms of pupil ability, apparent potential or parental support. The other was that the level of provision coupled with the educational background of schools, varied dramatically. Only by creating artificial catchment areas and adhering ruthlessly to them could one achieve a balanced intake, and only by positively discriminating in favour of inadequately housed schools could one achieve any real parity of esteem. In practice neither remedy was effectively applied and there was already some polarization around the schools with the 'best' academic reputations situated in the most affluent areas.

Falling rolls made it necessary for authorities who cared about a comprehensive system to exert themselves still more to maintain balanced intakes. They were effectively prevented from doing this by the exaltation of the doctrine of parental choice. Clearly defensible in theoretic terms, in practice parental choice was to destroy the comprehensive pattern, for some schools flourished while others decayed. The middle-classes got selective education without the worry of the 11 + . The fate of schools had nothing to do with the quality of education they offered. It was determined by examination success and transport and social factors. Just to make certain that the system was as divisive as possible, the government legislated to ensure that examination results were published and that HMI reports were available. This was a quaint procedure supposing that government is equally concerned about the education of all children, but understandable if the education of some children is considered more important for the state than others.

This policy produced some sink schools in which the rising tide of disorder could scarcely be contained, and may others in which, thanks to falling rolls, a flight from the inner cities and polarization through parental choice, a broad curriculum could not be sustained without additional staffing support and in which sixth forms became uneconomic and very restricted in what they could offer. By 1980, 90 per cent of 'A' level entries involved only twelve subjects.

Not content with this the Thatcher government found other ways to wreck the comprehensive policy. It introduced the Technical and Vocational Education Initiative (TVEI) funded by the MSC, partly to diminish LEA influence on schools, partly to concentrate expensive resources in a limited number of schools in the hope that dramatic change would be achieved, and partly to set up some schools that were seen to be radically different from other schools in the area. If there wasn't polarization already, there soon would be. What is more, the lavish resources were to be focused on a limited number of selected pupils, so damaging the comprehensive system within individual schools. Often the money provided annually by the MSC was more than three times the capitation grant for the rest of the school.

During the second half of this period the cause of independent education flourished. The 'assisted places' scheme was the most public way in which the government demonstrated its belief that independent schools were better than state schools. Also, by maintaining taxation arrangements that encouraged 'investment' in independent education, the state made it easy for a rival system to flourish. So it can be argued that by starving the state system of resources and demoralizing its teaching force the government made sure that spending money on independent education paid off.

Another attack on the comprehensive system was foreshadowed by Sir Keith Joseph's successor in September 1986. It consisted of a plan to fund twenty 'technical colleges' (CTCs) financed directly by the Ministry, to cream off even more pupils from the remaining comprehensive schools. Ill-conceived and probably ill-fated, this 'plan' was projected as an answer to 'inner city truancy'. If admission to such institutions were in reality to be based on a proven truancy record it would present a fitting finale to a sorry chapter in the history of the English educational system!

The other miserable element that has led to intense frustration in this period has been the glaring under-resourcing of schools. To what extent this has been deliberate policy is questionable. Its causes are manifold. Part of the reason lies in the way schools are financed through local government. Three harmful factors have been simultaneously at work. The prime one has been the ruthless method used by central government to curb local government spending. This has had an exaggerated effect on education which consumes in most areas up to half the budget. Secondly, in most LEAs, expenditure on capitation allowances has not kept pace with inflation. It has to fall behind in only one year for this shortfall to be both perpetuated and enhanced. Thirdly, managing a contracting service is bound to be less cost-effective than servicing an expanding one because much expenditure is unaffected by smaller numbers using the same plant. This includes the rates on schools, the cost of heating and cleaning them, the telephone rentals, the hire charges on capital equipment and the interest on building loans. Smaller numbers in schools often involves a less economic use of staff. As a consequence savings were commonly sought on maintenance programmes and capitation allowances.

The environments of most schools have declined disastrously, and this has encouraged graffiti and vandalism, for neglect invites contempt. There has been a sharp decline in working conditions, with heating systems failing, and a consequent harm to discipline, for children do not behave so well when cold. Some schools have been forced to close in bad weather, and this, combined with the effect of strike action, has undermined established routines. In some areas the undermanning of education offices and their loss of the direct control of services resulting from the Bains Report, has added to the sense of frustration, for headteachers witness the decline and are unable to do anything about it, being denied access to the fount of power.

In the classroom there has been a dramatic decline of the book as a teaching tool. Few schools can still afford to issue books on loan to pupils for the year. Instead there has been a massive rise in the production of worksheets, coupled with a decline in setting homework. However, because teachers, as is their wont, have reacted positively to these privations, it is hard to estimate how seriously they have affected what is taught in schools. For example, worksheets have been justified as aiding autonomous learning, and the high cost of wood and metal has been masked by discovering it is better to teach design than craftsmanship. Similarly nutritional theories have enjoyed a vogue at the expense of cooking.

When teachers withdrew their goodwill in 1985, it was something more than a trade union ploy. The goodwill they withdrew was for most of them the real thing. They no longer saw why they should pour out their spirit to have it wasted and scorned. If the nation wanted to write down the value of their job, and write it down also in the form of a contract, they would do what they were supposed to do, and nothing more. That was the mood of teachers at the start of their action, and by the end of 1986 when the time had come to settle their contractual terms, it had hardened still more.

The settlement marked a major change in the ethos of all our schools. It represented the triumph of those who see the education service in materialistic terms, believing that they can measure its success accurately and increase it by abrasive methods. It may herald the end of our liberal traditions in state education, which will be left to the tender mercies of the independent sector. At least, this appears to be the logic of the present situation.

But one would accept this logic only if one looked at the public face of education and confined oneself to what has been newsworthy during this period. There has been another reality at work, itself worth recording, though in some ways unremarkable, and, if one has been involved in the education service, only to be expected. The good news is that 1973-86, though it has been a period of lost opportunities, frustration and the fading of what seemed to be realistic hopes, has not been a period of decline. Rather there has been much quiet endeavour and unheralded advance.

This owes much to the professionalism of teachers and the need they have to seek job satisfaction. It has a lot to do with the independence of the individual teacher who is devoted to circumventing orders. The history of British education is the story of how teachers have provided a better service than governments intended. In the old elementary schools, many teachers provided much more than the three 'Rs'. Secondary modern teachers introduced 'O' level courses though they were not intended to, and they started up sixth forms, illicitly taught in free time and cloakrooms. Vocational studies were mounted in comprehensive schools often against the advice of LEAs, based on borrowed typewriters and self-financed RSA entrants. I have described how teachers beat the artificial limit on CSE entry, and already determined moves are afoot to defeat any similar restrictions in GCSE courses. If the syllabuses prove too demanding for the below average pupil, schools will develop systems of unit accreditation, and coupled with the production of records of achievement spread across the whole ability range, will prevent the system proving as divisive as intended. In practice the advent of TVEI has proved less harmful than was feared, for many schools have used the money to do what they intended to do anyway, within the traditional education system. They have just been better resourced, while other schools, lacking the money, have managed to keep pace with most developments. You will find, for example, courses in control technology established in non-TVEI schools, and indeed in non-TVEI authorities, and there is every sign that the education service will tame the MSC and will go on its own sweet way, which is often a much sweeter way than can be planned in remote offices. Many schools started their computer study courses without computers, and there is little doubt that teachers want to move faster into the twentieth century than most government agents would credit.

There is no evidence that there has been any decline in educational standards during this period. There have probably been some small advances. Nor has there, as yet, been any sign that teachers are prepared to restrict their pastoral concern for pupils. Indeed, there have been striking developments in pastoral terms. There have been real advances in counselling individuals, shielding them from the ravages of often rapacious schools and helping them cope with an increasingly divided social structure and the poverty that stalks our streets, and also in providing caring school environments with a positive and significant pastoral curriculum.

There have been enormous advances in the last thirteen years in seeking to raise the self-respect of all pupils so that they can cope with a world in which drugs are easy to obtain, where the old taboos have disappeared and where boys and girls at an increasingly early age need to develop standards about sex, based on knowledge and not hearsay. If they choose experiment rather than abstinence, they should know how to avoid conception, and, if this fails, what options are open to them. In handling these problems most schools have been in advance of public opinion, though recently the impact of AIDS has made openness respectable.

Enormous strides have been made actively to counter prejudice. Much more time is spent in opposing racism and sexism, and in explaining that homosexuality is an acceptable state with nothing sinister about it. This has not been done in hugger mugger. There have been positive attempts to involve parents more in the running of schools, not just through governing bodies or PTAs but by discussion of the curriculum and, in primary schools, by encouraging their help in the classroom.

The 1981 Act assumed that there were 18 per cent of pupils already in mainstream schools who had special needs. During this period much progress has been made in integrating them more fully. Remedial classes have disappeared and support teaching in small groups is now offered to pupils who find the going difficult. Since 1981 there has been a slow transfer of pupils from special schools into the mainstream.

In most secondary schools corporal punishment has been phased out, in spite of the increased challenge teachers have all felt from pupils driven to despair by adverse home circumstances. The futility of caning pupils suffering from depression, or high on glue or low on sleep, has done more to convince teachers that the cane should be abandoned than any ruling of the European Court, or the 1986 vote in Parliament. In spite of declining social conditions the ethos in most schools has become more relaxed and companionable, and more rooted in mutual respect.

Some areas of the timetable have undergone notable transformations. In most schools, beyond the third year, physical education has ceased to be compulsory, and a wide range of leisure pursuits have been introduced, embracing almost everything one can think of, from ice-skating to yoga, from golf to squash, from health food weight-watching programmes to gardening.

Religious education has become transformed, often illegally, as four-fifths of our schools have defied the 1944 Education Act and have turned

their backs on a daily religious service for all pupils. As befits a multicultural society most schools teach something about world religions, they
discuss the philosophic basis for atheism, and they go in for community
service and some practical application of spiritual beliefs.

Teaching overall has become much less narrowly academic, with a
greater emphasis on the practical application of acquired knowledge, and
on understanding and problem solving rather than on handling information and approved opinions. Even in modern language teaching and music,
two areas that have not been developed on the scale one would have
wished, there is now greater emphasis on the spoken word and on playing
instruments. There is in fact no innovation envisaged by the GCSE that has
not been foreshadowed by experimental work already taking place on a
wide scale in the classrooms of our schools.

Now none of this could have happened unless the country had a
committed and skilled teaching force, and there is no doubt that whatever
follies governments may yet commit and however foolishly they write
down in restrictive and proscriptive terms the limits of a teacher's
obligations, these will continue to be exceeded, for a teacher's job is
unbearable, shorn of satisfaction. It is often what a teacher chooses to do
above the norm that gives most pleasure.

If the country is to avoid in the next thirteen years wasting again the
spirit and enthusiasm of its teachers, which may come flowing back should
salary settlements be negotiated, then what is needed is a government
that eschews coercion, and local government leaders, both elected and at
officer level, who see themselves as enablers and facilitators rather than
crusaders. Much of this chapter has consisted of an account, not of how
schools have failed, but of how necessary progress has been frustrated, in
part by bad policy, in part by meanness and lack of resources, and in part
by administrative failure. The purpose of all good educational administration is to enable the skill, the initiative and the energy of those doing the
job to be released and channelled into constructive endeavour. Inasmuch as
this chapter is a record of blighted hopes and unachieved ambition, there is
much to be done. Inasmuch as time has been wasted, it needs to be done
fast, and it will therefore prove costly. Because of advances in technology,
because of deteriorating social conditions, because of the lost opportunities,
more is expected of the service than ever before. One has to move faster
than ever even to stand still, and some of the small overall advances have
been gained at the cost of disproportionate endeavour. The challenge to the
education service is to reassert the superiority of education over training, to
refuse to allow competitive examination systems to sour the scene,
to contrive to offer relevant teaching in catering both for increased leisure
and changed working needs and in so doing to recover from its recent
crippling experiences. The challenge to government is to accept that
without a grand new investment in the service we will move ineluctably
into a period of retreat.

Notes

1 Department of Education and Science (1965), London, HMSO.
2 179,000 in 1945; 459,000 in 1976.
3 From two years to three years for the non-graduate teacher.
4 See MIDWINTER, E. (1974) 'Teachers centres: The facilitators', *British Journal of In-service Education*, 1, 1, and PEDLEY, R. (1978) *The Comprehensive School*, London, Penguin, p. 12.
5 Because the number of above-scale posts was determined by a points system heavily weighted in favour of staying on at school.
6 Even though in England and Wales in 1971/72 in the public sector 68.7 per cent of male teachers and 85.5 per cent of female teachers were non-graduates. See *Facts in Focus*, 2nd edn, Penguin, p. 104.
7 The Certificate of Secondary Education was introduced in 1965.
8 See GATHORNE-HARDY, J. (1977) *The Public School Phenomenon*, London, Hodder and Stoughton, p. 377.
9 Leeds, for example, spent much of their ROSLA money on building middle schools.
10 The first Black Paper edited by C. B. Cox and A. E. Dyson, published by *The Critical Quarterly*, appeared in 1969.
11 See CROSSMAN, R. (1976) *The Diaries of a Cabinet Minister*, Vol 2, London, Hamish Hamilton and Jonathon Cape, p. 637.
12 The Houghton Report (1974) was to mark the high-water mark of teachers' salaries. See *Education*, 166, 4, p. 78.
13 The number of postgraduate awards in the social sciences at UK universities more than trebled between 1967 and 1972. It rose by no more than 50 per cent in any form of engineering. See *Facts in Focus* 2nd edn, Penguin, p. 109.
14 Basis for Choice was a product of the Further Education and Curriculum Review and Development Unit (FEU) and was launched in June 1979. Like City and Guilds 365, it involved a profiling system that has now fallen into disrepute. Neither were designed for schools' use.
15 For an account of the 'N' and 'F' proposals see *Secondary Education*, 8, 3, pp. 14–16.
16 DEPARTMENT OF EDUCATION AND SCIENCE (1977) *Education in Schools: A Consultative Document*, Cmnd 6869, London, HMSO.
17 See RAE, J. (1986) in the *Sunday Observer*, 23 November.
18 Mark Carlisle, against the advice of every teacher association, planned in 1980 to oblige all schools to publish their examination results. See *Education*, 156, 24, p. 546.
19 See CROSLAND, C. A. R. (1956) *The Future of Socialism*, London, Jonathan Cape, p. 275.

Chapter 5: Special Schools

Patricia Rowan

Patricia Rowan has been Deputy Editor of *The Times Educational Supplement* since 1978, and on the staff since 1972. She chairs the governing body of an Inner London comprehensive school and is also a primary school governor. She is author of *What Sort of Life?*, (1980) a paper for the OECD project 'The Handicapped Adolescent', giving an account of strategies in nine local authorities in the UK to aid transition from school to adult life and work, and was Editor of *Integration in the School* (1981) published by the Centre for Educational Research and Innovation at OECD.

★   ★   ★

For children and young people with disabilities, 1973 was the turning point, a time of hope and expectation. After years of pressure, including a Plowden Report recommendation seven years earlier, the Warnock Enquiry into special education needs was announced.

The strength of feeling which led to Warnock was part of a whole new climate of thinking which needs to be set into a wider context. All over the world, attitudes, concepts and policies on special education had been changing for a decade or more as social and political aspirations to create a fairer and more integrated society began to be expressed in national policies for minorities, the disadvantaged and those with disabilities.

It was a natural development of the progressive climate of the sixties which nurtured comprehensive schooling that the principle should be extended to those groups that society had deemed handicapped—though often it was society itself that did the handicapping.

In many countries, traditional patterns of living and of education were being challenged by human rights and civil rights movements, and by the pressure groups and consumer organizations which were beginning to feel their strength. Among them, disabled people themselves were putting their claims to equality of education, opportunity and esteem; the common message was that they had the same essential rights and aspirations to as normal a life as possible as everybody else.

It was in 1975 that the United Nations declaration of the rights of disabled people stated that: 'whatever the origin, nature and seriousness of their handicaps and disabilities, disabled people have the same fundamental rights as their fellow citizens of the same age'.

A working party, under the chairmanship of Lord Snowdon, was to put the case simply and eloquently when it reported in 1976 on *Integrating the Disabled*[1]:

> Integration for the disabled means a thousand things. It means the absence of segregation. It means social acceptance. It means being able to be treated like everybody else. It means the right to work, to go to cinemas, to enjoy outdoor sports, to have a family life and a social life and a love life, to contribute materially to the community, to have the usual choices of association, movement and activity, to go on holiday to the usual places, to be educated up to university level with one's unhandicapped peers, to travel without fuss on public transport.

But if children with disabilities were isolated in separate streams which cut them off from their peer groups throughout schooling, they were likely to be outsiders for the rest of their lives. The question was how far integration in schooling could lead to integration into society, and central to that debate were the new definitions of both handicap and integration that were being developed.

Disability was essentially different from handicap, the new reasoning went: disabilities might impose limitations on the individual, but it is the physical, cultural or social obstacles in the way of access to society or classroom, which create the handicap.

For somebody in a wheelchair, a staircase need not be an obstacle if a way can be found to circumvent it; but an examination-oriented, academic curriculum can have the effect of handicapping somebody with learning difficulties, or whose schooling has been interrupted by ill-health.

It is a matter of the interaction between the child and its environment. A disability may not be a handicap if help is forthcoming which makes it possible to take on the challenge of the ordinary class-room successfully. An integration policy can provide the framework for meeting individual special needs in this way.

Integration, however, means different things to different people. Although the Warnock Report[2] called it 'the central issue in special education', and defined quite clearly the different degrees of integration which were possible, the Committee avoided an unqualified recommendation for an integration policy. It chose instead to make its central thrust a call for a new definition of special need that would replace categories of handicap.

Confusion has continued to this day as to what integration means, whether it has to be all or nothing, whether Warnock had really backed it, and most of all, whether it could work without extra money.

The story of the wasted years in special education is the story of Warnock and of the hopes that rose and fell with the fate of the Report. Thirteen years after the announcement of the Enquiry, the whole political and social context was shifting away again from attitudes that could easily accommodate the new concepts of disability and integration. The international mood was back to basics and bench-marks—as in the United States *A Nation at Risk* report and the Education Secretary's legislation for a national curriculum in the United Kingdom—and away from the common school which could stretch to include everyone. Everywhere, economic constraints put a brake on the resources needed for positive discrimination policies.

In this country, many of the early hopes and expectations remained unfulfilled, dashed by a thousand statements, struggling for expression through a prickly hedge of practical, professional and ideological conflicts as the dedicated and the bureaucratic amongst our service providers sought alike to make sense of policies in the absence of any clear lead, financial provision, or even monitoring, from central government.

Although there were some signs that attitudes and practices were changing, it was by now evident that we were still only at the beginning of a very long, slow process.

History and Statute

Special education grew up as a parallel stream to the rest of the system as a result of a variety of medical, historical and legal factors, which all still affect provision and possibilities for change.

The Warnock Report summed up this background, which provided the starting point for the Committee's work:

> As with ordinary education, education for the handicapped began with individual and charitable enterprise. There followed in time the intervention of government, first to support voluntary effort and make good deficiencies through state provision, and finally to create a national framework in which public and voluntary agencies could act in partnership to see that all children, whatever their disability, received a suitable education. The framework reached its present form only in this decade.

The first schools for blind and deaf children were started in the eighteenth century, to be followed more than fifty years later by homes and asylums providing limited schooling or training to physically or mentally handicapped youngsters. After the Forster Education Act of 1870, public provision began patchily with the new school boards and, alongside the voluntary effort, opened up new open-air, day and boarding schools.

Legislation built up piecemeal, but a solid statutory basis was provided by the 1944 Education Act. Section 8(2)(c) laid a duty on local authorities to have regard 'to the need for securing that provision is made for pupils who suffer from any disability of the mind or body by providing, either in special schools or otherwise, special education treatment'. Section 34 said they must ascertain 'what children in their area require special education treatment'; and section 33(2) obliged them 'to provide for the education of a pupil with a serious disability in an appropriate special school, or any other suitable school where this was impracticable or the disability was not serious'.

Categories of handicap were subsequently laid down for England and Wales: blind, partially sighted; deaf; partially hearing; educationally subnormal, epileptic; maladjusted; physically handicapped; speech defective; delicate. Similar categories were listed for Scotland (except that the Scots used what later became regarded as the more acceptable term 'mentally handicapped,' rather than 'educationally subnormal') and for Northern Ireland.

In 1970 one last group of children—those with such severe mental handicaps that they had previously been labelled 'ineducable' and looked after by the health authorities—were brought into the remit of the education service by a new Act of Parliament. The consequence when the Act was implemented two years later was the division of schools for severely subnormal children (ESN) into those for children with moderate (M) or severe (S) learning difficulties.

At the time Warnock reported, the national framework of special education was still heavily dependent on its independent, charitable and voluntary beginnings. In particular, a very high proportion of blind and deaf children were in non-maintained schools.

The pattern of provision was changing in response to the changing incidence and nature of handicap as much as to legislation. Improved medical and social services had led to the virtual elimination of polio and tuberculosis, and reduced the need for open-air schools for the delicate. Advanced medical techniques had made it possible to save the lives at birth of some severely and multiply handicapped children, but changing policies on testing for mongolism and spina bifida in early pregnancy and the possibility of readier abortions also had their effect on the population of special schools and hospitals. Meanwhile, the number of children diagnosed as maladjusted was rising steadily, along with the number of children with behavioural difficulties who either remained in the ordinary classroom, or were increasingly consigned to separate units.

Before the Warnock Committee had reported, however, or barely reached the halfway mark in its deliberations, another piece of relevant legislation had been slotted into place. Section 10 of the 1976 Education Act caused a considerable stir at the time because it preempted the Committee's own verdict on that central issue of integration. Hung on to an Education Bill about something quite different, as an amendment in the House of Lords (a habit with their Lordships even then), it was eloquently backed by Lord

Vaizey, amongst others impatient to see the principle established in statute.

Section 10 shifted the balance one stage further towards an integration policy by replacing section 33(2) of the 1944 Act, and obliging local authorities 'to provide for handicapped pupils in normal schools except where this is impracticable, incompatible with effective instruction, or would involve unreasonable public expenditure'.

The Warnock Report

It was Mrs Margaret Thatcher who, as Secretary of State for Education and Science, acknowledged the long campaign for a major review of special education by announcing in November 1973 that she proposed to appoint a Committee:

> To review educational provision in England, Scotland and Wales for children and young people handicapped by disabilities of body or mind, taking account of the medical aspects of their needs, together with arrangements to prepare them for entry into employment; to consider the most effective use of resources for these purposes; and to make recommendations.

She appointed to chair the Committee Mrs Mary Warnock, a senior research fellow at St Hugh's College, Oxford, and a former headmistress of Oxford High School for Girls, who from that time took her place as a regular, incisive member of that panel of the great and the good from whom all committee chairmen are chosen. It was her first-class, logical brain which effectively managed the Committee and witnesses, controlled a great weight of evidence, and presided over the writing of a well-argued Report that avoided emotional response to an emotive subject.

Before the other members of the Committee were appointed, however, a General Election and a change of government intervened, and in March 1974 Mr Reginald Prentice took over as Labour Education Secretary. It was not until the following September that he got the rest of the team together and they were able to start work.

It is doubtful whether the change in political power had made very much difference to the selection of Committee members. Indeed, it is a measure of the shift in attitudes which the Warnock Report itself helped to bring about that it would today be unthinkable to appoint a group of people so completely dominated by the professional and official voice to enquire into such a subject, and with so little room for the consumer or parent.

Mr George Cooke, County Education Officer for Lincolnshire, became Vice-chairman and his tireless commitment continued long after the Report's publication as he stumped the country proselytyzing on its themes; the rest of the educationists, administrators, paediatricians, psychiatrists, psychologists and other experts from the world of education and medicine were all dedicated and hard-working. But not one handicapped person was appointed to the Committee and only one parent, Mrs Winifred Tumim, mother of two deaf children, who was also Chairman of the Education Committee of the National Deaf Children's Society.

Mrs Tumim, a passionate and articulate advocate, has since confessed that—although she felt she had succeeded reasonably well in putting forward the parents' point of view wherever it seemed relevant—for the most part she had felt herself 'inevitably falling in with the ... professional preoccupations and values' of the rest of the Committee.

'My thinking was obviously coloured by traditional British attitudes towards educating handicapped children', she wrote in *The Times Educational Supplement* on 12 March 1982. 'These attitudes are based, implicitly at least, on a defence of expertise and professionalism.'

The Committee sat for four years; took written and oral evidence from nearly 400 organizations or individuals; coopted fifteen more members to add expertise to the four sub-committees looking at pre-school, normal and special schools, and at school-leavers; commissioned half-a-dozen research projects; sent small groups of members to visit the United States, Canada, Denmark, Sweden, Holland and West Germany; and made very many visits in England, Scotland and Wales to nursery schools, special nursery units, ordinary schools, maintained and non-maintained special schools, independent schools, hospitals, assessment centres, colleges of further education, colleges of education, and departments of education in polytechnics.

The philosophy of their Report may be summed up in three quotations from the opening chapter, 'The general approach':

> We hold that education has certain long-term goals ... They are, first, to enlarge a child's knowledge, experience and imaginative understanding, and thus his awareness of moral values and capacity for enjoyment; and secondly to enable him to enter the world after formal education is over as an active participant in society and a contributor to it, capable of achieving as much independence as possible. The educational needs of every child are determined in relation to these goals. We are fully aware that for some children the first of these goals can be approached by minute, though for them highly significant, steps, while the second may never be achieved. But this does not entail that for these children the goals are different. The purpose of education for all is the same; the goals are the same.
>
> Moreover, there are some children with disabilities who, through education along the lines we advocate, may be able to lead a life very little poorer in quality than that of the non-handicapped child, whereas without this kind of education they may face a life of dependence or even institutionalization. Education in such cases makes the difference between a proper and enjoyable life and something less than we believe life should be.

> Our concept of special education ... embraces the notion of any form of additional help, wherever it is provided, and whenever it is provided from birth to maturity to overcome educational difficulty.

With such a starting point, it is even easier in retrospect to understand why Committee members were dismayed at the precipitate amendment of the 1976 Act to encourage integration of handicapped pupils into the ordinary school. Not only did it preempt their own conclusions on this central issue, thus ensuring polarized reactions to the report in terms of whether it would be 'for' or 'against', but it also seemed to offer simplistic solutions on a very complicated issue.

In the end, the Committee worked its way logically out of the cul-de-sac into which it had been forced and laid out a wider, and wiser, new conceptual framework for special education.

Drawing upon thinking and developments in this country and elsewhere, the concept introduced in the Report embraced not just a wider group of children than those previously identified as handicapped, but recommended that categories of disability should be replaced with the idea of a continuum of special educational needs, to be met in a variety of ways. By removing the labels, it was focusing attention on how the needs of individual children were to be met, as much as where they should be educated.

One of the main intentions was to break down the habit of thinking of just two kinds of children: normal and handicapped. Looking at the whole spectrum, the Committee found, as many as one in five children might be expected to have special educational needs at some time in their schooling, and the majority of those were already in ordinary schools. At that time 1.9 per cent of children were likely to be in special schools, and another 5 per cent in special classes. Opening up the definition to take in between 16 and 20 per cent of the school population gave added force to the movement towards integration, but also emphasized the importance of qualifying the term.

> The wider concept of special education proposed in this report, embracing as it does all those children in ordinary schools who, though not at present accounted handicapped, need additional support in a variety of forms, is directly in line with the principle that handicapped and non-handicapped children should be educated in a common setting as far as possible.

Warnock distinguished three main forms of integration: locational, social and functional—'not discrete, but overlapping' and representing 'progressive stages of association'. Locational integration exists where special units or schools share the same site as ordinary schools, social where they share activities outside the classroom; functional is the fullest form, where social and locational lead to joint educational activities.

International studies suggest that most developed countries with an integration policy (including some believed to be much further along the road than us) adopt versions of these physical, social or functional approaches, rather than the assumed all-or-nothing model.

The report translates into practical terms the various alternatives along the continuum which might provide for different needs at different times:

1   full-time education in an ordinary class with any necessary help and support;
2   education in an ordinary class with periods of withdrawal to a special class or unit or other supporting base;
3   education in a special class or unit with periods of attendance at an ordinary class and full involvement in the general community life and extra-curricular activities of the ordinary school;
4   full-time education in a special class or unit with social contact with the main school.

The Committee saw a continuing place for special schools for some children and hoped that they could develop as centres of expertise and support for ordinary schools.

They recognized that resources might not be immediately available to provide for all their recommendations, but noted that some could be carried out within existing budgets. However, they also set out tough conditions to guard against integration on the cheap. These insisted on the need for the accurate assessment of all the physical, mental and emotional factors affecting a child's performance, full involvement for parents, and preparation and consultation for teachers.

> We strongly endorse the need for adequate staff and resources to be made available to ordinary schools to meet the needs of children assessed as requiring special educational help. These staff must have additional training or substantial experience in special education.

Fierce debate has continued to this day—and not just in this country—as to whether it is essential to have extra resources and adequate in-service training assured before embarking on integration policies, or whether it is a matter of political will and sufficient sense of direction to shift special education funding out of the segregated sector. On the one hand there is the spectre of unsupported isolation in the mainstream classroom; on the other a constant excuse for resistance to change.

The Warnock Report made 225 recommendations, but the central thrust of its wider concept of special educational need was to be found in the five relating to the scope of special education:

1 The planning of services for children and young people should be based on the assumption that about one in six children at any time

and up to one in five children at some time during their school career will require some form of special educational provision;

2 Statutory categorization of handicapped children should be abolished;

3 The term 'children with learning difficulties' should be used in future to describe both those children who are currently categorized as educationally subnormal and those with educational difficulties who are often at present the concern of remedial services;

4 In order to safeguard the interests of children with severe, complex and long-term disabilities, there should be a system of recording as in need of special educational provision those children who, on the basis of a detailed profile of their needs prepared by a multi-professional team, are judged by their local education authority to require special educational provision not generally available in ordinary schools;

5 Section 8(2)(c) of the Education Act 1944 and Section 5(1) of the Education (Scotland) Act 1962 (as amended), which defines the duties of local education authorities in relation to the provision of special educational treatment and special education respectively, should be amended to embody a broader concept of special education related to a child's individual needs as distinct from his disability and a wider description of children which includes those with significant difficulties in learning, or with emotional or behavioural disorders, as well as those with disabilities of mind or body.

Even before spelling out the requirements of this wider concept of special educational needs, which was to become central to its implementation, the Report had, however, identified three areas for priority action: provision for children under 5 with special educational needs; provision for young people over 16 with special needs; and teacher training.

None of these 'three areas of first priority' was to figure to any significant extent in the legislation which eventually followed, as we shall see later, nor yet could subsequent changes in provision or policy be taken as unequivocal signs that the government was taking on board the spirit of Warnock. Far from it. Department of Education and Science ministers were also to spend some time and energy ducking and weaving to avoid giving parents the rights of appeal and access to information recommended in the Report; dodging the issue on the proposal for a named person who might provide a point of contact at critical times to guide parents and handicapped young people through a confusing maze of services; side-stepping the implications of recommendations designed to promote better relationships and coordination between professionals and services, and to sort out the overlapping and sometimes competing responsibilities of education and social services and of area health authorities.

The Warnock Report was completed in March 1978 and by this time Mrs Shirley Williams was the Secretary of State for Education. She was a member of a Labour government existing on the slenderest of majorities, under instructions from the International Monetary Fund, and heading for the Winter of Discontent.

Mrs Williams did what many an Education Secretary has done before her (and which action men like Lord Young, Sir Keith Joseph and Kenneth Baker have derided ever since) and in place of response embarked on rounds of extensive consultation with special interest groups, local education authorities, and in short virtually everyone who had given evidence to the Warnock Committee in the first place.

The Report and its new concept of special educational need had in fact been warmly received on the whole, even by those section 10 proponents who had feared in advance that it would duck the integration issue. The new Conservative government which took office in May 1979 had other priorities, however, and the first piece of legislation introduced by Mr Mark Carlisle as Secretary of State was the 1980 Act delivering new rights and choices to parents (except where their children had special needs). Implementation of Warnock had to wait its turn until the following year.

The Warnock Committee had warned in a parting shot that organizational changes and additional resources would not be sufficient to achieve their aims, unless they were accompanied by changes in attitude. It was a message that the government accepted selectively. Attitudes came cheaper than resources.

The 1981 Education Act

The 1981 legislation, when it was eventually introduced, did the bare minimum to provide a new legal framework for special education, without spending any extra money at all. Lady Young, the junior Education Minister, explained that changing attitudes was what mattered, and you couldn't legislate for that. Nor was it felt that Warnock's three priority areas for action could most appropriately be dealt with by legislation.

The overriding constraint was the government's implacable refusal to allow that extra resources were necessary to shift organization as well as attitudes into a different direction. Another brake on desirable development was the reluctance of the DES (although the 1983 guidelines were issued jointly with the Department of Health and Social Security) to take action on proposals that might involve stepping into the territory of another department, particularly that dangerous ground where services and professionals stand entrenched behind their own bristly defences.

The result was an Act that essentially extended the comprehensive principle (something of an historical irony in Mrs Thatcher's first government), but which in an exercise of statutory hypocrisy sought an attitude shift without obligations; which gave new rights to parents, but raised expectations without providing the statutory right to claim the necessary resources.

The Act accepted the central thrust of Warnock's new concept of special educational need, abolished categories of handicap, and laid a new general duty on local education authorities to place as many children with special needs as possible in normal schools. The balance of law was thus shifted a notch further in favour of integration, though weasel words about efficient use of resources, and the provision of 'efficient education' for other children, remained.

The needs of children with severe learning difficulties were to be safeguarded by the introduction of a new 'statement', a record describing their special needs and how they were to be met.

Key definitions offered in the Act to assist in this process proved to be unhelpfully circular in nature. 'A child has special educational needs', it says, 'if s/he has a learning difficulty which calls for special educational provision to be made'. And: 'a child has a learning difficulty if s/he has significantly greater difficulty in learning than the majority of children of his age, or has a disability which either prevents or hinders him from making use of educational facilities of a kind generally provided in schools ... for children of his age'.

The Warnock concept that approximately one in five children have special educational needs at some time was not translated into statute, and the lack of definition of the target population has resulted in wide variations in interpretation.

Although both Warnock and the Act were explicit about the need to end labelling, the instant result of the abolition of categories such as 'speech defective' or 'educationally subnormal' was the creation of a new label: SEN, for special educational need. And when, more than three years after implementation, the House of Commons Select Committee began to invite evidence on progress, debate still seemed to be bogged down in definitions and interpretations: when does a learning difficulty become a significant learning difficulty?

By the time the Act was implemented on 1 April 1983, parental involvement in the assessment and placement of their handicapped child had become a far more important feature of the regulations than it had been in the original Bill or, in spite of many attempts to amend it during the Special Standing Committee stage and in the House of Lords to improve parental rights to information, in the final version that went on the statute book. Perhaps in the end the government was sufficiently convinced by its own rhetoric to accept that clear right of access to all recorded information about their own children could not logically be withheld from parents of disabled children.

The regulations spell out that statements of special need must include, verbatim, all professional advice prepared during assessments—educational, medical or psychological.

Although the Circular emphasizes the importance of consulting parents, and gives them valuable new rights to see drafts of statements and to appeal against provision offered, delivery of these rights has proved both uncertain and uneven, as will be shown later. In any case, new rights were often to prove illusory without that last vital statutory right to the resources to meet them.

As Peter Newell commented in a Special Education Handbook[3] written for the Advisory Centre for Education as a guide to implementation of the 1981 Act:

> The new law on special education is a hesitant step along the road to providing adequate safeguards, rights and duties for all those involved in the education of children with special educational needs, and to ensuring their right to integration into the life and work of the community, and its 'ordinary' institutions.
>
>   It is a pale reflection of similar legislation already in force in other countries (for instance the Education of all Handicapped Children Act in the US).

The main difference was that the American legislation, aimed to ensure education 'in the least restrictive environment', gave parents the right both to expect support in the ordinary classroom as a consequence of an individualised education plan (IEP) and also to delivery of the necessary services, whatever it cost. Public Law 94.142 has given rise to court cases, endless trouble and expense for administrators at state level, and regular attempts at federal level to reduce the financial commitment of 'title' money (a form of specific grant). It has been suggested that this sort of litigation–happy system would not suit parents here, but there isn't much doubt that it has helped the movement of both attitudes and integration policies in the US, although practise varies between states.

Another issue on which there was a vigorous lobby at the committee stage of the Bill was the case for a National Advisory Committee, strongly recommended in the Warnock Report to monitor progress, advise, coordinate services and disseminate good practice.

Constantly wary that a watchdog might turn into a quango, the government refused to change course on that one, and has remained adamantly opposed to the concept, in spite of renewed pressure. HMI could monitor progress, said the DES, and three major research projects were later to be commissioned to collect information on progress and disseminate good practice. In the event, the exercise by HMI was not to be conducted until 1987, the year when the three research reports on policy and provision, in-service, and support in the ordinary school, were due to be published, and when the House of Commons Select Committee was also to consider progress since the 1981 Act (in proceedings truncated by the General Election).

The net result of government refusal to set up a permanent watchdog was that from 1983 to 1987 it was virtually impossible to get any national picture of implementation, a situation compounded by lack of central guidance and by the DES inability to find a satisfactory way even to collate statistics without the old category standbys.

As to the three high priorities for action set out in Warnock; the Act and its regulations made some movement on the under-5s, in that the duty of an education authority to provide statements was extended downwards to include children from the age of 2, and that the health authority was given a duty to identify children's special educational needs from birth, to inform the parents and the education authority, and to give the parents details of voluntary organizations which could give advice and help. A welcome multidisciplinary approach to identification and assessment at this stage was required.

But the Warnock Committee's main concern as to children under 5 had related to early, unsegregated, educational opportunities. The explicit recommendation was for 'A substantial extension of nursery education for all children', in the hope that opportunities for nursery education for young children with special needs would be correspondingly extended. Appointed so soon after publication of Thatcher's *Framework for Expansion*, that must have seemed a reasonable proposition, though it has since been criticized as a rather naive basis on which to expect action. Certainly the hoped-for expansion of nursery education has not materialized.

The most comprehensive betrayal of Warnock, however, was to do with provision for young people over 16, both in further education and in adult training and day centres. Making the case for vastly improved access to education for handicapped youngsters once they had passed the school leaving age, the Report emphasized:

> Local authorities have a duty, which is not widely recognized, to provide for all young people who want continued full-time education between the ages of 16 and 19, either in school or in an establishment of further education, though not necessarily whichever of the two the individual prefers. It is essential that they should fulfil this duty and ensure that adequate numbers of places in schools and establishments of further education are available to and taken up by young people with special educational needs.

It was further recommended that education in ATCs and day centres should be provided by education departments, with separate programmes run for young people. These last were difficult propositions to handle in our compartmentalized system, since both ATCs and day centres were run by the social services departments, and catered for adults of all ages. The day centres to which physically handicapped youngsters were sent from 16 onwards—if provision were made at all—were dominated by the elderly and the diseases of the aged. Continuing education or training for young people was rarely to be found in a day centre, and difficult to arrange as a separate programme, given the limited numbers of school leavers in each centre.

The ATCs were regarded as the natural destination for severely mentally handicapped school leavers, though again their commitment to adults frequently meant a bottleneck for new entries; and once inside the training offered by instructors was often of the minimal, production-line variety.

It was at this stage that many handicapped young people, sometimes just below employability level, were likely to fall through the yawning gaps in the net between the departments of education, social services, employment and the area health authorities. Some young people with learning difficulties have shown that—given appropriate training and further education—it is possible to progress to a job, self-respect and independence. But the lack of co-ordination between the services, and the fact that it has seldom been clear which of them has a statutory obligation to provide a service to over-16s, has meant that such planned progression remains the exception.

School leavers with very severe physical disabilities but real intellectual potential were even more likely to be doomed to an empty life without stimulation in a day centre, or isolation at home. There is little evidence of change in provision for this group since Warnock reported in 1978. The 1981 Act, perhaps because the DES was reluctant to introduce legislation that would have involved real co-ordination with another department, did not transfer responsibility for education in adult training or day centres.

As to further education, the DES lawyers were particularly doubtful about the Warnock definition of rights. Statutory provision for the special educational needs of 16-19 year-olds was better postponed, it was said, until the hazy business of a legal basis for further education as a whole was sorted out. DES ministers and officials then embarked on what can best be described as a cynical waiting game, to see whether any parent would be prepared to take court action to establish the right of a handicapped teenager to further education. If no-one was prepared to go to the considerable trouble and expense involved, perhaps the 1944 Act could be left in its usefully ambiguous state.

It was clear enough that handicapped young people had the same rights as others to education between the ages of 16 and 19, but not necessarily in their own choice of school or college. The difficulty was that their choices were very much more circumscribed by lack of suitable courses. Although some special schools kept their pupils past the age of 16, and statements were to be required up to the age of 19 for those still in school, there was growing agreement that many young people with special needs could be better prepared for an independent life, and perhaps work, if they had the chance to leave the protective care of the special school and take on the challenge of a more adult life-style in college. It was certainly arguable that young people whose schooling had been interrupted by ill-health or hampered by learning difficulties needed the right to education up to 19 (or 21 as in other countries) more than their contemporaries.

In the absence of national or regional policy, however, provision was scarce and patchy. It depended where you lived, whether there was a suitably tailored course available locally, access to a regular course, or progression from one to the other. Some local authorities were developing their own successful projects. Some courses began as the personal initiatives of college staff. Organization and training for lecturers often developed *ad hoc* out of experience, but usually in isolation. It could easily happen that no suitable course was available for a disabled young person of 16 in either school or local FE college. Some ATCs were doing their best to meet needs by employing teachers themselves or running link courses, but by no means all. Was an ATC place an acceptable alternative to FE?

The further education legal basis (FELB) project proceeded on its slow and bureaucratic way. A test case was threatened in Oxfordshire, but averted after DES pressure and the resourceful organization of a suitable course by the Oxfordshire Chief Education Officer. The FELB files were left to gather dust and eventually shelved.

Since then the numbers of handicapped students in FE have vastly expanded, however, perhaps as much because of the attitude changes engendered by Warnock as by DES policy. At the time the Warnock Committee reported there were thought to be fewer than 1000 students with special needs in post-school education. But by 1985 evidence of increasing numbers was coming in from all sides. Professing himself encouraged by this news Sir Keith Joseph, then Education Secretary, commissioned the National Bureau for Handicapped Students to carry out the first ever national statistical survey of students with special needs in further and higher education.

The NBHS report, *Catching Up?*,[4] found that numbers of students with special needs in post-school education and training had grown to 43,540 in English colleges, but fewer than 10,000 were full-time students, and the chances of getting on a course varied dramatically across the country, as did the provision of in-service training.

In the north-west, more than thirty students in every 1000 were physically and/or mentally disabled, compared with just over thirteen per 1000 in East Anglia. Three out of five FE and tertiary colleges were unable to cope with the needs of physically handicapped students and only 36 per cent had physically handicapped students on mainstream courses. Nearly two-thirds were likely to deny them places because of access problems or lack of support staff.

One in five FE colleges had no special needs students and where provision was made, most disabled students were on special courses, with only 3400 integrated—with support—into ordinary classes. Fewer than one in five colleges had a formal policy on admission.

Catching Up? highlighted the need for more integration into mainstream courses, and more concerted programmes between local authorities and colleges. It was clear that there was a groundswell of concern and effort to improve provision, which deserved more support from local and central government. Perhaps only a statutory obligation to provide education beyond 16 for young people with disabilities, together with the resources that would have to follow, will make sure of the service they need, though joint funding and joint training between the services would help.

When the Warnock Committee chose teacher training as the third of its three priorities for action, it recommended that: All initial training courses should have a compulsory 'special needs element'; all existing teachers should have access to a short awareness course; and that training facilities should be increased so that a recognized qualification should be made a requirement for all teachers with responsibility for children with special needs.

Although teacher training was one of the areas left untouched by the Act both Sir Keith Joseph, as Secretary of State, and the then Chief HMI for Teacher Training, Mrs Pauline Perry, had made up their minds by the time the Act came into force that training teachers to handle special needs in the ordinary classroom was a different proposition to training to teach in special schools.

When the Council for the Accreditation of Teacher Education (CATE) was established, a compulsory special needs element in all initial courses was duly laid down as one of the criteria for course approval, a measure that is beginning to have an effect. Progress is often hampered, however, because the necessary staffing is not available. That is a position likely to deteriorate rapidly as a result of new in-service funding arrangements, according to Professor Peter Mittler, Director of the Centre for Educational Guidance and Special Needs at the University of Manchester's Department of Education, and Co-director of the team delivering the DES-funded research project on in-service training for special needs.

Sir Keith's introduction of specific funding for selected government priorities has been used to provide direct funding for in-service courses to help teachers in ordinary schools to deal with handicapped children. Another under-resourced move in the right direction. Progress on short awareness courses has been patchy, depending on school and local authority priorities.

The government remained unconvinced of the need for a mandatory qualification for all special needs teachers and was only with difficulty persuaded to retain them for teachers of children with sensory impairments. Having insisted on phasing out initial training for teachers of children with severe learning difficulties and sensory impairments, the government was eventually persuaded that one-year, full-time INSET courses should be obligatory, but left open the question of the necessary resources.

Higher education departments have increased the number of short courses and broadened their scope to cover a wider group of children; in particular, there has been a growth since 1983 in one-term, full-time courses for teachers with responsibilities for special needs in ordinary schools. Around 500 teachers have taken these innovative courses, but that doesn't go far to cater for 23,000 primary schools and over 4000 secondary schools, and there has hardly been a start on further education.

The reality is that funds available under specific grant and under the new grant-related in-service training (GRIST) arrangements due to operate from April 1987 are grossly inadequate to meet the in-service training implications of the 1981 Act. Nor has it helped that earmarked funds have gone to local authorities, but not to higher education to fund new training initiatives and staff.

The admirable intention of GRIST is to involve schools and local authorities more in in-service decisions to meet staff development needs, and investment in school-based courses has been one of the first results. What concerned Professor Mittler and his colleagues was the resulting massive reduction in one-year secondments, by as much as 90 per cent in some authorities.

For the universities and polytechnics, the consequent loss of students and funding produced an immediate crisis since it placed in doubt the very existence of the departments which ought to provide the knowledge and experience base to service the special needs element in initial training.

One strong department in danger of being wiped out by the loss of full-time students was Professor Mittler's own, although its PGCE courses had so impressed HMI that the then Chief Inspector had wanted it to be a national resource, providing short courses for staff responsible for introducing special needs elements into initial training.

Professor Mittler, the man selected by the DES to conduct the major research project in the field, had warned the Secretary of State that direct ministerial intervention was essential to provide earmarked or direct funding for the extra tutors needed in HE, and stressed the urgent case for coherent national and local teacher training strategies. His personal plea for leadership, initiative and resources received a dusty answer from DES officials.

Statements of Special Educational Needs

There is not much room for doubt that, whatever the intentions of Warnock and those who framed the 1981 Act, its main effect has been to focus effort and attention on the production of statements.

Writing in *The Times Educational Supplement* on 1 April 1983, the day the Act came into force, Margaret Peter (Editor of the National Council for Special Education's *Special Education: Forward Trends*) warned of counter-productive bureaucracy and expense:

> The Act threatens greater divisiveness because it prescribes time-consuming, paper-laden and labour-intensive procedures for helping the more severely impaired two per cent. These are likely to divert the time and energy of teachers, psychologists, administrators and other personnel away from the other 18 per cent in ordinary schools.

Table 1: Number and Proportion of Children with Statements of Special Educational Needs as at January 1986 (Form SEN 2 1986)

	Number of pupils with statements	Percentage of school population with statements
Avon	6454	4.2
Barking	352	1.4
Barnet	676	1.4
Barnsley	457	1.2
Bedfordshire	1576	1.7
Berkshire	2252	1.8
Bexley	739	2.2
Birmingham	3517	1.9
Bolton	632	1.3
Bradford	1381	1.6
Brent	—	—
Bromley	794	1.8
Buckinghamshire	2661	2.5
Bury	576	1.9
Calderdale	345	1.0
Cambridgeshire	1928	1.8
Cheshire	3373	2.1
Cleveland	2276	2.1
Cornwall	1109	1.5
Coventry	1019	1.9
Croydon	854	1.7
Cumbria	1235	1.5
Derbyshire	2919	1.9
Devon	2918	2.0
Doncaster	124	0.2
Dorset	1681	1.8
Dudley	912	1.9
Durham	1646	1.6
Ealing	654	1.5
East Sussex	1747	1.8
Enfield	769	1.9
Essex	4674	1.9
Gateshead	608	1.8
Gloucestershire	217	0.2
Hampshire	5303	2.2
Haringey	547	1.8
Harrow	571	1.8
Havering	615	1.6
Hereford & Worcester	52	0.04
Hertfordshire	3446	2.0
Hillingdon	565	1.5
Hounslow	417	1.3
Humberside	2319	1.6
ILEA	7241	2.2
Isle of Wight	337	1.8
Isles of Scilly	1	0.4
Kent	4934	2.0
Kingston upon Thames	381	1.8

Table 1: (Continued)

	Number of pupils with statements	Percentage of school population with statements
Kirklees	1027	1.5
Knowsley	389	1.3
Lancashire	4154	1.8
Leeds	1554	1.3
Leicestershire	1725	1.2
Lincolnshire	1972	2.2
Liverpool	1676	1.9
Manchester	248	0.3
Merton	58	0.2
Newcastle upon Tyne	864	1.9
Newham	738	2.0
Norfolk	1695	1.5
North Tyneside	602	1.8
North Yorkshire	1748	1.6
Northamptonshire	1754	1.7
Northumberland	874	1.7
Nottinghamshire	2531	1.5
Oldham	664	1.6
Oxfordshire	968	1.1
Redbridge	708	2.1
Richmond upon Thames	294	1.3
Rochdale	682	1.8
Rotherham	871	1.9
St Helens	640	1.9
Salford	742	1.8
Sandwell	1066	2.0
Sefton	641	1.2
Sheffield	1368	1.7
Shropshire	1145	1.6
Solihull	133	0.4
Somerset	1319	1.8
South Tyneside	422	1.6
Staffordshire	2628	1.5
Stockport	889	1.8
Suffolk	1598	1.6
Sunderland	1002	1.8
Surrey	3355	2.0
Sutton	347	1.4
Tameside	789	2.1
Trafford	404	1.2
Wakefield	943	1.7
Walsall	734	1.4
Waltham Forest	726	2.1
Warwickshire	1639	2.0
West Sussex	1254	1.2
Wigan	218	0.4
Wiltshire	1862	2.1
Wirral	1081	1.8
Wolverhampton	758	1.6
TOTAL: ENGLAND	135303	1.7

One year later, her fears that the needs of most of the children the Act was designed to help would be submerged under a welter of bureaucracy were being amply confirmed. Some local authorities took on new educational psychologists or advisers; some stretched existing staff to breaking point; others were failing to meet their new obligations. There was little sign that the Act was promoting integration or helping the 18 per cent.

Three years on Mr John Fish, the HMI who saw through both Warnock and the Act, told a conference despairingly that he wished as much effort went into meeting special needs as into producing the statements that identified them.

One authority which shares that philosophy is Oxfordshire, where the policy is to keep statements to a minimum and put the resources into assessment and integration. Some critics question this course, since it could put at risk the rights of those most severely handicapped, and DES officials worry about the fine print, if not the spirit of the Act.

In fact, such DES statistics as there are show wide variation between authorities as to the proportion of children with statements (table 1), and even then the figures reveal little about policy. A percentage way above 2 per cent (such as Avon's 4.2) could mean the deliberate inclusion of more of Warnock's 18 per cent or—more likely—a when-in-doubt-statement scatter technique. A much lower figure could mean another transfer of resources from paper-pushing to provision, or neglect of the statutory safeguards.

Yet again, lack of central guidance and monitoring both confuses the picture and inhibits transfer of experience, and the figures reveal as much as anything the uncertain start to statementing. Since regulations were published only a few weeks before the 1 April deadline in 1983, some authorities could claim they were simply not ready: Hereford and Worcester and the London Borough of Hounslow had not begun implementation a year later; Brent did not establish formal procedures until the end of 1986.

It has been said that there are as many interpretations of the Act as there are LEAs, and surveys indicate what heavy weather most are making of what they regard as complex, cumbersome and time-consuming new procedures.

An estimate quoted by the Society of Education Officers shows that educational psychologists need nine more hours for each child to meet the requirements of the 1981 Act compared with previous procedures and, although one of its main consequences seems to have been the appointment of extra educational psychologists (when they can be found) these extra demands obviously affect the level of service. The time taken to complete a statement can vary from eight weeks in one authority to thirty-two weeks in another.

Any such policy change is bound to be greeted with mixed feelings by officers and professionals, especially when budgets can't be stretched to help things along. The more critical questions are how far the new law has succeeded in bringing about the hoped-for shift in professional attitudes: whether the new rights of disabled children and their parents are being delivered; and whether the Warnock concept of a continuum of special needs to be met, with individual support, in a variety of ways is any closer to reality. So far the answers to these questions are not encouraging.

The Spastic Society's Centre for Studies on Integration in Education conducted two surveys in 1986 to find out how the new partnership between parents and professionals was coming along, but discovered that most authorities were still determined to keep control in their own hands.

The first of these surveys, *Caught in the Act*,[5] confirmed the feeling of many parents that they were not only still being excluded from the decision-making process, but that the odds were against them even getting to first base.

It found that half of all local education authorities failed to give parents adequate information on the assessment and statementing procedures; only a third told parents they had a right to be fully consulted and to receive all relevant information; only one in seven referred to the concept of parents as partners, most failed to provide details about sources of support and advice and almost half did not give information on appeal arrangements.

The second survey, *Guiding the Professionals*,[6] looked at the instructions that authorities gave to their own staff and found that: (a) more than a third failed to spell out their duties under the Act to heads, teachers and educational psychologists; (b) less than a half told staff of parents' rights under the Act; (c) only half made it clear that attention had to be focused on the child rather than the disability or referred explicitly to the need to integrate children with special needs into ordinary schools; (d) no less than 45 per cent made it clear that professionals were not to discuss possible placement with parents.

Bromley and Surrey put it in capital letters: 'NO PROFESSIONAL ADVISER SHOULD DISCUSS WITH PARENTS THE PROPOSED SCHOOL IN WHICH THE SPECIAL EDUCATIONAL PROVISION MIGHT BE MADE FOR THE CHILD. THIS IS A MATTER FOR DECISION BY THE DIRECTOR OF EDUCATION'.

Some authorities bypass the Act by encouraging staff to attach 'informal' advice to reports, which parents will not see; many exclude them from case conferences. All these stratagems make it more difficult for parents to challenge decisions, and in any case authorities are not bound by Appeal Committee decisions about special needs placements in the same way as for ordinary school choice.

Derbyshire is one authority which has gone out of its way to involve parents fully, to allow them to attend case conferences, or to give educational psychologists the power to decide on placement or delivery of services.

In general, however, the CSIE story of parents unable to exercise their rights because of lack of information was confirmed in October 1986 by another of the three DES-sponsored national surveys. The report on policy and provision since the 1981 Act,[7] written by a team at the University of London 'Institute of Education led by Professor Klaus Wedell and Dr John Welton, was based on detailed studies in five authorities and answers to a questionnaire sent to all English LEAs. It indicated marked differences in local policies about the role allowed to parents, and noted that authorities found it even harder to listen to parents than to inform them.

It also found that professionals may tailor their advice in statements to coincide with the resources that they know are available, either from education, health or social services: 'It was admitted that, in some cases, professional advisers were under pressure not to write down what a child really needed because of the lack of resources.'

Perhaps their most significant finding was that—far from detailing the individual support a child would need to survive in the ordinary classroom, as might have been expected to advance a genuine integration policy—the most likely effect of the statementing procedure was to perpetuate segregation: 'it was still true that in most authorities a statement can be equated largely with a decision to make a special school placement'. Only a quarter of LEAs placed 22.9 per cent or more of their children with statements in mainstream schools.

'In some cases, parents felt that the statutory assessment had been forced upon them because the LEA was unable to meet their child's needs adequately in mainstream'. In others, parents, 'would have preferred education in an integrated setting, with support, if the LEA had been willing to provide it'. 'Some reported attempts ... to manipulate them into accepting provision, which they did not really feel was right for their child, by withholding information about alternatives'.

Uncertainty has been increased by a Court of Appeal ruling that statements only had legal validity in special schools; but the real Catch-22 situation has been captured by a High Court ruling that a statement specifying speech therapy had no legal validity since it was not an educational requirement, and a 'dichotomy' existed between the education and health authorities over who was obliged to pay. Parents have been driven to the courts because of the inadequacy of the appeals procedures, but such legal niceties make a mockery of the necessary multidisciplinary approach, and problems are only compounded by the acute shortage of (underpaid) speech therapists. VOCAL, the charity for the speech-impaired, concluded from a recent survey of 128 health authorities that not one NHS region in Britain achieves the recommended target of one speech therapist to every 100 children needing help.

The Slow Process of Integration

One consequence of the professional preoccupation with statement production for Warnock's 2 per cent has been to divert attention away from obligations to the 18 per cent paid such scant attention in the 1981 Act.

However, a National Foundation for Educational Research study on support for the ordinary school[8] (the third of the national surveys commissioned by the DES in the wake of the Act) found a modest expansion in services providing support for this large group with learning difficulties, but without the benefit of a statement. Some radical rethinking had led many authorities to drop the name 'remedial' for such support services, though 38 per cent still used the label. There was an unresolved debate as to whether the traditional method of withdrawal from the classroom for help in a small group was still best, as many junior school teachers firmly believe, or whether support in the ordinary classroom was a more effective way to achieve integration, as a strong body of opinion now insists.

Either way, support services are threatened by financial pressures. A 1985 survey by Croll and Moses of special needs in primary schools[9] found a majority of headteachers believing that cuts in part-time teachers, rather than a direct decrease in special needs support, was responsible for a decline in the quantity and quality of provision.

Nevertheless, the message of Warnock has prevailed to the extent that many schools do now appoint a head of special needs department and, although the London Institute research presents an admittedly confused pattern, analysis of their data appears to show that—where change has taken place in provision—there is some decline in the proportion of children attending residential schools in other authorities and some movement towards units or mainstream placements for children with special educational needs.

Answers to the Institute's questionnaire showed 68 per cent of authorities reporting an increase in the proportion of children with special needs being placed in mainstream settings, though the movement is regarded as very slow.

DES statistics showing children with statements in ordinary schools (table 2) do not differentiate between those in special classes and those in ordinary classes, but evidence from the Institute survey and elsewhere suggests that most integration in this country is into units, or what Warnock called locational integration. The assumption has to be that this is seen as a necessary preliminary to more functional integration eventually, but little policy information is available.

The lack of any sense of national purpose or direction on the issue at the DES (where the sceptical neutrality of the special needs section isolates it from relevant decision-making about teacher training or curriculum within the department as well as from special needs outside) may be one reason why few LEAs have developed authority-wide policies on special needs provision, as Warnock recommended. The Inner London Education Authority has adopted one of the most radical and far-ranging plans for switching special needs provision to support in the ordinary classroom but it could take a very long time to reach fruition.

One paradoxical reason for this is the strength of its existing special needs sector. Experience shows that it is often the professionals who have invested most time and experience in their work and careers who are most resistant to change. Frequently the key obstacles to a switch to integrated policies are not shortage of resources but a vigorous special schools lobby, professional inertia and fears of teacher resistance in ordinary schools. To that the London Institute researchers on policy and provision would add the inability of competing professionals to cooperate within and between services or to bring

Table 2: Children with Statements of Special Educational Needs in Special Classes and Units and Ordinary Classes in Ordinary Schools as at January 1986 (Form SEN 2 1986)

Avon	3933
Barking	37
Barnet	122
Barnsley	102
Bedfordshire	125
Berkshire	280
Bexley	137
Birmingham	507
Bolton	15
Bradford	131
Brent	—
Bromley	209
Buckinghamshire	673
Bury	104
Calderdale	18
Cambridgeshire	517
Cheshire	1560
Cleveland	419
Cornwall	727
Coventry	113
Croydon	150
Cumbria	586
Derbyshire	1043
Devon	600
Doncaster	19
Dorset	320
Dudley	133
Durham	288
Ealing	59
East Sussex	38
Enfield	48
Essex	694
Gateshead	11
Gloucestershire	57
Hampshire	357
Haringey	19
Harrow	97
Havering	65
Hereford & Worcester	10
Hertfordshire	844
Hillingdon	46
Hounslow	63
Humberside	580
ILEA	566
Isle of Wight	41
Isles of Scilly	1
Kent	818

Table 2: (Continued)

Kingston upon Thames	41
Kirklees	231
Knowsley	47
Lancashire	183
Leeds	416
Leicestershire	321
Lincolnshire	504
Liverpool	83
Manchester	15
Merton	10
Newcastle upon Tyne	94
Newham	61
Norfolk	588
North Tyneside	84
North Yorkshire	310
Northamptonshire	197
Northumberland	163
Nottinghamshire	133
Oldham	63
Oxfordshire	1
Redbridge	60
Richmond upon Thames	35
Rochdale	97
Rotherham	177
St Helens	39
Salford	26
Sandwell	96
Sefton	75
Sheffield	361
Shropshire	445
Solihull	46
Somerset	475
South Tyneside	60
Staffordshire	146
Stockport	188
Suffolk	613
Sunderland	170
Surrey	415
Sutton	51
Tameside	147
Trafford	150
Wakefield	19
Walsall	105
Waltham Forest	186
Warwickshire	7C
West Sussex	103
Wigan	70
Wiltshire	855
Wirral	190
Wolverhampton	126
TOTAL: ENGLAND	26423

in the voluntary sector—one reason why follow-up research will focus on joint planning and training.

Resourcing remains a critical integration issue, however, and—even accepting that what is needed is an act of political will—Wedell and Welton warn central government that relocation of resources is not enough without some pump-priming or short-term topping-up until other resources can be freed, and that policy-makers will have to decide what part of the school population the extra resources are to be redistributed from. Barry Taylor, Chief Education Officer for Somerset, warned in a *Times Educational Supplement* article[10] that the same diseconomies of scale operate as with falling rolls: moving a few children, with support, to the ordinary school does not allow you to close down special schools at once, or reduce their specialist staff. The difficulties in the way of changing pre-existing patterns of provision cannot be underestimated.

One crucial factor affecting the quality of education offered in an integrated setting is the curriculum, an issue neglected in the Act and, indeed, in Warnock. Some current secondary school developments such as profiles, records of achievement, modular examination courses, equal opportunities and computer-assisted learning, could help to stretch the common school to include every-one, but bench-marks and selection threaten rejection. Integration is a challenge both to the curriculum and organization of the school, but where it is recognized that the interaction between child and school is more important than the disability, the results can benefit everybody.

And in spite of everything, there are examples in many local education authorities, schools and colleges of imaginative programmes developed to accommodate children with special needs in units or regular class of mainstream schools. Despite the government's lack of recognition of resource needs, the lack of leadership from the centre, low morale, and continuing fear and ignorance about integration, there is eagerness and willingness for change to be found.

The changing climate of ideas which led to the Warnock Report and its pale shadow, the 1981 Act, had begun to shift thinking and provision. The critical question now is whether the Conservative Government's market-place education philosophy, with the emphasis on parental choice, competition and selectivity foreshadowed by Mr Kenneth Baker's Great Education Reform Bill (Gerbil), will mark the end of the Warnock era by introducing a climate in which integrated provision for special needs can no longer grow and flourish.

Notes

1 SNOWDON WORKING PARTY REPORT (1976) *Integrating the Disabled*, London, National Fund for Research into Crippling Diseases.

2   DEPARTMENT OF EDUCATION AND SCIENCE (1978) *Special Educational Needs* (The Warnock Report) Cmnd. 7212, London, HMSO.

3   NEWELL, P. (1983) *ACE Special Education Handbook*—'The new law on children with special needs', London, Advisory Centre for Education.

4   STOWELL, R. (1987) *Catching Up?: Provision for Students with Special Educational Needs in Further and Higher Education*, London, National Bureau for Handicapped Students.

5   ROGERS, R. (1986a) *Caught in the Act*, London, Centre for Studies on Integration in Education.

6   ROGERS, R. (1986b) *Guiding the Professionals*, London, Centre for Studies on Integration in Education.

7   WEDELL, K. and WELTON, J. *et al* (forthcoming). *The 1981 Education Act: Policy and Provision for Special Educational Needs*, London, Cassell.

8   HEGARTY, S. *et al.* (1987) *Meeting Special Educational Needs: Support for the Ordinary School*, Slough, NFER, (also summarized in *Educational Research*, June.

9   CROLL, P. and MOSES, D. (1985). *One in Five: The Assessment and Incidence of Special Educational Needs*, London, Routledge and Kegan Paul.

10 TAYLOR, B. (1987) 'Wanted—A sense of direction', *The Times Educational Supplement*, 6 February.

Chapter 6: Further Education

Frank Griffiths

Frank Griffiths is the Education Secretary of the National Association of Teachers in Further and Higher Education (NATFHE). He is a member of a number of bodies including the Council of BTEC and the Board of the National Advisory Body. Prior to working full-time for NATFHE he was a Senior Lecturer in the Department of Health Studies at Teesside Polytechnic. In the 1983 General Election he stood for the Labour Party in the Stockton South Constituency.

★   ★   ★

Writing on the origins of the English education system, John Rosselli made the point that, as early as the first half of the nineteenth century, its central and enduring contradiction was already discernable: 'it is a system of education provided for the bulk of the people by a minority who themselves educate their children by another means'.[1] This perceptive remark invites those who write or speak for a particular segment of that system to argue with passion and conviction that their slice exemplifies Rosselli's point, for the paradox referred to is something which has permeated the whole of English education, from the concept of the 'public elementary school' to that implied by the title of 'further education'. Moreover, its effects are cumulative and self-perpetuating: by the time a large—and now growing—fraction of an 'elementary school' cohort reaches the point of entry to 'FE', the effects of separate educational development are compounded into whole-scale social class consequences for leisure, work, consumption, marriage, health, and so on.[2]

Perhaps more than any other part of the British system, further education comprises a range of education experiences and institutional forms scarcely understood and certainly not experienced by those whom most people in this country would regard as properly and fully educated. The statistics are not readily to hand, but it can be predicted with reasonable certainty that hardly any member of what might popularly be called the 'British establishment' has ever had any direct contact with 'FE'. The disparities which are revealed by comparisons of the educational background of key leadership groups between public and state schools would be dwarfed by the scale of the imbalance in a comparison of those with and without experience of FE. Even in recent years when the sons and daughters of the middle class intelligensia have been packed off via conscience or principle to the neighbourhood comprehensive, it can be hypothesized—no more is possible without the data, and the position may be changing—that these young people have not in great numbers found their way into a college of further education, nor even its more exalted cousin, a polytechnic.

There is another sense in which 'further education' is uniquely affected by the class-riven nature of our society. For one thing it comes at the non-compulsory end of the state system where, traditionally, the understandable disinclination of 16-year-olds to expose themselves to, as they see it, yet more pupilage, has been reinforced by an official policy of limited access. With thirteen years left to this century, there is still not financial assistance available to the young adult to enable her or him to continue his or her education beyond sixteen. Indeed, it is surely no accident that the only financial inducements available at that point are either the payment of Supplementary Benefit for idleness or an allowance for entry into the Youth Training Scheme. Almost alone amongst any nation in the world purporting either to be or seeking to become an advanced industrial economy, ours positively rewards non-entry into organized education at the age of 16, and, via the residue of the Poor Law tradition, penalizes the unemployed, young and adults alike, should they actively seek education rather than what our culture defines as its opposite, 'work'.

Yet the staggering feature of further education is its enormous size and apparent popularity. It is a vast system covering well in excess of three and a half million student enrolments (plus many more unrecorded), provided in an array of settings, across the aspiration and achievement range, and reflecting diverse modes of attendance and provision. By 1984, for example, just over 25 per cent of the 16-18 age group were enrolled under FE regulations. However, before such a figure can be properly understood, it is important that some technical and legal points are clarified.

What is FE?

Clarity in language must come first. Thus, the figure of 25 per cent just cited is accurate enough but the phrase 'FE regulations' is capable of serious mis-representation. By law, institutions currently operating under 1975 FE regulations, include a vast array of centres of learning and instruction, including all polytechnics, several hundred 'colleges of FE' or 'technical colleges', colleges of higher education (formerly known as teacher training colleges), adult education centres, and a mixed bag of agricultural colleges, direct grant and voluntary institutions outside LEA control, and even an organization more noted for its trade union professional association functions, namely the Royal College of Nursing. Thus FE is provided in a bewildering and administratively chaotic array of institutions.

A further complication is that not all work carried out in institutions operating under the regulations is 'FE'. The official phrase governs the mode of Parliamentary funding of the institution and the nature of the employment contract of staff who teach (or 'lecture') in them, but 'further education' is not all they do. Sadly from the perspective of those who resent its relatively marginalized status in our system, 'further education' suffers from an official definition couched in essence in a strictly negative tone: 'non-advanced further education' (NAFE). Ironically, there are many who work in its more prestigious cousin's area of advanced further education (AFE), who resent the separation so implied from what they would prefer as an all-embracing (for them) designation of higher education, including, of course, universities.

The result of this semantic muddle means that, strictly speaking, the 25 per cent referred to above are 'NAFE' students, even though some of them will be studying in colleges alongside a substantial proportion of AFE students. One example may be instructive. Thus, Cheltenham and Gloucester College of Arts and Technology (know as GLOSCAT) had 35 per cent of its student population in 1986-87 classified as 'advanced further education'. As with all social institutions, the very language we use to describe them is part of the process by which they are socially located and perceived. In the case of further education a particularly interesting period of development has been evident since about 1973 through to 1986, since in this period of exaggerated and rhetorical vocationalism brought forth by political responses to entrenched economic crisis, intriguing attempts have been made to redefine the sector. For other reasons, notably the pressure upon the government and local education authorities from the consequence of falling school student numbers, the sector has been at the centre of the debate about sixth form versus tertiary colleges. Remarkably, despite all of this, the legal basis of FE remains shrouded in doubt and confusion.

When writing of other areas of English or British education, and especially in the context of missed opportunities and years of waste, an exercise in legal clarification would be irrelevant and probably tedious. The law, however, is a human invention and a social institution and, in the case of 'FE', the fact that it probably has no firm lawful status illustrates the ambivalence of our society's view of it.

Basically, the law relating to FE stems from the 1944 Education Act, where, in section 7, the overall system is defined as being 'organized' in three progressive stages to be known as primary education, secondary education and further education'. More specifically, section 41 appears to place a duty upon LEAs to ensure the provision of 'adequate facilities' for FE and, in section 42, this is somewhat fleshed out by linking the requirement to provide with one of preparing and submitting 'schemes of further education' to the

Secretary of State. Taken together, these two sections form the statutory basis for FE from which, for example, the FE Regulations 1975 (and subsequent amendments) are traceable.

The real difficulty, however, concerns the 'schemes' which, under the 1944 Act, were duly prepared by LEAs and submitted in the early 1950s to the Secretary of State. Stating the matter bluntly—and with the single exception of London[3]—they have not been subsequently revised, nor re-submitted to the Minister, nor has any Secretary of State been inclined to call for them. In short, whilst enormous changes in the nature and location of colleges have taken place, set against a background of reform in the compulsory years of schooling which, after all, provides the bulk of students for FE, the system has gone on almost in pretence that what exists in the present period is actually what was submitted to the government in the mid-fifties. It is doubtful if any other area of public sector provision on the scale, size, complexity and expense of further education, rests upon a basis where many quietly believe the courts could render it unlawful. In 1981, a working document[4] drawn up by the DES, Welsh Office and the local authorities, cogently argued that much of existing LEA provision was capable of being judged 'ultra-vires' by the courts.

In conclusion what we recognize as FE is a vast system covering well in excess of three and a half million student enrolments (plus many more unrecorded) provided in an array of settings, across the aspiration and achievement range, and reflecting diverse modes of attendance and provision.

Changes in FE 1973–86

Notwithstanding the level of official ignorance and indifference towards FE, the system has proved itself buoyant, dynamic, and responsive to 'need' during the years 1973–86. However, it is also evident that because there is no clear perception of either what it is or is capable of becoming, it remains vulnerable to both *ad hoc* political interference and more organized attempts by, for example, the Department of Employment, aimed at narrowing its role down to one of residual training. It is as if key decision makers in governments see further education in little more than the negative sense of what it is not, almost as if they were re-writing the 1904 Regulations for Secondary Schools. An extract from those regulations makes for timely reading. Thus:

> In order to arrive at a proper differentiation of functions, it is important for purposes of central and of local administration, and in particular for considering and properly planning courses of instruction, to distinguish secondary schools, on the one hand, from technical institutes and classes which devote themselves mainly to giving specialized instruction and training in certain subjects to young

persons and adults who should previously have completed a sound general education, and on the other, from evening schools and classes which, though they may offer instruction to some students in subjects of a general kind and to others in subjects of art or of pure and applied science, do not provide a consecutive and complete course of general education, to be followed by each student who attends the school.[5]

It would be untrue to argue that the characteristic of separate development in our education system can be traced from any one document, but it is clear from codes and regulations published at the point when it became lawful for LEAs to provide other than elementary schooling, that what we now understand as FE—or more sharply as work related non-advanced further education (WRNAFE)[6]—was never intended to be part of authentic mainstream education. The publication in January 1984 of the White Paper *Training for Jobs* can almost be regarded as having direct ancestry with the 1904 code and with much that went in the century before.

It was the 1984 White Paper which coined the unpronounceable acronym 'WRNAFE' and announced by the central government fiat a switch of funding from the rate support grant monies payable to local authorities to the Manpower Services Commission, of 25 per cent of the cost of supplying this provision. Despite the difficulty of even supplying a workable let alone meaningful definition to WRNAFE, that money has been switched each year since 1985. If paying the piper truly means calling the tune, at least a quarter, but in practice much more, of the central government's financial support for FE, has passed out of the hands of the Ministry notionally responsible for education.

In fact the volume of work and money in support of FE but emanating from the Department of Employment vote for the MSC, is now substantially greater than the 25 per cent announced in *Training for Jobs*. If due account is taken of course fees for young people and adults now paid by the MSC, and of the indirect costs of provision now met by the MSC in the sense of YTS allowances, payments to adults on schemes like the Community Programme, RESTART, and shortly the Job Training Scheme (JTS), plus the multitude of projects, and their related capital grants, the final result is that we now have one huge monopoly buyer of a form of educational provision ignored by the conventional educational system for generations. What remains unclear is how the 'vocationalization' of FE will affect the rest of the education system. In order to answer this question it is necessary to disentangle some of the statistics relating to FE since 1973, and to set out chronologically the key events as they have occurred. Tables 1 and 2 are extracts from the DES *Statistical Bulletin* published in 1986. The figures only cover that of Non-Advanced FE Establishment and adult education centres; AFE must be treated separately despite the fact, as pointed out above, that it falls legally and administratively under the same rubric.

In terms of bodies occupying chairs or taking up lab space, the figures are

Table 1: Enrolments on Non-advanced Courses in FE Establishments and Adult Education Centres analyzed by Mode of Attendance: November 1974 and 1978 to 1984. (thousands) – England

	1974	1978	1979	1980	1981	1982	1983	1984
FE establishments								
Full-time and sandwich	218	288	288	296	328	355	344	337
Part-time day:								
With release from employment	464	452	455	419	351	313	352	368
Other part-time day	155	173	156	166	216	241	247	272
All part-time day	619	625	611	585	566	554	600	640
Evening only:	728	660	583	573	573	596	635	642
All modes (numbers)	1,566	1,572	1,482	1,455	1,468	1,505	1,578	1,619
All modes (full-time equivalent)[2]	(431)	(493)	(486)	(484)	(501)	(521)	(524)	(526)
YTS/YOP[1] included above (numbers)	–	2	5	8	18	32	104	114
Adult education centres:								
Part-time day	..	358	347	316	334	365	429	429
Evening only		1,519	1,391	1,227	1,181	1,169	1,199	1,148
All modes (numbers)	1,720	1,878	1,738	1,543	1,516	1,534	1,628	1,577
All modes (full-time equivalent)	..	(235)	(217)	(193)	(190)	(192)	(204)	(197)

1 Youth Training Scheme (YTS) 1982 to 1984 and Youth Opportunities Programme (YOP) for earlier years; 16-18 year olds only included here.

2 The following weights have been used in calculating full-time equivalents: full-time (1.0); sandwich (0.75); day release (0.3); other part-time day (0.125); evening only (0.075).

Table 2: Percentage Enrolments on Non-advanced Courses by Mode of Attendance, Age and Qualification Aim: November 1984

Qualification aims of students	Full-time and sandwich				Part-time			
	16–18	19–20	21 and over	All ages	16–18	19–20	21 and over	All ages
ONC/OND	1	4	1	1	0	0	0	0
BTEC (Technological)	9	13	9	9	9	11	3	6
BTEC (Other)[1]	16	18	8	15	7	7	1	4
City & Guilds	20	10	10	18	34	28	9	18
Royal Society of Arts	3	4	9	4	5	4	4	5
College diplomas	3	8	6	4	0	0	0	0
GCE 'A' level	19	18	8	17	6	12	6	7
GCE 'O' level	10	4	4	8	11	13	9	10
Other specified qualifications	10	11	12	10	2	5	5	4
Unspecified examinable courses	5	5	11	5	7	7	7	7
All qualifications	94	93	79	92	83	80	44	60
Non-examinable courses								
Sciences	3	3	9	4	7	4	11	9
Social studies	1	1	4	1	4	2	4	4
Arts (including leisure)	3	4	7	3	7	6	41	27
All Non-advanced	100	100	100	100	100	100	100	100
Numbers (00s)	(271)	(27)	(39)	(337)	(381)	(136)	(765)	(1,282)

1 Including courses in business studies, administration, hotel and catering trades and the arts.
Source: DES *Statistical Bulletin* 5/86 'Enrolments on non-advanced courses of further education – November 1984' (March 1986)

impressive. Thus in 1984 just over 1.6 million people were enrolled in NAFE, a figure which can be then translated, somewhat erroneously, into so-called full-time equivalents (FTEs). Footnote 2 gives the various conversion weights, and is significant not so much for them, since they are to some extent arbitrary, but because it conveys succinctly the fact that in FE there are at least five modes of study. If account is taken of open and distance learning schemes, the number of modes is even greater.

It should also be noted that the figures understate provision to the extent that short courses are very frequently not included. The short course phenomenon, often arranged with little notice, frequently customer specific and increasingly conducted on employers' premises, is a growing feature of the new market responsive FE. Such is its short-run 'ad hoc' character it frequently escapes inclusion in the snap-shot methods of DES statisticians.

As absolute numbers those enrolled between 1974 and 1984 show little change. However despite an absolute increase of only 53,000, there have been important changes in the composition of the student population, and in the gender balance. Thus the real growth has occurred in the numbers of full-time and sandwich students which show a recorded increase of 119,000 over a period. Another key constituency which has emerged is the category 'YTS/YOP' reflecting the growth since the latter part of the seventies in mass youth unemployment. Statistically this phenomenon is significant but not such that the measurable system regards them as authentic students; they thus are shown as an addition to the total.

Apart from these notable areas of growth, the period also reveals a drop in certain modes of attendance. In one sense this is because patterns of take-up in FE have always reflected trends in the wider economy and its labour markets. Just as the new YTS clientele signifies the demise of employment opportunities at 16 and 17, so the decline in day release from employment and evening only attendance, graphically illustrates the collapse in much of British industry from which such students have traditionally been drawn. This tradition of part-time attendance is a long established one in the history of British education. The system of formal apprenticeship training was always an opportunity for those fortunate enough to have entered into it, to acquire not just a craft skill but also the elements of a broader education. Notwithstanding the delightful parody in Tom Sharp's comic novel *Wilt*, which conveys grotesque images of trainee butchers being force-fed medieval literature, it is an undeniable, if again statistically unrecorded, fact that many such students have gone on to acquire wider educational qualifications. Indeed one of the striking features of the FE tradition has been the tendency for the pedagogical relationship between teacher and student to reflect the master-apprentice pattern once dominant in industry, with many instances of the apprentice-learner going on to become the practitioner-teacher. An inspection of a typical CFE's staff list will show an enormous array of vocational qualifications, other than degrees, in fields like catering, welding and hairdressing, reflecting this biographical link between practice and pedagogy. As a consequence of apparent deindustrialization, this important form of provision looks to be in secular decline.

Or is it? Certainly the evidence regularly supplied by the MSC scarcely indicates any real decline in industry's demand for people with not only new 'hi-tech' skills but in many so-called traditional occupations. What the figures may therefore show is a growing reluctance by industry to bear the costs necessary in supporting their employees' training. In this regard the apocalyptic tones of *Competence and Competition*[7] and *A Challenge to Complacency*[8] are pertinent both as a forecast of economic (and social) doom and as a record of failure.

Ironically the decline in the numbers of students on part-time day release and evening only attendance, can be set against a general 'climatic' background of exaggerated vocationalism. Ever since James Callaghan's Ruskin speech in 1976, virtually all of education has been in a state of perpetual genuflection to something variously described but summable as 'the world of work'. In terms of course content and mode of delivery, pedagogical style, funding, planning and administration, 'FE' has been as genuflective as most and arguably more so. Yet against a setting of political rhetoric and action of an almost unparalleled intensity in terms of its narrow focus upon one particular purpose of education, the outcome is probably that industry itself is less prepared or able to support the students who might go on to colleges to study.

In this regard the category in the statistics 'other part-time day' is instructive. It is fairly inchoate as a category reflecting a very wide range of students and courses. One significant group which it includes are those students of all ages studying under the so-called '21 hours rule', whereby state benefits are still paid even though the individual is, for that period of a week, unavailable for paid employment.

The point about this example is that it illustrates the flexibility and responsiveness of FE (and its students) despite an official state fiction derived from the spirit of the nineteenth century Poor Laws, whereby, those unemployed must be deemed undeserving of benefits like free or heavily subsidized education, lest they develop the taste for it rather than 'work'. Hence the fact that for most of the years covered by this chapter the so-called 'twenty-one hours' provision has been associated with the mysteries and subterfuges of the 'black-economy'. Where the myth of availability of work collides most abruptly with the reality of mass unemployment, so has the system of FE gradually managed to provide meaningful educational opportunities. Yet it has not been without argument and conflict with central government departments and even now, with the advent of a new Job Training Scheme (JTS) retaining the old Poor Law ingredients of compulsion and less eligibility, the right of the unemployed to real education and training is again under threat. And all the while the 'discourse' in terms of which the whole area is endlessly conducted, is that of unyielding adherence to the needs of work and industry, of skills and competencies which are 'relevant' and so on.

Conclusion

More than perhaps any other sector of the education system, and subject to the difficulties of giving it a precise definition, 'further education' has the closest relationship with the state of the British economy. The connection is not merely one as of cause to effect but rather an interrelationship whereby the pattern of development within FE affects both industrial and commercial performance and crucially the perception education has of employment and vice versa.

If it is true as George Tolley argued recently[9], that British culture is antithetical to education, then the marginalized and officially undefined world of FE is central to us eventually changing such a lamentable state of affairs. Some real educational difficulties are though yet to be resolved, including the old question of whether it is possible or even desirable to attempt the mass schooling of our people in a predominantly 'academic' grammar school vein. The 'hands on' tradition of the secondary modern system lingers on in parts of the FE Sector especially attractive to those who would see the provision of colleges stripped down into 'units' or 'modules' of competence narrowly expressed in terms of training outcomes.[10] The emergence of the unemployed cohort of the early 1980s in schemes such as the YOP and then YTS was based on an *ad hoc* piece of political panic and has never risen out of the secondary modern mould in which its 'trainees' had been cast when they had been 'pupils'. Similarly with the onset of the Job Training Scheme, scheduled as it is for a throughput of a quarter of a million 'trainees' from the year commencing April 1987, there is little expectation that its content will resemble more than a 'postgraduate' in-fill to an earlier YTS experience. In fact, given that the key target constituency for the JTS is the young adult population of between 19 to 25 years, the demographic dimension of a shifting locus for the burden of mass unemployment from school leavers to this new group, seems almost too obvious.

Alongside the change in the nature of the student population, the big policy question is what to do about resolving the sixth form versus tertiary college debate, which as this chapter has tried to show, is more than a mere wrangle about buildings and the salary levels of the staff who work in them. At the heart of the issue is the challenge to British culture of resolving what for centuries has been a master-servant model of educational provision. The recent creation of a National Council for Vocational Qualifications (NCVQ) might have provided the basis for organizing the curriculum across this great divide. Sadly but not surprisingly it is set within a 'vocational' channel deliberately separate from the 'academic' remit of the Secondary Examinations Council (SEC) and with an in-built model of achievement levels peaking just below that encompassed by the university system and the elite professions such as law and medicine. In short, the British tradition of separate development in education looks set to dominate provision certainly to the end of the century and probably beyond.

Notes

1 ROSSELLI, J. (1981) 'Education: Church and state', *The Origin of the Social Services, New Society Social Studies Reader*.
2 REID, J. (1981) *Social Class Differences in Britain*, 2nd ed., London, Grant McIntyre.
3 The London Government Act, 1973, which, amongst other things created the Inner London Education Authority, and new Outer London LEAs, necessitated resubmission of the schemes.
4 DEPARTMENT OF EDUCATION AND SCIENCE (1981) *The Legal Basis of Further Education*, London, HMSO.
5 MACLURE, J. S. (1971) *Educational Documents*, 2nd Edn, London, Methuen, p 157.
6 DEPARTMENT OF EMPLOYMENT (1984) *Training for Jobs*, Cmnd 9135, London, HMSO.
7 NATIONAL ECONOMIC DEVELOPMENT COUNCIL/MANPOWER SERVICES COMMISSION, (1984) *Competence and Competition*, London, NEDO books.
8 COOPERS & LYBRAND ASSOCIATES (1985) *A Challenge to Complacency: Changing Attitudes to Training*, London, NEDO.
9 TOLLEY, REV. DR G. (1987) speech at a conference on 'Education for a change', Wolverhampton.
10 MANPOWER SERVICES COMMISSION (1986) *Review of Vocational Qualifications in England and Wales*, London, MSC.

Chapter 7: Higher Education

Peter Scott

Peter Scott is Editor of *The Times Higher Education Supplement*. Previously he worked for *The Times*. He is the author of *Strategies for Post-secondary Education* (1976) and *The Crisis of the University* (1984).

★   ★   ★

If higher education in Britain has ever enjoyed a golden age the summer of 1973 was it. The expansion of the universities that preceded, but was powerfully endorsed by, the 1963 Robbins Report[1] was approaching its crescendo. The new universities established during the 1960s and the promoted colleges of advanced technology (CATs) were settling into their bright new (or refurbished) campuses. Oxford and Cambridge had reformed themselves, to reasonable public satisfaction; the former by means of the 1966 Frank Report[2], the latter by a more gentle process of evolution. In the previous twenty years the civic universities established in the nineteenth century had reinforced their position as the bedrock institutions of the university sector. The former university colleges had shed the rather inward grammar school ethos that still clung to them in the immediate post-war years and firmly established themselves as large and respected multi-faculty institutions. The Scottish universities and the constituent colleges of the University of Wales had lost most of their provincial peculiarities (for so it seemed at the time) and had entered the mainstream of British university life.

Nor, of course, was this impression of beneficent expansion confined to the universities. By 1973 all the polytechnics had been designated and it was already clear that they were destined to make a distinguished contribution to the future diversity of higher education. University leaders had been disappointed that in 1965 the Labour Secretary of State, Mr. Anthony Crosland, abandoned the Robbins prescription for the creation of yet more universities and according to the so-called binary policy decided to build up instead large comprehensive institutions in the local authority sector.[3] But in 1973 they still did not imagine that the polytechnics would ever develop into serious rivals. The 1960s had also been a kind decade to teacher education. Many new colleges had been built and the others expanded out of all physical recognition. They had broken free from their former tutelage to universities and abandoned their rather Victorian title of 'teacher training colleges' in favour of the more up-to-date description of 'colleges of education'. Indeed, in the early 1970s teacher education enjoyed a glorious, but as it turned out, brief independence. The wholesale closure of many colleges and the painful incorporation of others in larger institutions still lay in the future.

The summer of 1973 also marked a golden age for higher education in its inner intellectual life. In discipline after discipline the early 1970s were a time of great excitement and optimism. Admittedly the balance between science and the arts anticipated by the Robbins Committee, and desired by every post-war government, had not been achieved—but in 1973 that was a matter of concern for the politicians not for higher education itself. Within science and engineering any disappointment about the failure to recruit enough students was more than compensated for by exciting progress in research. In physics and the biological sciences, in particular, this was a time of great scientific advance.

For the arts and social sciences, of course, the sense of academic well-being was even stronger. The humanities were an area that benefited from intense student demand, and the social sciences were approaching the peak of their popularity. The latter were comparatively new subjects in many institutions. The intellectual colonization of British higher education by social scientists from the London School of Economics was still a fresh memory in 1973.[4] Outside economics and politics most social science departments were recent creations. They were looking forward to the brightest of academic futures. The arts, of course, could not benefit from the same excitement of comparative novelty. But here too the preceding years had been marked by great academic change. Many arts subjects had begun to absorb the professional culture of the social sciences and the popular values of the university extra-mural tradition, and to attach these new influences to their traditional humanist and academic preoccupations with exciting intellectual results. Finally in 1973 the first stirring of ambition could be felt from the new professions—not only teacher education, but also social work, town planning and the rest. It was already clear that advanced training for such professions would soon become a significant presence in higher education alongside medicine, law and the other traditional professions.

The sky was not entirely unclouded for higher education in 1973. Perhaps the most menacing worry seemed to be the public's and so the politicians', distaste for student disorder. There were already those who argued that this phenomenon had led to a decisive decline in the popularity of higher education. The image had been sullied. The world of *The History Man*[5] was just round the corner. There were other apparently less significant worries. Britain's economic underperformance seemed to threaten the nation's capacity to fund an expanding system of higher education at previous levels of generosity. The under-recruitment of science and engineering students, and the consequent headlong expansion of the arts and especially social sciences, also seemed an ambiguous phenomenon.

But in 1973 such worries had done little to erode the self-confidence of higher education. They were blurs on the horizon. Higher education had been expanded with great success, and that expansion was expected to accelerate during the rest of the decade. Yet there appeared to have been no decline in the quality of the system, in terms either of student standards or research excellence. So social and educational objectives on the one hand, and academic and scientific objectives on the other, which in the nervous past had often been regarded as in competition, appeared to be in most perfect harmony. The battle against a narrow elitism seemed to have been won—or rather it had never needed to be fought. Self-confidence and success were the dominant characteristics of higher education in 1973.

Higher education thirteen years later is both recognizably the same and unrecognizable. It is the same first in a visual sense. The physical landscape of most universities, polytechnics and colleges has not changed much. A few new buildings have gone up, the once bright concrete is stained, the grass is no longer as well tended, but the environment is familiar. A visitor to most campuses in 1973 would still have no difficulty in finding his way about in 1986. The physical plant enjoyed by most higher education institutions is very much the plant created in the 1960s and early 1970s. Because of the obsolescence of buildings (many higher education buildings after all are of the same generation as those out-of-favour high-rise flats and comprehensive city-centre developments) and the growing sophistication of expert facilities and equipment, many institutions in 1986 face acute problems of physical renewal.

The system is the same in another sense. The slow-down of expansion, since the end of the 1970s in particular, has sharply reduced the turn-over of the academic profession. Many science and engineering departments have been unable to generate many extra academic posts because of their endemic failure to recruit more students. More recently arts and social departments have begun to suffer the same difficulties, partly because they have slipped into a less exciting middle-aged maturity, partly because their very rapid expansion between 1955 and 1975 left them with a bunching of similarly aged staff, partly because they have fallen into political disfavour. All departments, of course, have suffered from the cuts in higher education budgets. The trickle of new recruits into university and polytechnic teaching and the haemorrhage of older staff who have taken advantage of early retirement incentives have intensified the sclerosis of the academic profession. It is an exaggeration to say that higher education is still staffed in 1986 by the people already in post in 1973. The polytechnics and colleges in particular have been able to recruit extra staff; the catch has been that they have had to recruit many more students to justify these extra posts. But it is disturbingly close to the truth in too many universities. Again higher education in 1986 seems to be living off past accumulations of human, as it is physical, capital.

In another sense, of course, higher education today is unrecognizable from the system that existed in 1973. First, it is much bigger. The total number of students has increased by 20 per cent, a slower rate in growth than in the 1960s, of course, but starting from a much higher base.[6] In the past thirteen years the polytechnics and other colleges have expanded much more rapidly than the universities. Second it is much cheaper, or as the government might prefer, more efficient. The unit of resource, or income per student, has fallen significantly, although much further and faster in the public than in the university sector.[7] This process of attrition had begun in the 1970s but was accelerated during the 1980s by the Conservative government's determination to reduce public expenditure. Third, it is more diverse. Although higher education in 1973 had already begun to move away from the traditional model that had prevailed up to the time of Robbins, it was still a much more academic system. Today more students are part-time or enrolled on courses other than honours degrees. More candidates for higher education have non-standard entry qualifications. There has been an explosion of interest in continuing education, consultancy and short courses.[8] Many new subjects and forms of professional training have been incorporated into higher education. Some would argue that the academic integrity of higher education had been compromised, and maybe its intellectual effectiveness and critical independence as well. But more would welcome this broadening of higher education as a necessary transition to a mass system.

Fourth, and last, higher education is much less self-confident in 1986—self-satisfied some of its critics might suggest. Part of the reason for this decline in morale may be that the increasingly heterogeneous character of higher education makes it difficult to sustain the same confident allegiance that could be summoned up by a much simpler and more academic system. But a larger reason is that for seven years, and maybe more, higher education has been battered by cuts. It has fallen on hard times. Not only have these reductions in public support led to a large number of serious problems—how to do more with less, how to manage without planning horizons, how to cope with rates of change that inevitably lead to diseconomy, and so on—the cuts have also seemed to communicate society's verdict on higher education's record. And it is a negative verdict. Like Browning higher education in 1986 cannot look forward—'Never glad confident morning again!'

The history of higher education since 1973 has been shaped by the political and economic events of the past thirteen years. Both can be divided for convenience into four main phases. First came the oil price shock that was triggered off by the Middle East war of October 1973. The immediate effect was to push Mr Edward Heath's Conservative government into immediate and panicky cuts in public expenditure, from which higher education suffered alongside other services. The longer-term effect was to produce much higher levels of inflation, from which higher education again suffered grievously because its income dwindled inexorably in value. In Britain the inflation was made worse by the expansionist policies that were pursued by the new Labour government first elected in March 1974 and confirmed in power at a second general election later in that year. Only when these policies were abandoned and a much more restrictive economic regime reimposed under pressure from the International Monetary Fund in 1976 did this first phase come to an end.

The second phase was marked by public austerity but also by a return to stability. If its watchword was Mr. Crosland's memorable phrase of two years before 'the party's over', wage restraint and the consequent reduction in inflation did bring the chaotic conditions of 1973-76 to an end. For an activity like higher education with distant planning horizons and long lead-times this was an undoubted benefit. But any recovery of morale, let alone momentum, was difficult. Higher education was hit by retrenchment, first and actually in the colleges of education many of which were closed because of the falling demand for teachers, but more dangerously if only prospectively across the whole system as the shadow of future demographic decline fell across optimistic plans for further expansion. Although some confidence had begun to return in the late 1970s this second phase persisted until brought to an abrupt end by the defeat of the Labour Government at the 1979 general election.

The third phase covered the first two or three years of the new Conservative government, from the summer of 1979 until the middle of 1982. The full impact of the new government and its commitment to radical right policies on public expenditure were not immediately felt. The presence in the new Cabinet of a significant number of more traditional Tories, soon to be christened 'wets', acted as a brake on the immediate introduction of full-blooded policy changes. This brief pause was apparent not only in public expenditure, but also employment and foreign policies. However, in the end this pause may have made the impact of the cuts when they were eventually and inevitably imposed much worse. For they were imposed in a disorderly fashion that compounded the damage they caused. This pattern was apparent in higher education, especially with regard to the university grant.

The fourth phase began in 1982/83 and still continues. In one sense there has been a retreat from the disorganized rigour of the earlier cuts in public expenditure. Some cuts have been cancelled and alleviation offered in the case of others. But this relief has led to the institutionalization of resource levels, standards of efficiency, and managerial practices that would have been considered unthinkable a decade earlier. In the worst years of the cuts, the early 1980s, they may have seemed like a bad dream that would vanish with the inevitable awakening to normality. In the mid 1980s although the worst pressures eased such hopes have had to be abandoned. A new and apparently permanent order in higher education, as in the health service or local government, is being built that has a depressing credibility.

This general pattern fits the particular case of higher education well. The

1973–76 crisis hit the universities especially hard. Until that date they had been funded through the University Grants Committee in five-year blocks, the so-called quinquennial planning and funding system designed to insulate them from financial uncertainty and political pressure. Compensation for inflation during a quinquennium was regarded virtually as a binding convention. This was all swept away. As inflation rose towards 30 per cent in 1974, the promised revaluation of the university grant was cancelled. The UGC had to warn the government, for the first but sadly not the last time, that 'the prospect was one of insolvency for some institutions'.[9] Even in their review of 1975/76 the Committee complained that the universities had experienced a 'further year of extreme financial stringency, annual financing and short-term decisions'.[10] For the polytechnics and colleges the crisis of the mid-1970s was less severe—partly because they were still in an immature stage of development, partly because having enjoyed less privileged treatment in the past they had lower expectations, and partly because the means by which they were funded were confusingly entwined with local government finance as a whole. Expenditure on non-university higher education was still determined in terms of volume, so-called 'real' terms, in the 1970s in contrast to expenditure on universities which had always been to some degree cash-limited.

The second phase, the austere stability of the late 1970s, was marked by four new developments. The first was the accelerating closure of colleges of education;[11] the second, the first faltering steps towards the coordinated planning first of public sector higher education and then of the total system; third a reviving debate about the future shape of higher education as the twenty-year planning horizon established by Robbins in the early 1960s was approached; and fourth an attempt to restore effective planning and funding mechanisms for the universities after the collapse of the old arms-length quinquennial system. So an agenda was set that has endured. These four themes are still the dominant ones in higher education policy today. The troubles of the beleaguered colleges of education in the 1970s have broadened out in the 1980s into a much wider debate about institutional viability and the structure of higher education outside the universities, although the basic questions about the proper relationship between teacher training and the mainstream of higher education have lost none of their capacity to excite political controversy. Is there room for a 'third force' of smaller colleges and institutes of higher education alongside their 'Big Brother' polytechnics and universities? Is there any future in Britain for colleges with a strong pastoral tradition that try to emulate the liberal arts colleges so well entrenched in American higher education? Or should they aim at something closer to the model of the open-access community college?

A convincing argument can be made out that the second theme, the struggle to plan public sector higher education, has provided the real backbone of higher education policy in the last decade. The Oakes Committee of the late 1970s was the first sustained attempt to address this issue.[12] It was followed by the 1980 Report of the House of Commons Select Committee which was preoccupied by the problem of planning the polytechnics and colleges.[13] In the following year the DES lost patience with the rather convoluted constitutional arrangements which seemed to provide the only acceptable solution and attempted to cut the Gordian knot that tied polytechnics to their local authorities.[14] When this attempt ran into political difficulties, a consultation document was published to cover the DES's tactical retreat.[15] Finally the present National Advisory Body (NAB), as an *ersatz* UGC for the public sector, was established in 1982, according to a pattern very similar to that proposed by the Oakes Committee four years earlier. But throughout this sequence of confused episodes the basic questions remained essentially unchanged. Was it possible to reconcile local control of polytechnics and colleges with their effective planning as part of a national system of higher education? If it was possible, could a sensible planning framework be produced in which local authorities allowed their institutions reasonable autonomy and a reasonable balance between central and local government influence was maintained? If it was not possible, was it necessary to rethink the binary policy of the 1960s which divided higher education into an 'autonomous' university and a more accountable public sector? Until 1979 and after 1982 the attention of policy makers was concentrated on the second of these questions which assumed an affirmative answer to the first. Only for a brief period at the beginning of the 1980s was much attention given to the third which assumed a negative answer, before a new Secretary of State, Mr Kenneth Baker picked up Alexander's sword again in the 1987 White Paper.

The third theme, the search for a post-Robbins policy for higher education as a whole, was first expressed in the late 1970s within the narrow context of demographic decline. For much of that decade the DES was obsessed by the phenomenon of falling rolls, initially its impact on the demand for teachers which triggered the extensive programme of college of education closures and later the need to merge and close schools to maintain their viability and efficiency. It is hardly surprising that this obsessive thinking was carried over into higher education policy. How would higher education fare in the face of a 30 per cent decline in the number of 18-year-olds in the later 1980s and 1990s, an outcome which it seemed could already be accurately predicted in the 1970s? This appeared to be the issue which institutions, administrators and politicians had to confront. Of course the new pressure to restrain the growth of public expenditure intensified this restrictive policy climate. A range of strategies were advocated—from so-called 'tunnelling through the hump' (accommodating the early 1980s peak of student demand without providing matching resources, in the hope that this demand would diminish towards the end of the decade), to providing the extra resources and exploiting spare capacity left by diminishing demand from school leavers to develop higher education opportunities for mature students and continuing education. These strategies, together with the DES's most up-to-date projections of student demand, were laid out in a 1978 discussion document, the so-called Brown

Paper *Higher Education into the 1990s,*[16] and reiterated and revised in a similar paper a year later.[17]

However in the 1980s the focus switched from the future to the present, from the probabilities of student demand at the end of the decade to the certainties of public expenditure cuts that had been imposed by the new Conservative government. As a result the prospect of demographic decline, which had seemed such a serious threat under the previous government, was superseded by the here-and-now threat of savage cuts. This changed the nature of the debate about the future of higher education. Instead of being about how the system could be adapted to the hypothetical circumstances of the future, it was now about how universities, polytechnics and colleges could adjust their practices and their expectations to live within their newly restricted means. The problem was redefined and the timescale foreshortened. So when the panic provoked by the disorderly cuts of 1980–82 abated, the debate about a post-Robbins order for higher education had a different character. Value-for-money efficiency, managerial hierarchy instead of collegial consensus, performance indicators to enforce political accountability, the extension of the old customer-contractor principle beyond its original home in applied research to determine the future shape of all higher education priorities[18]—these were new elements in this debate which political circumstances had made obligatory. But a maybe unintended consequence was that the demographic shadow was lifted.[19] The present predicament of higher education may have appeared much worse under the Conservatives in the 1980s than under Labour in the late 1970s, but its future prospects almost seemed brighter. So the advice offered to the then Secretary of State for Education and Science, Sir Keith Joseph, on a future strategy for higher education in 1984 by both the UGC[20] and the NAB[21] was not entirely without hope, however preoccupied both bodies had become by present funding difficulties. Perhaps some credit for changing the climate of the policy debate from the fatalistic character acquired in the late 1970s to the more robust style typical of the 1980s, against all the external odds, should go to the two-year Leverhulme inquiry.[22] But a simpler explanation may be that by the 1980s the golden age of Robbins seemed so remote that it now appeared irrecoverable. A more cynical view, of course, is simply that higher education had got used to living with adversity. Certainly there was little in either the tone or the content of the government's 1985 *Green Paper*[23] to encourage an optimistic or expansive view of higher education's future.

The fourth theme was the struggle to create acceptable planning and funding mechanisms for the universities to replace the comfortable certainties of the old quinquennial system which had been swept away in the crisis of the mid-1970s. At first an effort was made to recreate the quinquennium itself. When Mrs Shirley Williams, the Labour Secretary of State for Education and Science from 1977 to 1979, established a rolling 'triennium', a fixed university grant for one year ahead followed by provisional grants for two subsequent years, it was widely interpreted as a half-way house on the way to restoring the old system. But this attempt at restoration, which was perhaps never feasible, even under Labour, was categorically abandoned by the new Conservative government in 1979. Although the new Secretary of State, Mr Mark Carlisle, promised that the universities would enjoy 'level funding', the government at the same time decided to charge overseas students 'full-cost' tuition fees which were far higher than the nominal fees charged to home students. Their intention was to end what they saw as a subsidy of overseas students by British taxpayers; their decision was to cut the grant paid to universities on the assumption that they would be able to recover this shortfall by their increased income from overseas students. By the mid-1980s most universities had managed to bridge this financial gap, but at the beginning of the decade it still seemed impossibly wide. Many universities were forced to adopt panicky strategies to balance their books, cutting costs through freezing vacant posts and imposing other emergency economies and increasing their revenue through recruiting practices that verged on the unscrupulous in order to increase their number of overseas students. In the end, of course, pressure from other government departments, in particular the Foreign Office and the Department of Trade and Industry, forced a U-turn on overseas students. Under the Pym aid and scholarships package of 1983, named after the then Foreign Secretary Mr Francis Pym, large-scale subsidy of overseas students was reintroduced. But it was too late to reverse the damaging financial and academic consequences for higher education.

In the autumn of 1980 the Prime Minister, Mrs Margaret Thatcher, succeeded in overbearing the doubts of the 'wets' in her Cabinet. The immediate result was a renewed assault on public expenditure. In these changed circumstances Mr Carlisle's promise of 'level funding' to the universities was broken. The UGC grant was cut substantially, by a planned 15 per cent over three years, despite the Committee's solemn warning to ministers that this would lead to diseconomy and chaos in the university system. The following July the storm broke when the UGC distributed this much reduced grant in a highly selective way; some universities like Bath and York were not cut at all while others like Salford had to absorb cuts of up to 40 per cent. Much controversy has surrounded this episode. Many blamed the UGC, first for not resigning *en masse* rather than agreeing to distribute a plainly inadequate grant, and second for not applying a policy of equal misery by spreading the cuts equally across all universities. Indeed some critics spoke as if it were the UGC not the government that was the source of the cuts. In reply the UGC, under its Chairman Sir Edward Parkes, claimed that a mass resignation would have passed virtually unnoticed: that the distribution of the university grant had always been a discriminatory process, so 'equal misery' would simply have perpetuated past selectivity; and that its highly selective distribution of the

1981 grant succeeded in making university funding a sensitive political issue. An 'equal misery' policy might have enabled universities to muddle through and so allow the government to deflect damaging public controversy. Whether intended or not, the UGC's policy in 1981 certainly turned university funding into a controversial cause. It also forced the government to address the urgent need to develop a coherent policy for universities. The drift of the Carlisle years, at first relatively benign but then increasingly malignant, was succeeded by the often tortured intensity associated with Sir Keith Joseph, who followed him as Secretary of State.

In 1982 higher education began to settle down. The government retreated from the brink of chaos to which it had been brought, in the case of the universities, by its precipitate increase in overseas students' fees and its deep cuts in the university grant, and, in the case of the polytechnics and colleges, by its ill-judged plan to break the historic links with local authorities. In the latter case the retreat was marked by the establishment of the National Advisory Body. In the case of the universities the retreat was marked by the concession of a £200 million 'restructuring' fund (which was used to persuade almost 4000 teachers and researchers to abandon their posts, thereby confirming the UGC's original warning about the diseconomy of the government's cuts), and by the 'new blood' initiative, which created 600 new posts in a half-hearted attempt to prevent the sclerosis of the academic profession. Another feature of 1982—although it is doubtful whether it can be regarded as evidence of the government's retreat—was the growing concern about the erosion of scientific research. In April a report on postgraduate education was published;[24] in May Lord Rothschild's verdict was delivered on the then Social Science Research Council (SSRC)[25] which was far from being the condemnation demanded by the DES a year earlier; in June came a report on the support of university scientific research;[26] in the following July a further report on research council support for in-house and university research was published.[17] Although on different subjects and offering sometimes contrary prescriptions, these successive reports did apply increasing pressure on the government. Research seemed to be at risk, and ministers seemed to be complacent. This concern about the erosion of Britain's research base, especially in universities, led in two different directions. The first was to encourage increased opposition to the government like the 'Save Our Science' campaign led by disgruntled scientists in the most famous universities frustrated by their inability to keep up with the international competition. The second was to increase support for greater selectivity in research. This policy taken up with enthusiasm by the UGC in 1986 when it divided the university grant into teaching and research components and graded university departments on a five-point scale from 'outstanding' to 'below average'. Another aspect of this intensified enthusiasm for selectivity was the drive to rationalize Britain's scientific priorities. Perhaps the most dramatic example of this was the debate about Britain's continued participation in the European high energy physics research centre, CERN, at Geneva.[28]

If selectivity became established as one dominant preoccupation of higher education policy, access became another. In response to the 1980/81 cuts the UGC had ordered universities to cut their intake of students. The inevitable result was an almost corresponding increase in demand for places in polytechnics and colleges. So numbers rose in the public sector without any matching increase in resources. The polytechnic directors and others fought hard against this erosion of the unit of resource which they saw as undermining academic quality and compromising polytechnic claims to offer a higher education equivalent to that provided in the universities. The government, on the other hand, preferred to regard this erosion of resourcing standards as an increase in efficiency. The NAB, very much under the influence of local authorities preoccupied by the need to increase access to higher education, was caught in the middle. Its leaders were anxious to stick up for the public sector but were aware of the political advantages that could be gained by both a good record on maintaining access and also on increasing efficiency. Although it proved a difficult balancing act, it seemed to produce results when Sir Keith Jóseph's successor as Secretary of State, Mr Kenneth Baker, was manoeuvred into increasing the budget for polytechnics and colleges in the autumn of 1986. The public sector appeared to be collecting its reward for admitting the students displaced from the universities after the 1981 cuts, as much as for the greater relevance to industry of its more flexible style of higher education.

With the universities it was different. They too had their grant increased in the autumn of 1986, but as much in anticipation of future performance as a reward for past achievement. During the long period of debate that ran up to the 1985 *Green Paper* attention was concentrated more and more on the idea of a new 'concordat' between the universities and the government. The latter would increase the university grant if the universities accepted specific reforms, including greater selectivity in the support of research, the restructuring of the academic profession, greater managerial efficiency and increased scrutiny of academic standards. The UGC under its new Chairman, Sir Peter Swinnerton-Dyer, was a consistent, if not always enthusiastic, sponsor of such a 'concordat'. But the Committee of Vice Chancellors and Principals (CVCP) too was convinced that a new understanding with the government was necessary if a repetition of the chaos of 1979–82 was to be avoided. So the Committee not only established the Jarratt inquiry into university efficiency but also conducted its own investigation into academic standards chaired by Professor Philip Reynolds[29]. However this concordat, although perhaps successful in producing a more positive dialogue between universities and the state, remains difficult to characterize. Was it a draft contract under which universities abandoned their old autonomy, or simply political rhetoric of little long-term significance?

It may be too simple to describe the experience of the universities since 1973 as a thirteen-year descent from the freedom of the quinquennium to the dependence of the concordat.

Of course, the universities have lost their strategic, if not operational, independence. Thirteen years ago whether they were free, individually and collectively, to set their own direction could at least be argued. Even as late as 1981 it was still an open question. For in that year the UGC undoubtedly made up its own mind about the distribution of the recurrent grant without any reference to the government. Today that question has been closed. Never again will the UGC be able to act on an important policy question without consulting ministers. Never again will the universities be able to regard themselves as a semi-independent estate of the nation. It was to adjust the constitution and operation of the UGC to reflect this changed relationship between universities and the state that the Croham Committee was established.[30]

But two important qualifications have to be made. The first is that this government has made no attempt to manage the universities in the detailed administrative manner in which the polytechnics and colleges have been managed. Probably no future government will make this attempt. The one attempt by the DES to make detailed allocations directly to universities, the so-called 'switch' initiative to provide extra places in science and technology in 1984, was not judged to be a success and is unlikely to be repeated. So the detailed operation of the universities will remain a matter for (one-sided) negotiation between the UGC and individual institutions. The second is that not all the consequences of this centralization and politicization of university policy making were bad. Some would argue that by cutting student intakes to protect what were still generous staff/student ratios according to international standards, the UGC's traditional concern to protect the unit of resource which had been intensified by the instability of the 1970s, the Committee failed to give sufficient weight to the needs of the nation. So the politicians may have been right to trim a power that appeared to be exercised in such a selfish, or at any rate inward, manner. By breaking the old donnish dominion institutionalized in the UGC they may have made it more likely that Britain would develop a mass, or at least modern, university system.

Sadly that prospect still seems remote under present Conservative rule. In the last seven years the universities have been disorganized by the cuts and demoralized by their loss of independence and apparent loss of public esteem. So the losses are plain. The gains are more difficult to discover. The government would claim that the university system had been made more efficient and more relevant and that its quality had been improved. All three claims are doubtful. Any formal gain in efficiency has been bought at a fearful price. Universities have moved to less generous staff/student ratios by letting go many of their most active and able academic staff. They have learnt to live with less generous resourcing standards by deferring essential maintenance or exploiting overseas students. They have accepted tougher management practices by suppressing the spirit of collegiality on which successful academic enterprise so crucially depends.

With relevance it is the same, although here much less has changed than ministers pretend. The universities that have developed strong and sustained links with industry are the same universities which once were criticized for compromising their academic independence. The star of university-industry collaboration in 1986, Warwick, was condemned for just this vice in 1969 in a book written by the historian, Edward Thompson, with the evocative title *Warwick University Ltd.*[31] A phrase intended to condemn has been transmuted into praise. What has really happened is a significant shift in public attitudes to university-industry collaboration, now almost as acceptable on the left as on the right, rather than vigorous intervention by the Conservative government that has been in office since 1979. Indeed it could be argued that the disproportionate cuts inflicted on technological universities like Salford, Aston and Bradford in 1981 for which ministers were ultimately responsible hindered, rather than helped, such collaboration.

But it is the third issue, that of quality, which is crucial to the government's claim to have reformed the universities. Of course competition among school leavers to get university places has become much tougher. But this is the result of the UGC's independent decision in 1981 to cut student intakes because the university grant was insufficient, and of demographic pressures created by the early-1980s bulge in the number of 18-year-olds. In any case many of the displaced candidates enrolled in polytechnics instead; ministers publicly disapproved of the UGC's restrictive policy and claimed desperately that the 'Robbins principle', that mystical measure of accessibility, had not been broken; and it is generally accepted that 'A' level scores are a poor measure of future academic potential. So it is difficult to argue that the higher formal entry qualifications demanded by universities in the 1980s can reasonably be represented as evidence of increased quality.

Nor does the shape of the university system produced by seven years of cutting and cajoling by the Conservatives, support ministers' claims to have improved its quality. For although stratification has been encouraged, its motive has been economy not quality. Since the UGC came under categorical DES supervision when Sir Peter Swinnerton-Dyer succeeded Sir Edward Parkes as Chairman, universities have been punished for being 'expensive' rather than for being of lower quality. The Committee's controversial decision to grade the quality of the research in every university department, cloaked the much more significant drive towards cost-effectiveness, which in practice and of necessity has been interpreted as levelling down to the lowest defensible cost base. The result has been that UGC discrimination has not produced the elite stratification that might have been expected. Indeed Oxford and Cambridge have suffered disproportionately and London, which has also been unsettled by the inevitable pressure to rationalize this leviathan university, has also been hard hit. The big civic universities, which whatever view may be taken of the effectiveness of their management, produce the bulk of the system's scholarly and scientific work and also of its output of graduates, have not been especially favoured by the UGC. Nor have most of the Scottish universities, while the University of Wales, and in particular Cardiff, are not among the Committee's favourite institutions. The winners, to the extent that there have been any, have been a small number of smallish universities with extremely low unit costs. Bath, York, Loughborough and Warwick are typical. Cost not quality has been the decisive factor in shaping the university system under the intolerable pressures of Tory austerity.

The experience of the polytechnics has been different and arguably more hopeful. But it has not been sufficiently different to sustain optimistic theories about a 'rising' public sector of higher education and a 'declining' university sector. Morale in the polytechnics and colleges has been much less damaged than in the universities. One reason is that the cuts have been both less severe, an assessment that some would challenge, and different in character. On the whole polytechnics and colleges have been asked to teach more students, up to 20 per cent more, with the same resources. But this has been less difficult to accomplish than the task faced by the universities which was to adjust in too brief a period to a substantial real cut in their income. A second reason is polytechnics and colleges have lower expectations—some cynics would say this is the very intention of the binary policy—so they have been less seriously affected by the symptoms of rejection which have tormented the universities. A third is that higher education as traditionally practised in the public sector is more flexible. It is used to running part-time courses, providing continuing education, collaborating with industry. There has been no sense of any loss of academic integrity by engaging in such activity.

But it may be wrong to exaggerate the resilience of the polytechnics and colleges. They have been put under almost as great pressure as the universities by the public austerity imposed by the government. These pressures affect their teachers, who because of increased teaching loads have less time to develop new courses, engage in research, or recreate themselves through staff development. They can also be observed in the deterioration of the public sector's plant. Its logistics in their widest sense are being dangerously eroded. So it is a mistake to suppose that the condition of the polytechnics and colleges is radically different from that of the universities in the mid-1980s. Comparatively they may be better off: absolutely they remain worse off.

Nor should the institutional resilience and higher morale of the public sector conceal the fact that they are still caught up in a web of elitist assumptions, a hierarchy of assumed merit that ultimately favours the universities. Some interpret these assumptions and this hierarchy in the narrow terms of the details of the binary policy, the continuing dependence on local authorities and on the Council for National Academic Awards (CNAA). They regard such constraints on the financial and academic freedom of the polytechnics and bigger colleges as an anachronism. But an alternative, and maybe more subtle, analysis suggests that the power of hierarchy cannot be checked so simply. It might even be that with a dismantling of the binary policy the polytechnics and colleges would be subjected to even more intense subordination within a more homogeneous system. Their distinctiveness as part of local authority education and the academic shelter offered by a secure system of external validation may offer some slight protection against the full blast of university prejudice.

Even before the 1987 White Paper movement towards an arm's length relationship with local authorities seems inevitable.[32] For the most mature public sector institutions at any rate the confused aftermath of the Lindop report[33] has led to the substitution of accreditation for validation which should bring much greater academic independence. But the government itself has done little to encourage or to recognize the growing maturity of the polytechnics. Rather it has been an agnostic or even indifferent spectator. The growing autonomy of the public sector both from its local authority masters and its CNAA supervisors has owed much more to the subtle interplay of relationships between these external authorities and the institutions. The ambiguous result has been crab-wise progress towards a negotiated retreat by these external powers and a corresponding increase in institutional autonomy. But it would probably be a mistake to suppose that this had much affected the power of the larger hierarchy within British higher education.

The most difficult question of all to answer about the evolution of higher education from 1973 to 1986 is also the most essential. What influence has it had on the 'private life' of the system, the inner world of scholarly and scientific disciplines? One view is that there has been remarkably little influence, except in the limited external sense that shortage of resources has slowed development. But that seems too sanguine. Perhaps the most significant change is that this inner world is private no longer. Just as in schools the government has invaded the secret garden of the curriculum and pulled up the weeds (they would say) or trampled on the flowers (their critics would assert), so Conservative ministers have become embroiled in issues which in 1973 would still have been regarded as only yielding to academic judgments. This intervention has gone far beyond the more spectacular invasions, to root out alleged Marxist bias in the Open University's social sciences foundation course, to punish the Polytechnic of North London's sociologists, or to bully the former Social Science Research Council. The academic privacy of higher education has been destroyed. Again this is an ambiguous phenomenon. Many who resent this philistine assault from the right nevertheless believe that the intellectual priorities of higher education can no longer reasonably be regarded as a private matter in which lay people have no legitimate interest.

But more has been lost than gained in the new equation. It is not simply that the presented beleaguered and fearful state of higher education is an environment inimical to good scholarship. It is that the autonomy of higher education, which institutionalizes intellectual and critical freedoms of the first importance in a democratic society, has been dangerously eroded. The old order in higher education, which was still in good shape in the summer of 1973, could not have survived the strains of the succeeding years without radical modification. The old university club was bound to break up. But little effort has been made to care for the principles of intellectual freedom that these traditional arrangements represented however anachronistically.

Maybe the experience of higher education between 1973 and 1986 has simply reflected the sea–change in Britain's civic culture during these years. Higher education, in particular the universities, were a crucial component of that old aristocratic Whiggish liberalism which in the twentieth century merged into collectivist social democracy and so maintained its position as our civic religion. The universities with their subtle mixture of paternalistic populism and academic tradition both reflected and justified this civic religion. Like Anthony Trollope's Duke of Omnium[34] higher education embodies this tension between a tendency towards greater equality and the maintenance of aristocratic standards, a tension maintained by the powerful force of an austere code of public responsibility. Read Robbins if you doubt it.

In the last thirteen years all this has changed. Liberalism has been abandoned, aristocracy has become absurd, public duty appears sanctimonious or useless. We have witnessed the attempted destruction of the delicate values system that higher education both expressed and sustained. The moral shock waves have been much greater, much more significant than all the distress and diseconomy caused by the cuts. And in the end freedom may have been put at risk, because freedom in Britain may depend on awkward aristocratic institutions like the universities. No-one of course would seek to defend higher education as it was once satirised by the late Philip Larkin in a book review in *The Listener*, as a 'sleeping bag' for leisured intellectuals, a service once offered by the church. But few doubt that freedom depends on margins, margins for error that all too easily in a illiberal state can appear like margins of inefficiency and idleness. In Britain in the mid-1980s, as the experience of higher education clearly shows, those margins of freedom may have been dangerously reduced.

Notes

1 DEPARTMENT OF EDUCATION AND SCIENCE (1963) *Higher Education*: (The Robbins Report), London, HMSO.

2   *Report of an Inquiry into the University of Oxford* (The Franks Report) (1966) Oxford, Oxford University Press.

3   CROSLAND, A. (1965) Speech at Woolwich Polytechnic, April; CROSLAND, A. (1967) Speech at the University of Lancaster, January. The first is summarized and the second printed in full in ROBINSON, E. (1968) *The New Polytechnics*, Harmondsworth, Penguin.

4   HALSEY, A.H. (1985) 'Essay' in BULMER, M. (Ed) *Essays in the History of British Sociological Research*, Cambridge, Cambridge University Press.

5   BRADBURY, M. (1975) *The History Man* London, Secker and Warburg.

6   *Government Expenditure Plans* (annual), White Papers on public expenditure.

7   DEPARTMENT OF EDUCATION AND SCIENCE (1984) *Higher Education: Funding Comparisons Across Sectors*, London, HMSO.

8   UNIVERSITY GRANTS COMMITTEE (1984), *Report of a Working Party on Continuing Education*, London, UGC. ational ADVISORY BODY (1984), *Report of the Continuing Education Working Group*, London, NAB.

9   UNIVERSITY GRANTS COMMITTEE (1975) *Annual Report*, London, HMSO.

10 UNIVERSITY GRANTS COMMITTEE (1976) *Annual Report*, London, HMSO.

11 HENCKE, D. (1978) *Colleges in Crisis*, Harmondsworth, Penguin.

12 DEPARTMENT OF EDUCATION AND SCIENCE (1978) *Report of the Working Group on the Management of Higher Education in the Maintained Sector* (The Oakes Report), London, HMSO.

13 HOUSE OF COMMONS SELECT COMMITTEE ON EDUCATION, SCIENCE AND THE ARTS (1980) *The Funding and Organisation of Courses in Higher Education*, London, HMSO.

14 DEPARTMENT OF EDUCATION AND SCIENCE (1981). 'Early draft of a proposal to establish a national commission for polytechnics and colleges', published in the *Times Higher Education Supplement*, 30 January, page 1, and 6 February, page 2.

15 DEPARTMENT OF EDUCATION AND SCIENCE (1981), *Consultative Paper on Higher Education in the Maintained Sector* (Models A and B), London, HMSO.

16 DEPARTMENT OF EDUCATION and SCIENCE/SCOTTISH EDUCATION DEPARTMENT (1978) *Higher Education into the 1990s: A Discussion Document*, London, HMSO.

17 DEPARTMENT OF EDUCATION AND SCIENCE (1979) *Future Trends in Higher Education*, London, HMSO.

18 COMMITTEE OF VICE-CHANCELLORS AND PRINCIPALS (1985) *Report of the Steering Group on University Efficiency* (The Jarratt Report), London, CVCP; NATIONAL ADVISORY BOARD (1987), *Report of the Working Group on Good Management Practice in Public Sector Higher Education*, London, NAB

19 DEPARTMENT OF EDUCATION AND SCIENCE (1986) *Projections of Demand for Higher Education in Great Britain 1986-2000*, London, HMSO.

20 UNIVERSITY GRANTS COMMITTEE (1984) *A Strategy for Higher Education into the 1990s*, London, HMSO.

21 NATIONAL ADIVISORY BODY (1984) *A Strategy for Higher Education in the late 1980s and Beyond*, London, NAB.

22 Final report of the Leverhulme inquiry into the future of higher education (1983) *Excellence and Diversity*, Guildford, Society for Research into Higher Education.

23 DEPARTMENT OF EDUCATION AND SCIENCE (1985) *The Development of Higher Education into the 1990s*, London, HMSO.

24 ADVISORY BOARD FOR THE RESEARCH COUNCILS (1982) *Report of the Working Party on Postgraduate Education*, London, ABRC.

25 DEPARTMENT OF EDUCATION AND SCIENCE (1982) *An Inquiry into the Social Science Research Council*, London, HMSO.

26 ADIVISORY BOARD FOR THE RESEARCH COUNCILS/UNIVERSITY GRANTS COMMITTEE (1982) *Report of the Joint Working Party on the Support of University Scientific Research*, London, ABRC/UGC.

27 ADVISORY BOARD FOR THE RESEARCH COUNCILS (1983) *The Support Given by Research Councils for In-house and University Research*, London, ABRC.

28 ADVISORY BOARD FOR THE RESEARCH COUNCILS/SCIENCE AND ENGINEERING RESEARCH COUNCIL (1985) *High Energy Particle Physics in the United Kingdom*, London, ABRC/SERC.

29 COMMITTEE OF VICE-CHANCELLORS AND PRINCIPALS (1986) *Academic Standards in Universities*, London, CVCP.

30 DEPARTMENT OF EDUCATION AND SCIENCE (1987) *Report of an Inquiry into the Future of the University Grants Committee* (The Croham Report), London, HMSO.

31 THOMPSON, E. (1969) *Warwick University Ltd*, Harmondsworth, Penguin.

32 NATIONAL ADVISORY BODY (1987) *op cit.*

33 DEPARTMENT OF EDUCATION AND SCIENCE (1985) *Academic Validation in Public Sector Higher Education* (The Lindop Report), London, HMSO.

34 TROLLOPE, A. (1876) *The Prime Minister*, (reprinted 1938) London, Oxford University Press.

35 DEPARTMENT OF EDUCATION AND SCIENCE (1987) *Higher Education: Meeting the Challenge*, London, HMSO.

Chapter 8: School Teachers: Salaries and Conditions of Service

Rene Saran

Rene Saran has worked in industry, commerce and as a lecturer in adult and higher education. She is now Honorary Visiting Fellow in policy studies at the University of London Institute of Education and a Research Fellow at the City Polytechnic, where until recently she was principal lecturer in politics, teaching decision and policy-making courses. Rene Saran's earlier policy research resulted in *Policy-Making in Secondary Education* (1973) and an Open University course unit *The Politics of Educational Policy-Making: Pressures on Central and Local Government* (1979). Her Social Science Research Council financed investigation into the Burnham salary negotiations since 1945 appeared as *The Politics behind Burnham* (1985) and she also contributed 'The use of archives and interviews in research on educational policy' to the book *Strategies of Educational Research* edited by R. G. Burgess (1985).

★ ★ ★

Introduction

School Teachers and Their Unions

This chapter deals with teachers employed in the maintained, not the private, school sector, nor with those working as lecturers in colleges and universities. Attention is given primarily to teacher unions and their negotiating role in protecting and improving salaries and conditions of work. The chapter seeks to evaluate the years 1973–86 for teacher unions and their members in respect of national negotiations of salaries and conditions. At the time of writing this chapter (December 1986) teacher unions (as well as their employers, the local authorities) were threatened with the loss of negotiating rights over salaries and conditions of service. With such a cloud hanging over them, no teacher union could approach New Year's Day 1987 with much joy. Perhaps, then, the years 1973–86 have been 'wasted years'.

On 8 December 1986 the Teachers' Pay and Conditions Bill—which had been announced in the Queen's Speech in late November—was given its second reading. The committee stage was commenced two days later. The opposition accused the government of 'railroading' the Bill through. Under the Bill the Secretary of State for Education and Science would acquire the power to impose the government's own proposals for salaries and conditions, within the financial limits set by the government, in place of the negotiated draft agreement which had been signed by the employers and four of the six teacher unions on the Burnham Committee which negotiates pay.

The unions were balloting their members prior to ratification. By the time the Bill was introduced, the two smallest of the four unions which had signed the draft agreement had withdrawn their support. But the ballot of the third largest teacher union (Assistant Masters and Mistresses Association (AMMA)) showed a two-to-one result in favour of the draft agreement. Talks between Mr Kenneth Baker, the Secretary of State, some of the unions, as well as the employers, continued week-by-week, despite Mr Baker's draconian intervention. He argued that a two-year dispute, accompanied by much disruption of schools, deep parental concern and a divided profession, had to be resolved. And resolve it he would, if the employers and unions failed to come up with terms acceptable to himself.

But the Bill went much further than empowering the Minister to impose on one particular occasion his preferred plan for salaries and conditions. Under it the Burnham Committee will be abolished, to be replaced by an Advisory Committee appointed by the Secretary of State; the unions (and employers) would be able to make representations to this new Committee, but their right to negotiate with each other would disappear. Furthermore, the recommendations of the Committee were to be purely advisory, the Secretary of State was not bound to accept them. No wonder the teacher unions were united in opposing the establishment of such an Advisory Committee, whatever else might divide them. Jointly with the employers—and under the auspices of ACAS—they had agreed that a National Joint Committee, to negotiate both pay and conditions, take the place of the Burnham Committee which dealt with pay alone. While some of the constituents on both sides would have preferred a different settlement to the one which had emerged, it was preferable to one imposed on employer and employees alike.

Meanwhile, teachers had protested outside the House of Commons during the second reading and the National Union of Teachers (NUT) was preparing to complain formally to the International Labour Office that the government's plan would deprive teachers of their pay negotiating rights; the General Council of the TUC and the local authority employers sought an early meeting with the Prime Minister over the Bill.

The Dual Role of Teacher Unions

In contrast to their 'union' interests, teacher unions also have other, mainly 'professional', concerns. For example, their members are involved in subject organizations, and until the Schools Council was abolished, teacher unions were represented on its various bodies. Indeed, in the earlier years teacher representatives had a majority on the Schools Council. As pressure groups teacher unions often try to influence educational policy at both local and national level. Although occasionally unions play an initiating role, more usually their support is given (or opposition expressed) when an issue has already reached the political agenda.

Whether attempts to influence policy are motivated by professional or union interest, or—more likely—by a mixture of the two, is a moot point. The NUT, for example, stated (House of Commons, 1976, p. 141) that its activities combine professional and trade union interests, and that the two do not conflict (what is good for teachers is good for children and vice versa). Such a view is unlikely to convince people outside teaching, especially at a time when protection of jobs has been a major issue. Lodge and Blackstone in examining the NUT's record (in McNay and Ozga, 1985, pp. 221 and 231) noted the example of the union's opposition to the employment of nursery assistants in nursery classes, as well as to the organization of playgroups and the involvement of parents.

Expansion Gives Way to Contraction

1973 was the year of the oil crisis. This marked a major economic turning point changing attitudes to public expenditure. It happened to coincide with a declining demographic trend which had profound consequences for the education system. Apart from the post-war 'bulge' in births, which peaked in 1947, it was 1964 that produced the highest number of births (876,000 in England and Wales); thereafter each year the numbers fell, to a trough in 1976 (584,000). But it took time before the concept of contraction entered public consciousness. The 1972 White Paper (DES, 1972) still appeared under the title *Education—A Framework for Expansion*, whereas by the 1980s new preoccupations were reflected in titles like *Falling Rolls in Secondary Schools* (Briault and Smith, 1980) and *Education in Jeopardy: Problems and Possibilities of Contraction* (Dennison, 1981). Numbers admitted to initial teacher training were axed; total numbers enrolled (England and Wales) had risen from nearly 70,000 to nearly 120,000 between 1964 and 1972, but by 1980 there were fewer than 36,000 (Thomas, 1985, p. 78). The total number of teachers continued to rise until 1978–79, but by 1982–83 had fallen from 441,000 to 414,000 (Walsh *et al.* 1985, pp. 262–3).

The repercussions for school teachers and their trade unions were immense. In the sixties jobs had been easy to get and promotion opportunities were good. By the eighties, jobs were much more difficult to find and there was little room at the top. Between 1948 and 1972, educational spending had risen from 2.8 per cent to 6.6 per cent of the gross national product (Dennison, 1981, p. 8), itself a demonstration that education held a significant place in public esteem. In those years the teachers, through their trade unions, had participated in the 'triangle of power', alongside the DES and the LEAs, making up the partnership which governed the education system. In particular, the leaders of two organizations—Sir William (now Lord) Alexander of the Association of Education Committees (AEC) and Sir Ronald Gould of the NUT had exercised considerable personal influence. Gould retired in 1970, Alexander in 1977, on the demise of the AEC. Gradually the system of educational sub-government was pulled more firmly into the wider local and national political system, a trend which was accentuated by local government reorganization and the development of corporate management after 1974. All this affected education and the dominant influence of the NUT.

By the seventies teacher politics had been transformed. In common with other white-collar professionals, teachers had become more militant and had, in the late sixties protested vigorously against midday supervision and staged strikes in support of their salaries claim. Gradually teacher unions were driven on the defensive and their union rather than their professional interests came to the fore. The two largest teacher unions had come out of their isolation by joining the TUC—the National Association of Schoolmasters (NAS) in 1968, followed by the NUT in 1970. Teacher unions thus gave recognition to the necessity to extend their activities into the wider political arena in order to protect the interests of teachers.

Burnham Representation and Power Relationships

The NUT has been, and still is, the largest teacher union, as well as being the oldest. But relatively speaking it has lost its claim to speak for the majority of the profession. In 1979 its membership (289,311 out of a total of 563,591 for Great Britain) still exceeded the combined membership of the five other unions represented on the Burnham Committee.[1] As shown in table 1, by 1985 NUT numbers had fallen to below half of the total (252,823 out of 579,820).[2] That proportionate fall notwithstanding it still represents significantly more of the teaching force than its rivals.[3]

In the early sixties the NAS (now NAS/UWT) and the National Association of Head Teachers (NAHT) had taken their seats on the Burnham Committee. Both had been breakaways from the NUT after the First World War, the NAS over the issue of equal pay, the NAHT on account of conflicts between classroom and head teachers. Until the early sixties the power of the NUT had sufficed to exclude both from salary negotiations. With Burnham representation won, there opened the era when the NUT could no longer ignore the activities and tactics of the NAS. Conflicts between teacher unions became a regular feature of Burnham negotiations, and in the course of time, with changes in union membership enrolments, the balance of power between the teacher unions changed. As shown in table 2, this affected representation on the Burnham Committee. The NUT with sixteen seats had an *absolute*

Table 1: Membership of School Teacher Unions (Great Britain)

	1979	**1981**	**1983**	**1985**
Assistant Masters and Mistresses Association (AMMA)	85,026	85,097	82,783	93,906
National Association of Head Teachers (NAHT)	23,063	23,472	23,397	29,218
National Association of Schoolmasters and Union of Women Teachers (NAS/UWT)	142,633	145,844	146,064	158,161
National Union of Teachers (NUT)	289,311	261,747	249,478	252,823
Professional Association of Teachers (PTA)	19,205	22,612	21,843	39,086
Secondary Heads Association (SHA)	4,353	4,433	4,839	6,626

Source: Certification Office for Trade Union and Employers' Associations

majority on the Teachers' Panel of the Burnham Committee until 1981; in that year the sixteen NUT representatives made up just half the total; finally, in 1985, NUT control of the Teachers' Panel was lost—the NUT retained only thirteen seats out of twenty-eight.

Salary negotiations were also affected by the shift of power towards the centre in DES-local authority relationships under the 1965 Remuneration of Teachers Act (RTA). This is the Act that will be repealed if the 1986 Teachers' Pay and Conditions Bill referred to above is enacted. It is all too easy for the Secretary of State to accuse the divided teaching profession for 'leaving him no choice' but to seek *diktat* type powers under the Pay and Conditions Bill. Under the 1965 RTA the DES had acquired direct representation on the employers' side of the Burnham Committee—the Management Panel. This meant that the unions were negotiating with the local authorities, the teachers' employers, as well as with the DES, and indirectly with the government. They were often faced by a disunited Management Panel, which did not smooth the path of negotiation. Indeed, the way in which the DES used its greatly enhanced power as a Burnham Committee member under the RTA frequently led to long delays during negotiations. The resolution of conflict through negotiation became more difficult all round—so many organizations were involved on the employer as well as on the union side.

Whilst the DES had only two out of a total of twenty-seven representatives on the Management Panel, the organizations making up the Panel (Association of County Councils (ACC), Association of Metropolitan Authorities (AMA), the Welsh Joint Education Committee (WJEC) and the DES) had agreed to much greater powers for the DES. The Concordat, concluded in 1965, remained confidential until published fifteen years later (*Education*, 19-26 December 1980, p. 571). It gave the DES a veto over global sums which might be offered by the Management Panel to the Teachers' Panel, as well as a weighted vote of fifteen over the distribution of the amount of

Table 2: Representation of Teacher Unions on Burnham Committee (Primary and Secondary) 1973, 1981 and 1985

Teachers' Panel	1973	1981	1985
National Union of Teachers (NUT)	16	16	13
National Association of Schoolmasters/ Union of Women Teachers (NAS/UWT)[1]	3	7	7
Assistant Master and Mistresses Association (AMMA)[2]	4	4	4
National Association of Head Teachers (NAHT)	1	2	2
Secondary Heads Association (SHA)[3]	2	1	1
Professional Association of Teachers (PAT)	—	1	1
National Association of Teachers in Further and Higher Education (NATFHE)	2	1	—

Notes:
1 Initially it was the NAS only which was represented on Burnham, but following the 1975 Sex Discrimination Act, the NAS became the NAS/UWT.
2 Initially the Assistant Masters Association and the Association of Assistant Mistresses had separate representation. They merged into the AMMA after 1975.
3 The Secondary Heads Association resulted from the amalgamation of the Head Masters Association with the Association of Head Mistresses after 1975. Before amalgamation, each had one Burnham representative.
Source: Saran, 1985, p. 11.

money on offer. For twenty years the use of the veto by the DES was a major cause of the protracted nature of the Burnham negotiations. Securing Cabinet approval for an increased employer offer delayed negotiations by a minimum of three weeks, by which time as likely as not union psychology made it unacceptable. The power of veto created a ratchet effect; the inability of the employers to settle quickly produced higher-priced final settlements. During the 1985 salaries dispute, which was extremely protracted, the local authority representatives, were so exasperated with the role of the DES on the Management Panel that they unilaterally tore up the Concordat.

Loss of the veto over global sums was hardly crucial because rate-capping introduced in 1985 ensured that the local authorities were, in any case, highly dependent upon central government finance. Furthermore, heavy penalties resulted from not following government guidelines. But loss of the weighted vote over distribution undermined DES power. The DES had often argued strongly in favour of differentials, which means putting more of the available money at the top than at the bottom. Relatively this favours teachers on higher rates of pay. It had been a conflict over distribution between the Secretary of State and the Burnham Committee back in 1963 which had resulted in imposition, by law, of the Minister's preferred distribution, followed by the 1965 RTA which greatly enhanced DES powers.

In 1986 it was again distribution, much more than global sums, over which Baker disagreed with the employers and those unions which supported the draft agreement negotiated under ACAS auspices. It is arguable that if the

Concordat had not been torn up in the previous year the DES voice (with its weighted vote) might have prevailed on the Management Panel. The Pay and Conditions Bill was Baker's way of reasserting, indeed further increasing, the power of the DES. It was the local authorities which had renounced the Concordat; thus there was much behind the 1986 Burnham crisis which could not be explained simply by pointing a finger at the divided teaching profession and their six unions. Power conflicts between the DES and the local authorities (many under Labour control, following the 1985 local elections) was an important dimension in the overall political complexities.

Salaries and Conditions: 1973–86

Salaries

School teachers in Britain are not well paid when compared with their counterparts in other European countries, like, for example, Germany and the Netherlands. The history of salary negotiations since the Second World War shows that teacher unions above all concentrated on cost of living and relativity issues. Changes in the salary structure have more usually been initiated by the employers, and the teacher unions have often been deeply divided over major structural reforms. Multiunionism has certainly not made things easy. Between them, the unions represent a range of sectional interests and unity is difficult to achieve whenever differentials are under discussion.

Teacher unions each have their particular historical origins; the pre-Second World War divisions of the schools' system into elementary and secondary helps to explain why several unions were well established by 1944, drawing members from these separate sectors. The strength of the NUT was in the old elementary schools, whereas the secondary teachers (in the main working in the pre-Second World War grammar schools, then called secondary) were organized in four associations—the Assistant Masters, the Assistant Mistresses, the Headmasters and the Headmistresses. Their membership was drawn from secondary schools in the state as well as the private sector.

Following the 1944 Education Act, the NUT became the leading union for primary teachers, and for some time the only one open to the majority of primary teachers who were women. By contrast, the male-only NAS recruited successfully in the rapidly growing secondary modern sector; until 1961 opposition to equal pay remained its main platform. Once equal pay was an accomplished fact, the NAS found other reasons for its separate existence—the new image was that of the union for career teachers. Organizations developed in one context tend to develop a life of their own: self-perpetuation becomes as much of a driving force as the original purposes in times past.

Until 1945, teachers in elementary schools were on lower scales of pay than those in grammar schools. The fifties and sixties witnessed conflict between grammar school teachers (a minority on the Burnham Committee) and primary and secondary modern school teachers represented by the NUT. Grammar school teachers sought a career structure which would favour their members, whereas the NUT pressed for improvements to the basic scale, which would benefit the majority of the lower paid. However, by the late sixties the grammar school unions were working much more closely with the NUT on the Teachers' Panel. Once they were joined by the much more abrasive NAS in the early sixties, it was NAS tactics which threw the Burnham Committee's work into disarray.

Entry of the NAS into the Burnham circle transformed Burnham politics. Gone were Burnham conventions about confidentiality during negotiations. The practice of a single spokesperson to put the Panel's case in the full Burnham Committee was challenged. As a minority—often overruled within the Teachers' Panel—the NAS wanted its voice to be heard by the Management Panel. Membership competition between unions made compromise and agreement on the Teachers' Panel extremely difficult. The NAS fairly rapidly grew into the second largest teacher union. Then, in 1970, another new union was established—the Professional Association of Teachers (PAT). Its members subscribed to a policy of no strike action. Ten years later PAT was recognized by the Secretary of State, and given one seat on the Burnham Committee. The old-timers, including by then the more militant NAS, opposed the newcomer.

In 1971 a new salaries structure of five overlapping scales was introduced. With minor amendments, this has remained the structure until 1986. The NUT with its absolute majority on the Teachers' Panel had opposed its introduction, wanting to retain the basic scale plus graded post structure which had been agreed in 1956. Both the NAS and the four secondary associations favoured the structural proposals of Management. But as a negotiated settlement was barred by NUT opposition, the Burnham Committee found itself in deadlock. The dispute was then resolved by arbitration, in favour of the employers' case. In fact none of the important landmarks in teachers' salaries during the seventies were the result of normal Burnham Committee negotiations. Structural reform in 1971 was achieved via an arbitration award; two large increases in salary levels, to restore teachers earnings following periods of bad slippage, were the outcome of independent reviews: the first by the Houghton Committee, the second by the Clegg Comparability Commission. And during the mid-seventies there was a period of statutory pay policy, following the oil crisis and the explosion of public expenditure.

However, the early seventies in the pre-Houghton period presented the teacher unions with opportunities which were unfortunately missed, probably because of the massive Houghton increases. On the employers' side control of the secretariat was in the process of being taken over from Alexander and the AEC by the Local Authorities Conditions of Service Advisory Board (LACSAB). New minds were at work and there was considerable interest in discussing new approaches to teacher pay. After all, the LACSAB staff were experienced in the wider field of public sector pay negotiations.

Meanwhile, the two largest teacher unions had both turned to outside research agencies to assist them in preparation of their salaries policies. The NAS had commissioned reports from the Economist Intelligence Unit in 1967 and 1970, using the results in their publicity campaigns. The NUT had turned to the newly established Trade Union Research unit at Ruskin College, Oxford, in 1973. By then the NUT was involved in the TUC, yet the Director of the Research Unit found teachers to be a very isolated group of public sector local authority unions. He recommended the NUT to engage in quite radical rethinking, linking pay demands to educational policy, instead of continuing to use the usual very restricted arguments of the cost of living. Work was done on career paths for teachers, suggesting possible joint patterns covering schools and further education, and schools and the civil service. Then along came the Houghton award, and tragically all this work was abandoned. The Director sadly commented 'after all, it takes a long time to persuade people to look at their situation afresh; if a big windfall comes your way, you cease to bother' (Saran, 1985, p. 154).

Conditions and Structural Reform

Another aspect of opportunities missed is the scope for mutual benefit to employers and unions alike through 'trade-off' bargaining. For historical reasons teachers' salary negotiations were conducted entirely separately from those on conditions of service. This limited the Burnham Committee negotiators, and failed to provide a setting which would have compelled teacher unions to think simultaneously about pay *and* conditions. Both independent reviews of teacher pay had commented on this anomaly in their reports. The Clegg Report (1980, paras 25 and 30, pp. 9–10) noted that the employers sought clarity over what assumptions had been made about 'the professional obligations of teachers when considering their pay', whilst the Teachers' Panel held that 'management were acting improperly in asking us to include any statement on teachers' conditions of service in our report'. In the event, the Clegg Report (para 86, p. 30) throughout 'took account' of the many professional activities which are part of teachers' obligations to pupils, parents and schools, although the recommendations covered only pay. The earlier Houghton Report (1974, para. 264, p. 65) had stated: 'It is normal in most forms of employment for pay and conditions of service to be negotiated within the same machinery... The parties should examine this inconsistency.'

By the late seventies, the fall in school rolls was causing considerable problems; unions and employers recognized the pressing need to review the salaries structure. The 1971 structure had been devised in an era of expansion whereas meanwhile the education service faced contraction, resulting in fewer promotion opportunities. In 1981 a joint working party was established to undertake a salaries review. Major reviews are always time consuming, but over some three years considerable progress had been made. Then, instead of reaching a negotiated agreement, for which a provisional outline had been worked out, the teacher unions immersed themselves in the prolonged salaries disputes of 1984 and 1985, with extensive industrial action which disrupted the schools. Furthermore, as the parties could not agree to seek arbitration, that route to resolving the deadlock was barred. The conciliation facilities of ACAS were summoned. What had gone wrong?

The introduction of major structural reforms is always expensive. The second Thatcher government's anti-inflationary policies made it very difficult for the employers to secure a pledge from the DES and the Treasury that adequate funds would be forthcoming. In the summer of 1984, the Secretary of State (Sir Keith Joseph) indicated that if the Burnham Committee agreed a new salaries structure which was also acceptable to him, he would spare no efforts to try and persuade his Cabinet colleagues to find the necessary finance. One of Sir Keith's preoccupations meanwhile had been to emphasize improvement in teacher performance. The idea that better teachers should receive better financial rewards was in the air. Late in 1984 the Management Panel published a draft scheme under which teacher assessment (or appraisal) could be linked to the proposed new salaries structure, no doubt believing that this might impress the Secretary of State whose financial backing was essential. In protest against the linkage of assessment with pay, the NUT then walked out from the joint working party on structure, and there ensued bitter exchanges between the Leader of the Teachers' Panel and the Secretary of State, during which much doubt was cast on the Secretary of State's promise to seek Cabinet support for the amount of essential cash for structural reform. (Saran, 1985, p. 153).

A Single Forum for Salaries and Conditions?

In order to understand better some of the drama of teacher politics in the first half of the eighties it is essential to turn to the debate about a joint forum for negotiating salaries and conditions. Reference was made above to 'trade-off' bargaining; the Houghton increases in pay had been given without any pledge or commitment about conditions of work. By the late seventies the employers became insistent that pay increases be made subject to acceptance of certain contractual obligations.

Initially what had particularly concerned the local authorities was lunchtime supervision. The 1968 School Meals Agreement had been seen as a union victory, because it had placed lunch-time supervision by teachers on a voluntary footing. Under previous Regulations, LEAs had been able to require teachers to supervise pupils taking school dinners. Back in 1968 both sides had assumed that a sufficient number of volunteers would be forthcoming. The Agreement had left headteachers with 'overall responsibility for the conduct of the school meal', placing a professional responsibility 'on the teaching staff as a whole' to support the headteacher in ensuring the safety and welfare of pupils during the mid-day break (Working Party on Teachers and the School Meals Service, 1968).

By the late seventies, the use of industrial sanctions by teacher unions during salary disputes often took the form of withdrawal of goodwill. Schools and their headteachers faced difficulties over lunch-time supervision in particular, but also over other issues like cover for absent colleagues and activities outside normal school hours. In 1979 the NAS/UWT took the provocative action of working a 'statutory five-hour day', an extreme form of sanctions not supported by the other teacher unions. That year the two headteacher associations (NAHT and the Secondary Headteachers Association (SHA)) warned local authorities and the Secretary of State that after each withdrawal from lunch-time supervision fewer teachers were willing to return to these duties. Increasingly it came to be questioned whether reliance could continue to be placed on teacher professionalism, or whether the job of teachers had to be defined in contractual terms. The Houghton Report had still upheld the professional view of a teacher's job, which should not be 'compressed into a rigid structure of prescribed duties, hours or days' (para 294, p. 73).

Gradually, and somewhat reluctantly, the employers came to accept that the granting of salary increases had to be conditional on acceptance by teachers of certain contractual obligations. From the late seventies onwards, through the Council of Local Education Authorities/School Teachers (CLEA/ST), they tried to negotiate an appropriate contract. Again and again either the NAS/UWT or the NUT walked out of the talks—neither union seemed in a position to 'sign a contract' for fear of being denounced by the other one. In principle, the NAS/UWT declared itself willing to negotiate a contract, but only if the money was right. In 1986, as in earlier years, the NAS/UWT did not consider the money on offer adequate for surrendering the voluntary nature of duties, and with it the important union power to disrupt schools without strike action. Teacher unions have never found the financing of strikes an easy matter.

When the employers became desperate, they tried to win government support, from 1980 onwards, for reform of the Burnham machinery, so that salaries and conditions of service be negotiated within one forum—to facilitate 'trade-offs' between the two. Mr Mark Carlisle, the Secretary of State, had eventually lent a sympathetic ear to these overtures. By 1981 the DES had worked out draft proposals for new machinery, following discussions to which the teacher unions had in due course been invited. Not that the teacher unions were enamoured by the idea but Carlisle had been persuaded that the Burnham Committee should be replaced by a single negotiating body for pay and conditions. However, even Carlisle had insisted that the employers must carry the unions with them. And ministers come and go; when Carlisle gave way to Sir Keith Joseph, reform of Burnham machinery was placed in governmental cold storage until, five years later, the Teachers' Pay and Conditions Bill was tabled by yet another Secretary of State.

Sir Keith stated that he was not convinced that the existence of two forums prevented a salaries package from being agreed conditional on acceptance of a contract. The employers tested out Sir Keith's view, but all attempts at trade-offs between salaries and the contract failed—until 1986—by which time the impact of Baker's intervention drastically changed the negotiating climate. It seems likely, therefore, that Sir Keith's unwillingness to act contributed materially to the long-drawn out disputes during the mid-eighties, when industrial sanctions in the form of withdrawal of goodwill were used by the teacher unions.

Had the reform of Burnham been carried through five years earlier, the climate would have been different, and the working party to review the salaries structure could have addressed also the question of contractual obligations. In the absence of a negotiated contract, court rulings began to fill the vacuum. Some local authorities started to deduct pay when their teachers refused to cover for absent colleagues. When the NUT brought cases against some of these LEAs, arguing that provision of cover for absent colleagues was voluntary, Justice Scott ruled in May 1986 that cover was part of teachers' professional duty, part of their contract, even if there was no explicit written contract to state this (*Education*, 30 May 1986, p. 481). Thus by 1986 it was clear that if the teacher unions continued to refuse to negotiate a contract, their conditions of employment would in due course be defined for them by the courts. However, at that point in time Baker intervened with his Pay and Conditions Bill, thus threatening to impose pay scales and a contract favoured by him, as well as removing from teacher unions and their employers negotiating rights over pay and conditions.

Conclusion

One way of concluding this chapter is to use the word 'if' in capital letters. IF the government had reformed the Burnham negotiating machinery five years ago; IF the teacher unions had agreed to the merging of negotiations for salaries and conditions five years ago; IF Sir Keith had extracted adequate funds from the Cabinet to finance a reformed salaries structure; IF employers and unions had agreed the new structure as well as a contract at an earlier point in time than the eleventh hour of 1986—if all these things had happened, then the various parties, including the teacher unions, would have made their contribution to preventing the 1986 Burnham crisis and the Baker diktat.

Given that these things did not happen, what explanations for why this did not happen are there which are reasonably convincing? One of the simplest statements about politics is that 'politics is about power', about gaining, retaining or losing power. *The Politics Behind Burnham* (Saran, 1985) showed that power relationships were altered by changes in negotiating machinery. Not that the power of either employers or unions can be precisely quantified. But it is possible to establish what effect changes in negotiating machinery have on the balance of power between the parties. The 1965 Remuneration of Teachers Act greatly enhanced the power of the DES; the 1986 Teachers' Pay and Conditions Bill, if enacted, will further increase the power of the Secretary of State, thus tilting the balance of power heavily against teacher unions as well as against the local authorities, depriving both of negotiating rights. Even the mere threat of such a drastic shift of power away from the negotiating parties meant that unions and employers had their backs against the wall. There is always the ultimate power of the Secretary of State, provided that the support of the Cabinet and Parliament is assured. In face of such an ultimate power the unions and the local authorities can only appeal to the wider public who make up the electorate which confers power on a government.

Indeed, it is more than tempting to interpret the 1986 Burnham drama in electoral terms. Poll evidence had shown that education was high on the political agenda. Whilst many parents had sympathy for the badly paid teachers, especially those on the lower scales, two years of disruption in the schools caused parents much anguish and anxiety. In some areas parents and teachers campaigned jointly for improved teacher pay; the feeling gained ground that perhaps it was the unyielding Sir Keith Joseph who was to blame for the protracted dispute, rather than the unyielding and divided teacher unions or their employers, the local authorities.

Suddenly Sir Keith was removed and Kenneth Baker speedily secured more money from the Cabinet. Largesse is often associated with the approach of a general election—the same had happened in 1970, when a drawn out and bitter salaries dispute was suddenly settled by direct intervention of the Secretary of State, with a larger sum of money than had been available before. In 1986 Baker's tactics of intervention surely rested on his assumption that public support would be forthcoming for his decisive action to solve a long-standing dispute. Baker argued that Burnham affairs were in disarray, that teachers and employers had not put their own house in order, that he could not allow the dispute to remain unresolved, and that central intervention was the only way to resolve it.

This could just turn out to be a miscalculation. After all, government power can be used to impose a settlement. But what parents (the electorate) are really interested in is peace in the schools and the provision of a good education for their children. Peace may result from the ministerial intervention, but high quality education depends ultimately on inspiring leadership and inspired teaching in the schools. A profession which has had to submit to superior power, its contract of employment imposed instead of freely negotiated, may go through the motions of teaching, marking work, attending parents meetings, covering for absent colleagues. But the spark of enthusiasm, the high morale which fosters good work, is likely to be missing. Teachers may receive a substantial increase of pay, but enthusiasm is not usually bought with money. Teachers are looking for recognition, doing a professional job which is valued.

Teachers deserve a better fate than what has befallen them in recent years. Their unions must work together and put aside the rivalries over membership and organizational power. Their varied sectional interests reflect a past era. School reorganization has produced new overlaps in union territory, each union drawing its members from a wider section of the profession than used to be the case. Divided, they have easily been made the scapegoat; only through cooperation may some of the ground be regained.

Perhaps, rather tragically, the last fifteen years have been wasted years—but the history of events briefly summarized above provides a source for many lessons. All participants, union and local authority negotiators, local and national politicians, the teaching profession and certainly parents and the electorate at large, need to go away to do their homework. Above all, the question to which all parties must address themselves is that the children's right to the opportunity of a good education should rule supreme.

Postscript—June 1987

This chapter was completed at the end of 1986. In 1987 the Teachers' Pay and Conditions Act abolished the pay negotiation rights of the teaching profession and imposed conditions of service and a new salaries structure. The full consequences of these measures which have aroused widespread opposition among both teachers and local authorities have still to be measured. Whilst in nuance the analysis might have been slightly different had we known the outcome of Kenneth Baker's 1986 intervention, this knowledge would not have changed the substance of the argument.

Notes

1 The membership of the National Association of Teachers in Further and Higher Education (NATFHE), which used to be represented on the Burnham Committee for Schools, has been excluded from these calculations. NATFHE is the largest college lecturers union, not a school teacher union. It has been the main union represented on the Burnham Further Education Committee.

2 The figures in table 1 are for Great Britain, as given by the Certification Office for Trade Union and Employers' Associations. This information does not give separate figures for Scotland. As the NUT, in contrast to the other 'Burnham' teacher unions, does not recruit in Scotland, its

relative strength in England and Wales would be slightly greater than in Great Britain.

3 Jeremy Sutcliffe, in his article, 'NUT suffers dramatic fall in membership' published in the *Times Educational Supplement*, (3 July 1987) reported that during 1986 the NUT lost 24,000 paying members, 'more than a tenth of its active membership'. Almost all who left were women teachers—but then 70 per cent of the NUT's members are female. NAS/UWT also lost, but only 3 per cent. AMMA, and to a lesser extent PAT, were the gainers. In terms of paying members AMMA had in fact overtaken NAS/UWT 'as the second largest teacher union', though if honorary, retired and student members are counted, then NAS/UWT still had larger numbers. *Education* of the same date reported the NUT blaming 'the shrinking number of teachers now being employed plus the long – running industrial action' for its dramatic fall in membership. (This Note was added at proof stage).

References

BRIAULT, E. and SMITH, F. (1980) *Falling Rolls in Secondary Schools*, Windsor, NFER.

DENNISON, W.F. (1981) *Education in Jeopardy*, Oxford, Blackwell.

DEPARTMENT OF EDUCATION AND SCIENCE (1972) *Education: A Framework for Expansion*, Cmnd. 5174, London, HMSO.

House of Commons (1976) *Policy Making in the Department of Education and Science*, Tenth Report from the Expenditure Committee, session 1975–76, London, HMSO.

HUGHES, M., RIBBINS, P. and THOMAS, H. (Eds) (1985) *Managing Education: The System and the Institution*, London, Holt, Rinehart and Winston.

LODGE, P. and BLACKSTONE, T. (1985) 'Pushing for equality: The influence of the teachers' unions—the NUT' in MCNAY, I. and OZGA, J. (Eds), *Policy-making in Education: The Breakdown of Consensus*, Oxford, Pergamon Press in association with the Open University, pp 217–32.

MCNAY, I. and OZGA, J. (Eds) (1985) *Policy-Making in Education: The Breakdown of Consensus*, Oxford, Pergamon Press in association with Open University.

SARAN, R. (1985) *The Politics Behind Burnham: A Study of Teachers' Salary Negotiations*, Sheffield Papers in Education Management No. 45, Sheffield City Polytechnic.

THOMAS, H. (1985) 'Teacher Supply: Problems, practice and possibilities', in HUGHES, M., RIBBINS, P. and THOMAS, H. (Eds), *Managing Education: The System and the Institution*, London, Holt, Rinehart and Winston, pp 68–98.

WALSH, K., DUNNE, R., STOTEN, B. and STEWART, J.D. (1985) 'Teacher numbers: The framework of government policy', in MCNAY, I. and OZGA, J. (Eds) *Policy-making in Education: The Breakdown of Consensus*, Oxford, Pergamon Press in association with the Open University, pp 251–71.

WORKING PARTY ON TEACHERS AND THE SCHOOL MEALS SERVICE (1968) *Report*, DES, 13 March and published, for example, by the NUT (1968).

Chapter 9: Teacher Education

Professor Denis Lawton

Professor Denis Lawton became Director of the University of London Institute of Education in 1983. He taught in a Kent grammar school and at a secondary modern school in South London before joining the Institute in 1963. He is widely recognized as a pioneer in the study of the curriculum and an authority on educational writing. He has given advice on curriculum planning in many parts of the world and is the author of numerous books including *Class, Culture and the Curriculum* (1975) and *The Politics of the School Curriculum* (1980).

★   ★   ★

Introduction

To understand the wasted opportunities for teacher education it will be necessary to go further back than 1973. Some aspects of nineteenth century history are important, and they will be dealt with very briefly; it is also impossible to understand the present state of teacher education, including the control of the system, without reference to the 1944 Education Act and the 1944 McNair Report on the recruitment and training of teachers and youth leaders. Most of the chapter will, however, be concerned with the 1970s and 1980s.

Background

Nineteenth century education in England was dominated by two features: (i) the religious conflict; and (ii) social inequality. The religious question has now almost completely disappeared, but social class is still a dominant factor, closely followed by inequalities of gender and race. In the nineteenth century social inequality was exemplified by two contrasting kinds of schooling (i) high status boarding schools for the upper classes; and (ii) low status elementary schools for the children of the poor. The teachers provided for these two systems were quite different, socially and intellectually. Masters in the 'public' schools were normally graduates from Oxford or Cambridge who were thought to require no special professional training; on the other hand, the typical elementary school teacher was a successful product of that system, who became a pupil-teacher, apprenticed to a headteacher, and if successful in a highly competitive examination, spent two years at a college of non-university standard, with a narrow and rigid curriculum. Schoolmasters at public schools were 'gentlemen'; elementary school teachers were poorly paid and were accorded low social status.

The 1902 Education Act made it possible to develop state secondary schools, but these were modelled partly on the obsolete standards and curricula of public schools. Part of the history of teacher education and training since then is related to the convergence of the elementary and secondary systems. In general, however, it has tended to be a process of levelling down rather than levelling up, and the private ('public') school sector still remains in isolation, thus preventing a more healthy total convergence. For most of the time the education and training of the teachers for the majority of children has been deliberately cheap and functional.

From 1890 to 1914 one important aspect of the convergence referred to above was produced by attempting to associate universities with teacher training. This was recommended by the Cross Report of 1886, after which university day training colleges developed rapidly. Compared with the narrow and rigid teacher training colleges, the university day training colleges possessed a number of advantages: they were non-denominational, provided a more general education, and offered the possibility of a degree at the end of the course. A common route was also possible for elementary and secondary teachers, in the period following the 1902 Act.

After 1914 some improvement in the non-university training colleges took place, but the standard of education of future elementary teachers was generally considered to be low, and the concentration on training was reflected in the title of the colleges. Many teachers in county secondary schools and most in independent schools continued to be untrained graduates.

Post-War Developments

The 1944 Act abolished elementary schools and ended the distinction between elementary (now primary) and secondary teachers, but of course nothing was done to disturb the independent schools, despite the Fleming Report (1944). The McNair Report (1944) recommended a central training council to co-ordinate teacher training, and eventually Area Training Organizations (ATOs) were established to encourage university participation in teacher training through the university institutes of education. The McNair Report also made a number of recommendations for improving the supply and quality of teachers. But in the immediate post-Second World War years one of the most urgent problems was the acute shortage of teachers—quantity rather than quality was the dominant factor. The school population rose dramatically, and the annual output of teachers increased from 6000 in 1939 to 40,000 by the early 1970s. Despite the difficulties involved, the length of training was increased from two to three years in 1960. When Anthony Crosland became Secretary of State for Education in 1965 he still saw the shortage of teachers as the major problem to be solved, (Crosland, 1982).

The Robbins Report (1963) had been concerned with higher education generally, but a good deal of attention was paid to teacher education. The following recommendations were made:

(a) even higher targets for teacher training;
(b) training colleges should be elevated in status by the symbolic change of name to 'colleges of education';
(c) four-year BEd, courses were recommended for a minority of students (by 1972 one in nine of the students completing their courses were BEd graduates);
(d) colleges of education should be constituent parts of the university.

The last recommendation was rejected by the Conservative government. Instead the Council for National Academic Awards (CNAA) was established in 1964; and in 1965 the binary system became Labour Party policy: Crosland, then Secretary of State for Education, announced the government's acceptance of a plan to develop a system of higher education within the further education sector, separate from universities. The Crosland plan was based on the different traditions of the two systems, and the need to raise the status of LEA colleges through separate funding. In 1966, the White Paper *A Plan for Polytechnics and Other Colleges; Higher Education in the Further Education System* led to the establishment of thirty polytechnics over the next six years. Colleges of education were generally encouraged to move into the 'public sector' of higher education rather than develop closer links with universities. It is also important to note that during the early 1970s teacher training became compulsory for new graduate teachers in state schools.

Despite the shortage of teachers since 1945 and the massive increase in numbers, in general the status of teaching had improved in the post-Second World War period. There were, however, some complaints about the quality of recruits to the profession, including the low entry qualifications required for training colleges (five 'O' levels, compared with two or three 'A' levels for most routes into higher education); there were also criticisms of the quality of training, the irrelevance of much educational theory, and the unsatisfactory relation between theory and practice, including the arrangements made for teaching practice in schools. Practising teachers were often among those most critical of the 'theoretical' aspects of teacher education.

Plowden and After

The Plowden Report (1967), had recommended a full enquiry into teacher training; this was confirmed by a Parliamentary Select Committee. The change of government in 1970 produced a Secretary of State, Margaret Thatcher, who demanded speedy action on teacher training; she set up a Committee under Lord James, who was known to be critical of teachers and teacher training, which reported in 1972. The James Report (DES, 1972a) expressed dissatisfaction with the existing quality and structure of the teacher training system. A new three-cycle system was proposed: a two or three-year period of personal higher education; followed by a one-year period of pre-service professional training; then continuing professional education for the rest of the teacher's career, including study leave of one term in seven years. The James Report also recommended the abolition of Area Training Organizations (ATOs), thus weakening the university connection but supposedly encouraging greater autonomy for the colleges. The three cycle structure was not accepted, but the abolition of ATOs was.

Later in 1972 the government issued its own White Paper *Education: A Framework for Expansion* setting out plans for the next ten years. An all-graduate profession was planned, but BEd concurrent courses were preferred to the James recommendation of a 2 + 1 or 3 + 1 consecutive pattern. By 1970 the 'bulge' in the birthrate had passed, and DES planners were beginning to develop strategies for the reduction in size of the school age population. The falling demand for teachers would be coped with by encouraging colleges of education to 'diversify'—that is, to develop non—education degrees and other courses for non-teachers. The framework of 'expansion' soon became a massive programme of college closures and amalgamations. The policy of contraction was further encouraged by the economic problems of the 1970s.

In 1975 ATOs were abolished, but no effective replacement was set up to co-ordinate teacher education on a regional basis.

Current Problems

Since the mid-1970s the dominant theme in teacher education has been the demand for 'quality'. Within that general theme there are three interconnected issues which it may be useful to examine separately:

(a) The fall in demand for teachers and the contraction of the teacher education system.
(b) The demand for quality used as a means of increasing central control over teacher education.
(c) The real search for quality by non-governmental agencies and some of Her Majesty's Inspectorate (HMI).

The Contraction of the System

It is worth noting that falling rolls in secondary schools does not simply mean fewer teachers, but also tends to produce a demand for different kinds of teachers. Thus teacher education became linked to policies about the core curriculum and the idea of an entitlement curriculum. Teachers are likely to be required to teach more than one subject (and therefore their training ought to reflect this). The debate is a complicated one, but unfortunately financial cuts were the first priority; thus important opportunities for real reforms were missed. In particular, the DES has consistently ignored the problem of staffing comprehensive schools adequately. This was understandable in the 1950s and 1960s when there was a general shortage of teachers, but with the declining pupil numbers in the 1970s there was a real opportunity to plan for the staffing of comprehensive schools in accordance with the comprehensive curricula which were then developing. Instead, the DES ignored the fact that the comprehensive curriculum was necessarily very different from that of pre-war grammar schools, and merely seized the opportunity of falling rolls as a chance to reduce the numbers of teachers. Cost reduction was their major concern.

Falling rolls in primary and secondary schools resulted in an overall reduction in teacher training places, but the reduction has been selective and has changed the overall pattern. In the past, universities tended to be associated with the one-year Postgraduate Certificate in Education (PGCE) route to secondary schools, whereas colleges of education were largely concerned with the BEd route into primary teaching. In recent years this has become less and less accurate as a generalization. The DES and HMI have encouraged the expansion of PGCE primary courses; and universities which incorporated colleges of education (for example, Exeter and Warwick) have become involved in BEd primary work on a very large scale.

The overall decline in the size of the teacher training system has been very great indeed—from about 81,000 in 1976 to about 18,000 ten years later. Colleges and departments have been closed, and large numbers of staff have been encouraged to take early retirement. But the contraction has not been uniform: universities have contracted less than the polytechnics and colleges of higher education in the public sector. Universities have, indeed, increased their primary work at a time when the public sector was declining very sharply. This was the result of a policy by the DES and HMI, who may have been acting on the assumption that quality would be improved by concentrating more work in the universities; the suspicion also remains that the DES has a preference, in planning terms, for one-year courses compared with four-year B.Ed. degrees, since a shorter planning period is involved, and miscalculations can therefore be more easily rectified.

The smaller size of the system, however, has the effect of reducing its impact on quality; the percentage of new teachers entering the profession is now very small; moreover some 'new' teachers appointed by LEAs do not come directly from the training institutions but are recruited from the so-called 'pool of inactive teachers' (the PIT). Thus the profession is not only an ageing one but is more stagnant than it should be—this is important in terms of coping with innovations such as computers in the classroom, and other kinds of curriculum development. The DES has shown itself to be little concerned with this problem. Moreover, in both universities and public sector colleges, education departments have tended to be treated less favourably than other departments in terms of staff/student ratio and resource allocation. At a time when the demand for teachers was declining the opportunity existed for real improvements to be made and to give staff more time for educational research (an area of considerable need but widespread neglect). Instead, departments were encouraged to allow the staff/student ratio to deteriorate even further. As is so often the case, the slogans of 'quality' and 'value for money' masked the real intention of spending less money.

Central Control

I have described elsewhere (Lawton, 1984) the process of centralization as applied to local authorities and the school curriculum, but it is equally apparent in the field of teacher education. I suggested that the three groups within the central authority (the Conservative politicians, the DES bureaucrats, and the HMI professionals) have distinctive but overlapping educational ideologies. I tried to be more specific by dividing ideologies into beliefs, values and tastes in the following way:

Figure 1: *Three Educational Ideologies*

	Beliefs	**Values**	**Tastes**
Politicians	Market	Freedom of choice	Independent schools Fees/vouchers
Bureaucrats	Good admin	Efficiency	Central control Exams/tests
Professionals	Professionalism	Quality	Impressionistic evaluation

One of the strange features of the political debate about education is that Conservative politicians tend to be very critical of teachers (or rather of teachers in state schools), despite the fact that teachers are generally Conservative voters and, until recently, have been only moderately active trade unionists. On closer analysis, however, it is not quite so strange. Teachers in state schools occupy a number of positions which are in direct conflict with current Conservative ideology, and, in particular, they appear to enjoy security of employment and are not susceptible to 'normal' market forces. In Conservative eyes the state schools also tend to be seen as second-best, cheap alternatives for those who cannot afford independent schools, but they are, nevertheless, expensive. Thus the Conservative solution has been to cut the system down in size and make it more cost-effective. Teachers should be assessed, and teacher training must give better value for money. Teachers are seen not as professionals but as routine workers who must be closely supervised. Similarly, teacher trainers need to conform to centrally prescribed standards, work harder, and have more regard for the practical world—above all, they must 'produce' teachers who have much greater concern for economic and industrial efficiency; research and scholarship became low priorities.

It has been convenient for the DES and (some) members of HMI to support this policy, partly because it increases their own power and influence. The DES bureaucrats, in the interest of efficiency and good administration, want a more uniform system with less autonomy for individual institutions; members of HMI, who see themselves as the professional experts on teacher training, want to modify the procedures so that their advice carries more weight.

The means of imposing 'quality' in teacher training has taken three forms. First, a series of surveys and reports by HMI, diagnosing the 'problem'—including the alleged inefficiency of the existing training system; second, recommendations from the Advisory Committee on the Supply and Education of Teachers (ACSET), prompted by papers from the DES and HMI but with the support of some LEAs and teachers; third, central control in the form of criteria prescribed by the Secretary of State and enforced by the Council for the Accreditation of Teacher Education (CATE).

The significant publications by HMI have included the following, in addition to the primary and secondary school surveys (DES, 1978 and 1979):

(i) *Teacher Training and the Secondary School* (1981). This publication stemmed directly from the HMI Secondary Survey, summarized its findings for teacher educators, and put forward suggestions that initial training should be more relevant, and that practising teachers ought to be more involved in initial training.

(ii) *The New Teacher in School* (1982) was a much more critical document claiming to show, from HMI evidence, that about 25 per cent of newly-qualified teachers lacked some of the skills needed in the classroom. Teacher trainers were blamed for a number of these shortcomings: for example, for not carrying out greater quality control at the point of entry (weeding out candidates unsuitable on personality grounds); for not concentrating more on the practical requirements of schools; and for inappropriate educational theory. It was also suggested that national guidelines would be needed. Teacher trainers did not carry all the blame, however: LEAs and schools were criticized for employing new teachers in unsuitable ways—being required to teach subjects for which they were not qualified, for example.

(iii) *Teaching in Schools: The Content of Initial Training* (1983). This publication stressed the need for greater care in selecting students for teacher training as well as the desirability of eliminating more students during training. Much of the document is concerned with the kind of degree content that would be regarded as suitable for future teachers. One principle which it would be difficult to oppose, was that any teacher should have appropriate subject–matter to teach, but the formula for deciding appropriate content seemed to be rigid and bureaucratic. Once again the notion of 'partnership' with practising teachers was emphasised.

Another interesting aspect of the 'partnership' story was the rise and fall of the advisory committees on teacher supply and training. In 1949 the National Advisory Council on the Training and Supply of Teachers (NACTST) was set up to advise the Minister of Education on the training, qualifications, recruitment and distribution of teachers. By 1965 the Council, consisting of fifty-eight representatives of various educational groups, had produced nine reports on aspects of the problem of teacher supply. In its later years the Council was, however, increasingly an embarrassment to the DES, making recommendations which were in conflict with the Department's own policies. Using the excuse of internal disagreements within the Council, the DES abolished it in 1965. For eight years the DES existed without the benefit of advice from a national advisory committee, but in 1973 a new Committee was formed with the title Advisory Committee on the Supply and Training of Teachers (ACSTT). ACSTT lasted until late 1978. It was then replaced (in April 1980) by the Advisory Committee on the Supply and Education of Teachers (ACSET) which was less concerned with the problem of teacher supply than with advice about quality. By this time there was, according to the DES, a danger of teacher over-supply, and central government was less interested in improving the teacher/pupil ratio than in undermining the teaching profession by discussions of teacher competence. In 1983 ACSET recommended that there should be new machinery to advise the Secretary of State on the accreditation of courses, as well as the criteria which should be met by all teacher training institutions. The machinery was to consist of a central council (later called CATE) which would be advised by HMI. The criteria included a longer PGCE course (thirty-six weeks), greater involvement by practising teachers, specified amounts of school experience, as well as subject and age group requirements. To some extent the ACSET advice was upstaged by the government White Paper *Teaching Quality* which was published in March 1983. The White Paper was, however, followed by a DES Circular which referred back to the authority of the ACSET report.

The result of this elaborate exercise in negotiating the kind of advice the DES wanted was a much tighter control of teacher training. The following changes were implemented:

(a) Approval of initial training courses in universities and the public sector became conditional on accreditation by the Council for the Accreditation of Teacher Education (CATE).

(b) Before CATE approval could be sought, a course had to be supported by a local committee consisting of practising teachers, representatives of LEAs and other members of the local community, as well as the institution providing the course.

(c) Before consideration by CATE took place, HMI had to be invited to visit the institution. CATE would not begin the process of accreditation before a report from HMI had been received.

(d) The minimum length of BEd and PGCE courses was specified together with periods of school experience.

(e) Practising teachers must be associated with the selection of students as well as involved in the teaching of the course and assessment of the students.

(f) Teacher trainers involved in the BEd or the PGCE must have enjoyed recent success as teachers of the age range to which their courses are directed.

The Real Search for Quality

It could well be argued that the emphasis on the machinery of control, described above, has served to confuse the real issues of quality. The professional debate about quality in teaching education preceded the DES centralization campaign by many years. Essentially it is concerned with the relationship between theory and practice, and the nature of educational studies. Hirst (1985) described the history of educational studies in the following way. Four different approaches may be identified:

(a) Separate disciplines (for example, psychology and sociology of education).
(b) Disciplines in symposia taught through topics or issues.
(c) Integrated courses.
(d) 'The analytic study of specific practical situations, or generalizations about practice, the concern being not with broad topics or issues, but with specific practical judgments and the practical principles that are currently being used or advocated in schooling'.

Hirst suggests that in recent years there has been a significant move away from (a) and (b) towards (c) and (d). Hirst's article expresses not only his own view of initial training, but also the view that has been adopted by the University Council for the Education of Teachers (UCET) as their policy for the future. As early as January 1979 UCET published an interesting document along these lines about PGCE courses, describing the view of a committee which included public sector members as well as university teachers. Kyriacou (1986) has also described the development of a similar approach to theory and practice from a psychological point of view.

I will not attempt to summarize the UCET document or Hirst (1985) here, but it may be useful to emphasize some of the common concerns:

(a) The PGCE course should be regarded only as an initial course of professional preparation, not as adequate preparation for the whole of a teaching career.

(b) The PGCE and the BEd should not be regarded as providing even an introduction to the disciplines relevant to a teaching profession (philosophy, psychology, sociology, history of education) although these disciplines may illuminate such courses.

(c) Educational theory is not a process of translating theory derived from the disciplines into practice; educational theory is necessarily generated from practical experiences, some of these principles being arrived at intuitively or at the level of common sense.

(d) At PGCE level it is not possible to do more than offer a glimpse into the world of educational theory. The purpose of PGCE must be to concentrate on professional competence which relies on practical principles without attempting to trace their theoretical lineage.

(e) Even at later stages of professional development, the introduction to educational theory is difficult. Ideally, educational theory would involve an understanding of the contributory disciplines such as philosophy, psychology and sociology, but it is impossible in most cases to give practising teachers on in-service courses an adequate theoretical understanding of those disciplines.

(f) The generation of educational theory is complex, involving dialogue between practising teachers and those involved in the training of teachers and work on the contributory disciplines.

(g) A mode of discourse is needed to facilitate communication between those concerned with the disciplines, those concerned with more practical aspects of teacher training, and practising teachers in schools.

(h) The implications of such a view of educational theory go far beyond the view of teacher professionalism included in *Teaching Quality* (DES, 1983b), but it is only through that kind of partnership that real professionalism in education is likely to develop.

Conclusion

The tragedy of the last ten years has been that the attention of teacher educators has been diverted away from real questions of quality to bureaucratic issues of time and content requirements which seem to have taken on almost theological importance. For example, no-one disputes that one academic year is far too short a time for an adequate PGCE course (and UCET and others have argued for a two-year course), but whether a one-year course should be thirty-five or thirty-six weeks is trivial compared with the real issues concerning the quality of teacher education.

Few would deny that there are real questions of quality relating to the teaching profession which need to be addressed. But these issues have been consistently neglected throughout the 1970s and 1980s. The central problem is the need to integrate initial training with the in-service education of teachers, but even that needs to be seen in a more general context. Recent Secretaries of State for Education have tended to see teaching quality simply as a question of better training courses or better school management: this is clearly far too limited. A more appropriate analysis would examine the teaching profession from a number of separate but related positions:

(a) It is important to do everything possible to improve the initial training of teachers, but it is even more important to look at problems of recruitment. There is evidence to suggest that teaching does not attract sufficiently high numbers of the best qualified young people. The reasons for this are not difficult to perceive: teaching is a badly paid and difficult occupation. Despite much comment in the media and elsewhere about 'long holidays', the conditions of service, as well as the salaries obtainable in state schools, do not compare well with equivalent levels in trade, industry or the civil service.

(b) The quality, or even good health, of the profession is not only a question of selection and training but also of retention. Again, there is evidence to suggest that, in the UK as well as in the USA, the most able recruits are less likely to remain in teaching. In recent years politicians have latched on to the issue of teacher appraisal—usually as a way proposed to weed out the ineffective. But this is less important than establishing a system of professional appraisal which would ensure the continuing development of teachers throughout their career. In that context teacher appraisal becomes not a bureaucratic device for promotions and dismissals, but a way of diagnosing the professional needs of individual teachers and providing the means of meeting those needs. Without the resources for implementation, however, even that professional kind of teacher appraisal will be treated cynically by both the appraised and the appraisers.

Faced with all this, the best that has been offered by the Conservative government was a new method of funding INSET from 1987 onwards. This measure purported to be a means of increasing resources for INSET, but in some LEAs it seems very likely that even less money will be available after 1987. The scheme is not without merit: for example, it exhorts all LEAs and all schools to develop INSET policies and programmes. This is excellent, but programmes without adequate funding may be worse than the status quo. They may raise expectations whilst the will to provide the necessary resources is lacking.

The James Report (DES, 1972a) recommendation that regular periods of study leave entitlement should be built into a teaching career was not accepted, and nothing remotely like it has been proposed since then. One of the current fears of the professional associations is that opportunities for serving teachers to be released for long courses such as one-year MA programmes will disappear without being replaced by any better alternative.

The ACSET proposals which gave rise to the DES policy on INSET funding seemed to be advocating the extension of in-service provision, but the immediate result may be even fewer opportunities for professional development. Teacher education is still seen as something which must be provided on the cheap.

Reference

CROSLAND, S. (1982) *Tony Crosland*, London, Jonathan Cape.

DEPARTMENT OF EDUCATION AND SCIENCE (1967) *Children and Their Primary Schools* (The Plowden Report), London, HMSO.

DEPARTMENT OF EDUCATION AND SCIENCE (1972a) *Teacher Education and Training* (The James Report), London, HMSO.

DEPARTMENT OF EDUCATION AND SCIENCE (1972b) *Education: A Framework for Expansion*, London, HMSO.

DEPARTMENT OF EDUCATION AND SCIENCE (1978) *Primary Education in England*, London, HMSO.

DEPARTMENT OF EDUCATION AND SCIENCE (1979) *Aspecs of Secondary Education in England*, London, HMSO.

DEPARTMENT OF EDUCATION AND SCIENCE (1981) *Teacher Training and the Secondary School*, London, HMSO.

DEPARTMENT OF EDUCATION AND SCIENCE (1982) *The New Teacher in School*, London, HMSO.

DEPARTMENT OF EDUCATION AND SCIENCE (1983a) *Teaching in Schools: The Content of Initial Training*, London, HMSO.

DEPARTMENT OF EDUCATION AND SCIENCE (1983b) *Teaching Quality*, London, HMSO.

DEPARTMENT OF EDUCATION AND SCIENCE (1985) *Better Schools*, London, HMSO.

DEPARTMENT OF EDUCATION AND SCIENCE (1986) *Better Schools: Evaluation and Appraisal Conference*, London, HMSO.

HIRST, P. (1985) 'Educational Studies and the PGCE', *British Journal of Educational Studies*, October.

HOUSE OF COMMONS (1986) *Third Report from the Education, Science and Arts Committee (session 1985/86) Achievement in Primary Schools*, London, HMSO.

KYRIACOU, C. (1986) *Effective Teaching in Schools*, Oxford, Blackwell.

LAWTON, D. (1984) *The Tightening Grip*, London, University of London Institute of Education.

LAWTON, D. and GORDON, P. (1987) *HMI*, London, Routledge and Kegan Paul.

RANSON, S. and TOMLINSON J. (Eds) (1986) *The Changing Government of Education*, London, Allen and Unwin.

SCHON, D. (1983) *The Reflective Practitioner*, London, Temple Smith.

UNIVERSITIES COUNCIL FOR THE EDUCATION OF TEACHERS (1979) *The PGCE Course and the Training of Specialist Teachers for Secondary Schools*, London, UCET.

Chapter 10: Adult Education

William Boaden

After working in civil engineering and in the pit **William Boaden** was awarded, at the age of 21, a Foundress Scholarship for mine workers at Ruskin College, Oxford. This was followed by work in the South Wales and Yorkshire coalfields. He later entered the Youth Employment Service and then qualified to teach in further education. After ten years teaching in East Anglia he was appointed first Education Secretary of the Association of Teachers in Technical Institutions (ATTI) (later NATFHE). He became Director of the Centre on Educational Disadvantage until it was closed by the Secretary of State. He has been engaged in various work with unemployed adults, including TUC Development Officer for 'Centres for the Unemployed'. Currently he is Development Officer for the 'Education for Unemployed Adults Project' in North Yorkshire.

★   ★   ★

The year 1973 has a particular significance for all those interested in adult education. It saw the publication of the Report of the Russell Committee, 'Adult Education: A plan for development'[1] following almost four years work on the part of a group of very distinguished adult educators and administrators under the chairmanship of Sir Lionel Russell. The Committee had the following terms of reference:

> To assess the need for and to review the provision of non-vocational adult education in England and Wales; to consider the appropriateness of existing educational, administrative and financial policies; and to make recommendations with a view to obtaining the most effective and economical deployment of available resources to enable adult education to make its proper contribution to the national system of education conceived of as a process continuing through life.

but the requirement to focus on non-vocational adult education was not narrowly interpreted and the Committee considered wide ranging issues in the education of adults. Its recommendations were, however, 'characterized on publication as a mountain which had laboured long and brought forth an overweight mouse, the Russell Report was not able to escape the slur of being altogether too modest.'[2] It was, nevertheless, the first such examination undertaken by an official body for over fifty years and much was expected, by those in the field, to follow the publication of the Report.

The hopes raised by the work of the Committee and the volume and quality of the evidence it received make it appropriate to consider the major recommendations as a basis for needs identified and developments proposed.

In its direct recommendations for governmental initiatives there was concern to see the revision of relevant sections of the 1944 Education Act, to strengthen both the adult education administration within the Department and the opportunities for HMI to devote time to adult education and for the establishment of a Development Council for Adult Education for England and Wales. Aspects of a clearer definition of the requirements for local authorities to provide adult education occupied the attention of many in the field for some time. In June 1981 the Department of Education and Science issued a discussion paper, *The Legal Basis of Further Education* to which many organizations responded. In the event nothing tangible emerged and the provision of education for adults is still very tenuous indeed in circumstances where financial resources are constantly under threat. The provision of additional administrative resource and additional time for HMI to devote to adult education has not been sustained and in the case of the Inspectorate the pressures of the 1980s have produced increasing frustration for those interested and committed to the interests of adults. The much more radical proposal for the establishment of a Development Council with a wide range of functions, and with membership including both providers and participants resulted in the establishment at the end of 1977 of the Advisory Council for Adult and Continuing Education (ACACE).

The Advisory Council had the following terms of reference:

> To advise generally on matters relevant to the provision of education for adults in England and Wales, and in particular:
>
> (a) to promote cooperation between the various bodies in adult education and review current practice, organization and priorities, with a view to the most effective deployment of available resources;
>
> (b) to promote the development of future policies and priorities, with full regard to the concept of education as a process continuing throughout life.

It had a widely representative membership with considerable commitment who gave much of their time in fulfilling the Council remit during the six years of its existence. It had very modest resources for its small secretariat and little finance with which to commission necessary work. Nevertheless, during the course of its brief life it produced reports and papers on matters of concern to the continuing education of adults, some commissioned by the Secretary of State. Included among the publications before its demise were *Continuing Education: From Policies to Practice*[3] and *Protecting the Future for Adult Education*[4] which were concerned to establish patterns for development to the end of the century.

The Advisory Council made some substantial contributions, particularly for practioners, but it was an advisory body and lacked the status and the resource which were envisaged for the Development Council. It was followed by the Unit for Development of Adult Continuing Education (UDACE). The Unit was also modestly resourced and had a different profile from that of the Advisory Council. It certainly did not in any way match the needs of the service or of the many millions of adults seen by the Russell Committee as potential participants in a continuing process of education.

The Russell Report recommended the development of regional cooperation and also the establishment in each local education authority area of a Local Development Council. Some Regional Advisory Councils for further education did in practice extend the functions of their existing adult education sub-committees and others established such a mechanism but without a national stimulus and responsive support from constituent LEAs the sub-committees had only modest functions. A few local development councils were established but they were the exception and often reflected an existing enthusiasm or an understanding within the LEA of needs in the education of adults.

The concern to see an expansion of local education authority provision particularly amongst non-traditional participants was negatived by continuous, and latterly increasingly, destructive pressures on financial resources imposed by national policies. This led to an almost obsessive concern with fee structures reflected in annual surveys undertaken by the Advisory Council in conjunction with the National Institute of Adult Education (later the National Institute of Adult Continuing Education, NIACE). It also produced administrative arrangements which whilst offering a higher degree of flexibility in determining a local programme also created a response to market forces which was often inimical to a balanced provision and certainly broke little new ground. It also contributed in some instances to arrangements which moved adult education from the responsibility of the education service and lodged it with leisure services or a similar branch of the administration.

Earlier reference has been made to the interest and concern for student fees and the Russell Committee recommended that student 'contributions', as they wished them to be known, could not discourage any significant number or category of people from making use of the provision'.[5] Movement towards such an objective was substantially retarded and subsequently reversed by successive reductions in rate support grant and competitive pressures on educational finance at local level. Thus the National Institute of Adult Continuing Education fee survey 1985/86[6] contains a wide range of varying hourly rates of fees charged to part-time adult students and considerable variation in the incidence of concessions.

Among variations identified in general terms are:

(i)   possibility of local variations within an LEA;

(ii) additional costs for some students for text books or craft materials which may range from £10–40 at 1986 prices, plus possible supplementary costs (for example, creche/playgroup fees) for women attending daytime courses.

(iii) wide variations in the treatment of students with 'discounts' in terms of the total income accruing to a class.

The categories of student eligible for fee concessions included senior citizens, registered unemployed people, unregistered unemployed people (the unwaged), physically disabled people, mentally handicapped people and basic education students. For each of these substantial sections of the population there are further sub-divisions between initially 'non-examination courses' and 'examination courses' with further divisions for each where LEAs have an automatic no-fee, automatic reduced fee, discretionary no fee and discretionary reduced fee policy. For each category and for each sub-division the 100 LEAs who provided information showed a varied pattern and a resultant lottery for students. In addition to the major groups mentioned above the following were noted as in receipt of fee concessions in one or more LEA:

—People receiving FIS (Family Income Supplement)
—People receiving Supplementary Benefit
—People aged 16-18 in full-time education
—Spouses of people on state benefits
—People on YTS (providing courses are not part of their training)
—Full-time FE and HE students
—Widows receiving widow's pension
—People receiving sickness benefit
—People receiving housing benefit, rate or rent rebates
—Single parents
—Under 16s
—Residents in homes for the elderly
—ESL students
—People on Community Programmes
—Married couples enrolling for same courses

With fees charged for non-examination courses ranging from 29–100p per hour and, in examination courses, GCE 'O' level from 18–100 p per hour and GCE 'A' level from 15p–£1.50 per hour the disincentives to participation are quite marked. The situation is further confused and inequalities reinforced by the operation of net-budget policies by local providers in over one-fifth of the LEAs.

The Russell Committee, recognizing the essentially pluralistic nature of British adult education, was concerned that the voluntary sector should be encouraged. It noted the uniqueness of the Workers' Educational Association (WEA) and made recommendations in respect of both the activities of the Association and the nature of the financial support which should be provided. The WEA, operating through its district organization and with the active stimulus and support provided by its local branches and their members, responded to the tasks suggested by the Russell Committee. It developed its existing work in the broad general context of political and social education and undertook additional work in the industrial context. This latter activity being developed in consultation with the Trades Union Congress (TUC) and with individual trade unions. In addition it undertook work with the socially and culturally deprived in the inner cities and also pioneered activity with a direct focus on working with women and with disadvantaged groups such as the mentally handicapped. Later, as the numbers of unemployed people, and particularly the long-term unemployed, increased they were given particular attention. This developmental work was often the responsibility of a tutor-organizer appointed with a particular brief to establish or extend work in the special area of concern. In some instances the appointment of such tutor-organizers was financially supported by the DES, often on a short-term basis. This arrangement had inherent weaknesses in that much of the work required permanent professional support and the finance for this could not obviously be obtained from many of the student groups involved and WEA branches and districts have limited resources. The DES was often unwilling to extend the period for financial support and much of this desirable, perhaps essential, work was, in consequence, less widely and actively developed.

The WEA and its districts were additionally influenced by financial constraints which severely curtailed their contribution as a result of government policies both in terms of direct grant provision and the financial pressures exerted on local education authorities which produced reductions in their grant aid. Thus, considerable time has been spent in recent years by WEA professional staff and their voluntary branch members and supporters in the task of survival, a deflection from the real educational purposes of the WEA and in terms of potential students and student groups, a wasted opportunity.

The Russell Committee also considered a more modest, though in the context of a developing service, important element of the voluntary sector; the long-term residential colleges. Among the recommendations made was one for consideration of the establishment of one further college in the northern half of England. This eventually emerged as Northern College and it has made a substantial and a unique contribution in the nature of some of its work. There must, however, be many of its students and potential students who would have wished that a more supportive climate and provision of resources could have resulted in the earlier establishment of the College. Those same concerns must be equally in evidence in the circumstances of recent financial limitations.

In considering special aspects of adult education the Russell Committee

identified some major areas for potential development which merit consideration. The concept of paid educational leave which offers opportunities for
release from employment for educational activity has been long recognized as
desirable. The Education Act 1944 included provision, not yet brought into
effect, for young people to have release from work primarily for vocational
education. Those benefiting from this opportunity never amounted to much
more than 40 per cent of the young men and about 10 per cent of young
women. Whilst the numbers involved over the age of 18 years increased to
about one-third of the total the proportion of the potential population
involved was always relatively small, and in the case of young women
unacceptably so. The provision was always almost exclusively vocational and
therefore seen as an acceptable part of training. An extension of the practice to
more general education provision and across the adult work force as a whole
has made little progress despite the efforts particularly of the TUC. Some
advance was made in the provision of courses for shop stewards and work
place representatives with the support of the WEA, appropriate university
departments and the colleges of further education. The TUC has also had
some direct grant aid to develop provision but latterly the financial support
for this has been curtailed. With the exception of patchy support from a
relatively small number of employers for pre-retirement education there has
been little development; another example of needs identified and massive
opportunity wasted. A further special aspect related to 'disadvantaged' adults
and was seen to involve those experiencing social and educational disadvantages as well as the other, often more obvious, physical and mental conditions.

Reference has already been made to work with mentally handicapped
and mentally ill adults and developments also occurred on a very limited
basis to meet the needs of deaf people. Attention to the educational needs of
women and of those whose mother tongue is not English has also occurred
and been well developed by some LEAs and some voluntary organizations
but in aggregate the response to the needs of the vast numbers involved has
been marginal. The one intervention and development which has achieved
substantial support and satisfactory outcomes and which illustrates the
value of consistent financial provision and commitment nationally is the
response to literacy needs. The remit of the agency primarily responsible
for stimulus has been extended to include numeracy and basic skills and
more recently English as a Second Language (ESL) but it nonetheless
affords a model which indicates what is possible with adequate support.
The following extracts from the British Association of Settlements (BAS)
publication *Adult Literacy: A Continuing Need*[7] serve to illustrate that
combination of practical support and commitment nationally which produced local responses and a substantial meeting of needs.

In May 1974, on the same day as an all-party Private Members Bill
was introduced by Christopher Price, MP, into the House of
Commons, BAS published a campaign document entitled *A Right*

to Read—Action for a Literate Britain. As the BAS campaign was gathering momentum, a number of other bodies were taking up the issue of adult illiteracy. The BBC, for instance, had for some time been studying the possibility of some input via its further education service to assist the campaign and the development of provision generally. It is certainly true that without the BBC's initiatives, progress towards nationwide provision would have been more limited despite any increase in campaigning at the grass roots. The BBC publicity faced many local education authorities with the prospect of student referrals on a level far higher than even the most inventive and comprehensive local publicity had stimulated. The BBC's programmes effectively sought to destigmatize adult illiteracy and the measure of their success lies in the number of adults who felt able to come forward for help.

Central government's response to these various campaign pressures came in the form of financial resources to 'prime the pumps' of providing bodies and encourage them to offer increasing provision. In June 1974, the government announced that £1m would be set aside for adult literacy work for a one-year period and subsequently asked the National Institute of Adult Education to establish the Adult Literacy Resource Agency as an agency of the NIAE to administer and allocate the funds available in the financial year1975/76.

The Adult Literacy Resource Agency (1975–78) became the Adult Literacy Unit (1978–80) and in 1980 was established as the Adult Literacy and Basic Skills Unit (ALBSU). Its work has been effective in stimulating, encouraging and supporting both practitioners and providers and it has won both national and international recognition. In its publication *Adult Literacy and Basic Skills: A Continuing Partnership*[8] the Unit reviews developments since 1975 and establishes a case for a continued and acknowledged period of operation. It is this sensible understanding of the longer term need for support which has been absent in so many of the other areas of concern.

There is, however, one other aspect of organization where the model presented by ALBSU and its predecessors has not been followed and to the disadvantage of the needs addressed. Although the Agency and Units were established as agencies of the NIACE they had their own management committee and a high degree of autonomy in operational terms and this latter practice has not been repeated in the early stages of the establishment of UDACE and in the case of the Adult Unemployed Programme (REPLAN) even in the initial form of an external committee has been dispensed with.

The Russell Committee obviously paid considerable attention to both accommodation and equipment and also to staff. In respect of both buildings and equipment some modest advances were made but the development was not sustained and allocations for adult education were amongst the first to be reduced or totally cut as financial pressures impinged on LEA budgets. In respect of staff conditions the gradual awareness of the need for staff training has been acknowledged and supported in some measure whilst the provision of a recognized and adequate salary negotiating machinery for part-time staff has, over time, made some progress. This was due in no small measure to the efforts of the Association for Adult and Continuing Education in conjunction with the National Association of Teachers in Further and Higher Education (NATFHE).

The consistent feature of this review of responses to needs in the education of adults in the past thirteen years is the absence of real commitment nationally either in terms of understanding and willingness to respond or in the provision of financial resources. Where that general pattern has not been followed the satisfactory results are readily seen and for those participating in such initiatives the years have not been wasted.

Mention has already been made in respect of shortcomings in responding to the identified needs of unemployed people and the ACACE Report *Education for Unemployed Adults*[9] provides ample evidence of the reluctance nationally to respond to real needs of a substantial and very disadvantaged section of the population. The request to ACACE to identify the general education needs of unemployed adults and to advise on the most effective means of responding was made by the Secretary of State (Mark Carlisle) in July 1981. In September 1982 the Report was presented to his successor (Sir Keith Joseph) and when ACACE ceased to exist at the end of the following year there had been no response.

REPLAN was eventually announced in 1984 and although the structure for implementation of initiatives suggested in the ACACE Report owed much to the successful model provided by the literacy units this pattern was not followed. An identifiable coordinating agency was not established and the organizational structure was therefore fragmented whilst the proposal for a Management Committee for the Programme produced only a Steering Committee with a civil servant as chairperson and even this was allowed to lapse at the end of 1985.

Perhaps this brief comment on responding to the educational needs of that most disadvantaged group of adults is a fitting conclusion to a catalogue of missed opportunity and wasted years.

Notes

1   DEPARTMENT OF EDUCATION AND SCIENCE (1973) Adult Education: A Plan for Development, Report by a Committee of Enquiry appointed by the

Secretary of State for Education and Science under the chairmanship of Sir Lionel Russell, London, HMSO.

2   CORBETT, A. (1978) Much to do about Education: A Critical Survey of the Major Educational Reports, London, Macmillan Education.
3   ADVISORY COUNCIL FOR ADULT AND CONTINUING EDUCATION (1982) *Continuing Education from Policies to Practice*, Leicester, ACACE.
4   ADVISORY COUNCIL FOR ADULT AND CONTINUING EDUCATION (1981) *Protecting the Future for Adult Education*, Leicester, ACACE.
5   DEPARTMENT OF EDUCATION AND SCIENCE (1973), *op. cit.*
6   NATIONAL INSTITUTE OF ADULT CONTINUING EDUCATION (1986) *Indicators of Fee Levels Charged to Part-time Adult Students by Local Education Authorities*, Leicester, NIACE.
7   BRITISH ASSOCIATION OF SETTLEMENTS AND SOCIAL ACTION CENTRES (1977) *Adult Literacy: A Continuing Need, The Final Report of the BAS Adult Literacy Project 1975–77*, London, BAS.
8   ADULT LITERACY AND BASIC SKILLS UNIT (1983) *Adult Literacy and Basic Skills: A Continuing Partnership*, London, ALBSU.
9   ADVISORY COUNCIL FOR ADULT AND CONTINUING EDUCATION (1982) *Education for Unemployed Adults*, Leicester, ACACE.

Chapter 11: Fee-Paying Education: The Favoured Sector

Clive Griggs

Clive Griggs left school at 15 years of age and worked in a signal box for several years before going to college to qualify as a teacher. He has taught in a technical school in London, a language school in Sofia and a comprehensive school in Sussex. He was education correspondent for Tribune (1975–82), has published articles in a variety of academic journals, contributed chapters to D. Rubinstein's *Education and Quality* (1979), K.D. Brown's *The First Labour Party 1906–14* (1985) and is author of *The Trades Union Congress and the Struggle for Education 1868–1925* (1983) and *Private Education in Britain* (1985). At present he is Senior Lecturer in Education at Brighton Polytechnic.

★   ★   ★

Introduction

During the 1960s fee paying schools had largely faded from the scene of political and educational controversy.[1] In the move towards comprehensive secondary schooling attempts to maintain selection by some form of 'intelligence testing' had been largely discredited. Selection by ability of parents to pay fees at such a time seemed positively archaic. Morale within the fee paying schools, with the possible exception of the top Headmasters' Conference Schools (HMC) was low. Numbers had fallen in these schools both in absolute and percentage terms although the total school population had risen. Yet by 1973 fee paying schools were on the offensive riding on the tide of growing criticism of local authority schools initiated by a newly-emerging Political Right, many of whom were contributors to the Black Papers, and amplified by the tabloid press.[2] Private schools seemed to be providing the very traditional setting and standards which Rhodes Boyson and like-minded critics claimed were needed in the maintained schools.

John Rae has written of a revolution in the public schools between 1964–79.[3] This is probably an exaggeration because sections of traditional vested interests maintained their grip of certain aspects of schooling in that period, especially was this true for curriculum matters in some of the lesser known schools. However he is correct in charting substantial changes, such as the introduction of girls into all boys' schools, the decline of prefect power and corporal punishment, the reduction in time given to the Combined Cadet Corps and the greater attention paid to scholastic results. By the 1980s a picture emerges of an increase in both absolute numbers and percentage of the pupils attending fee paying schools at a time when the secondary school age population had fallen drastically and the primary school population was only increasing slightly.[4] This was achieved in spite of steep increases in school fees which were generally below the rate of inflation up to 1980 but above that rate afterwards. The reasons for the improved fortunes of fee paying schools during the very time when maintained schools were struggling with reduced resources are numerous. At least three events can be singled out as having a major impact upon the fee paying schools: the establishment of the Independent Schools Information Service (ISIS), the abolition of direct grant grammar schools by a Labour government with Liberal Party support and the setting up of the Assisted Places Scheme (APS) by a Conservative administration. A further point which should be born in mind is the reluctance on the part of some middle-class parents to support the idea of a 'common school' for all children in the form of comprehensive schools but this is too nebulous an issue to pursue here. It needs to be remembered that at all times throughout this period, the HMC schools at least not only catered for the children of high income groups in general but were able to mobilize support for their cause among past generations of such pupils now often well established in the hierarchies of banking, industry, the armed services, the judiciary, the civil service and Parliament.

Independent Schools Information Service (ISIS)

Among the great variety of nearly 2500 fee paying schools[5] there already existed numerous organizations to which some belonged. The HMC (consisting of about 250 boys' schools[6] including the elite Clarendon Schools[7]), the Independent Association of Preparatory Schools (IAPS), the Girls' School Association (GSA), the Girls' Public Day School Trust (GPDST) as well as several smaller associations. However, many schools were in no organization at all. The fragmentation of what were sometimes rival vested interests was obviously a weakness when criticisms were made of private education. The important thing to do was to bring as many schools as possible into a single organization which could effectively promote a new image of private schooling. Such a pressure group was set up to cope with the perceived threat to fee paying education from the Labour Party, a threat later reinforced by forceful performances in 1973 from Roy Hattersley, Shadow Minister of Education, in both public speeches and a debate with Norman St. John Stevas on television.

ISIS had been established in 1972 with Joyce Cadbury of the Governing Bodies of Girls' Schools Association (GBGSA) as chairperson and John Lindsay, retired headmaster of Malvern College, its first Director. The Organization got off to a good start following consultations with Margaret Thatcher, Secretary of State for Education, and favourable reports from *The Times* and *Daily Telegraph*. It was to become over the next ten years or more the most efficient propaganda machine for the private education sector, especially after 1977 when Tim Devlin, ex-education correspondent of *The Times* took over as Director. He was able to exploit his links with Fleet Street and bring a professional touch to ISIS increasing membership from 1036 schools with 300,000 pupils to 1350 schools with 422,000 pupils by 1984 when he left to become Head of Public Relations at the Institute of Directors. This meant that he had succeeded in attracting to ISIS half the fee paying schools in the UK containing about 80 per cent of the pupils in this sector.

School Fees

ISIS set out to change the public image of the private sector of education by bringing some unity between the various groups, improving overall organization and producing a number of publications ranging from detailed statistical material to propaganda tracts. Its major task was to remove the idea of an affluent minority purchasing a privileged education and to replace this view with one of parental freedom of choice, even if the scale of school fees made this seem implausible, (see table 1). The five years of preparatory school, which became increasingly important for those who wished to follow the kind of curricula favoured by the leading HMC schools, when added to the fees of five or six years at the latter, together with the range of extras needed was always in total about the price of a three-bedroomed house. This has remained fairly constant throughout the years. In 1973 the top HMC schools were charging over £900 per annum for boarding; by 1986 Cranleigh had reacher £6045. Girls' schools were slightly cheaper but only marginally so. Many preparatory schools by 1986 were charging £3000 per annum. For parents considering such schools it was pointed out that items such as uniforms, sports equipment, membership of clubs and registration fees had to be covered as well. Wellington sought to clarify the situation for prospective customers: '... charges are inclusive of all the pupil's school expenses, including such items as haircutting, gymnasium, swimming pool, etc., which might normally be considered as extras, but are not obligatory or essential. They do not cover

Table 1: Fees for Major HMC Schools 1973 and 1986

School	1973 £		1986 £	
	Boarding	Day	Boarding	Day
Bedales	867	477	5490	3735
Blundells	—	—	5160	3150
Bradfield	867	—	5340	3738
Bryanston	828	450	5790	3860
Charterhouse	888	630	5670	—
Cheltenham	780	465	5430	3615
Clifton	849	486	5550	3780
Cranleigh	921	606	6045	4215
Eton	861	—	5310	—
Fettes	840	—	5310	3570
Gordonstoun	958	420	5478[1]	—
Harrow	849	425	5850[3]	4485
Lancing	900	540	5370	3645
Marlborough	942	—	5550	—
Malvern	930	600	5400	3900
Oundle	885	—	5535	—
Rossall	849	528	5397	3777
Rugby	996	450	5535	—
St. Edwards	861	585	5325	3990
Sherborne	930	570	5550[3]	4200
Shrewsbury	900	498	5460	3900
Stowe	867	—	5760	—
Tonbridge	837	531	5370	3720
Uppingham	900	—	5700	—
Wellington	903	594	5310	3840
Westminster	912	540	5625[2]	3600[2]
Winchester	972	648	5760	—

Key: [1] £3240 to £6360 according to parental means
[2] £6225 and £3975 for Boarding and day pupils respectively when entering at sixth form level
[3] 1985 Fees
— Figure not available or boarding only
Source BURNETT, J. (Ed.) (1973) *Public and Preparatory Schools Yearbook* and (1986) *Independent Schools Yearbook: Boys' Schools*, London, Adam and Charles Black

personal expenses, such as travelling, pocket money, or tradesmen's bills'.[8] As rapid inflation became a feature of economic life schools began to raise fees during an academic year.

Scholarships and Bursaries

Much has been made of the system of scholarships and bursaries available to poor but talented pupils but the various schemes that have been in operation at one time or another tend to have one thing in common. Whatever their intention may be pupils from socially disadvantaged backgrounds rarely gain such awards. There are numerous reasons for this, including the obvious one demonstrated monotonously by sociological studies over the past half century that academic achievement at school is closely related to the occupation of father and home background.[9] Scholarships available in the HMC schools, which in fact have the largest number due to endowments often dating from the foundation of the school, are fewer than might be supposed, frequently covering only a portion of the fees, often restricted to the sons of officers from the armed services, clergymen or old boys of the school and often gained by those who had already attended a prep school.[10] From the scholarships advertised openly in the *Public and Preparatory Schools Year Book*, it was shown that about ten of the HMC schools offered full unconditional fees, a similar number gave qualified offers of up to full fees, whilst about 50 per cent offered no significant scholarships at all. The most common pattern was to find schools offering one scholarship of two-third fees and perhaps two at one-third fees together with small awards of between £50 to £100, usually for talent shown in music. When the scale of full fees is considered it becomes clear that for most parents finding over £1000 even if twice that amount is offered by the school, to say nothing of the inevitable extras, has meant that parental choice has a hollow ring when applied to the majority of HMC Schools. How far this was true for the direct grant system or is true for the APS will be explored later.

Terminology

Supporters of fee paying schools tended to point to the HMC schools making up about 10 per cent of all private schools when it came to a matter of academic results and resources but to focus attention on the smaller schools when critics raised the question of social exclusiveness. Already the public relations system of fee paying schools had got to work with some success on the matter of terminology. Confusion arose from the various terms used at times by different writers. Public schools to which the public were denied access; private schools which had become public trusts, independent schools which were partly dependent upon financial contributions from local and national government. By the early 1970s the schools were increasingly using the term independent schools for themselves which not only provided an impression of a unified system for all fee paying schools with only minor differences between them, but just as important, could be useful in winning the battle of words in the disputes between supporters and critics:

> In the early seventies the heads of independent schools were anxious to bury the term 'public school' as quickly and decently as possible. This was partly because, in the face of political threats, the

old established schools decided to throw in their lot with all recognized independent schools. A more important, if less publicly acknowledged, reason for a change of nomenclature was the desire of heads to dissociate themselves and their schools from the overtones of snobbery and exclusiveness that to the British ear were immediately audible in the words 'public school'.[11]

Direct Grant Grammar Schools

Fee paying schools felt fairly safe in the years of the Heath administration but with Labour back in office in 1974 they had to face the prospect that after many years of rhetoric about integrating these schools into the maintained sector, the Party had promised not only to put an end to direct grant grammar schools, but also to withdraw tax relief and charitable status as a step towards removing some of the subsidies provided to these schools by local and national government. The direct grant grammar schools were a mystery to most people, but were in fact selective fee paying schools which received a direct grant from the government on condition that they offer at least 25 per cent of their places by examination to children who had attended local authority schools for at least two years. The most famous was probably Manchester grammar, but this academically excellent school was not typical of many of the schools of the time, for as the Donnison Report published in 1970 on independent day schools and direct grant schools had shown, '... the school which is ... highly selective, proud of its academic achievements and geared to the needs of the most able, ... is the sort of school which often springs to mind ... but no more than one quarter of the schools really fit this description ...'.[12] The staff were no better qualified than those in county grammar schools; in fact the latter had a higher proportion of teachers with first and second class honours degrees.[13] The social composition of the schools was similar to that of HMC schools; 'three out of four pupils come from homes of white collar workers, three out of five have fathers in professional or managerial occupations, ... only one out of thirteen comes from a semi-skilled or unskilled worker's family'.[14] The higher the percentage of boarders and the larger the sixth form, the higher the proportion of pupils from high income families: 85 per cent of boarding pupils were from professional and managerial homes compared with 57 per cent of day pupils.[15]

The Labour Party was opposed to selective secondary education and hence, supported by the Liberal Party, offered the direct grant grammar schools the choice of either joining the maintained sector or the fee paying sector in 1976; 117 out of the 178 schools went private thereby bringing about a considerable expansion in the fee paying sector. Department of Education and Science Circulars 12/76 and 6/77 followed leading to a reduction in local authority expenditure on buying places at these schools unless it could be shown that an authority could not provide suitable alternative tuition. Although leading Conservatives, such as Norman St. John Stevas, pledged the restoration of the direct grant system by a future Tory government, the realization that local authorities favouring comprehensive education could influence the financing of such schools led supporters of fee paying schools to consider alternative ways for the future of offering access to their schools to pupils whose parents might be deterred by the scale of the fees charged.

Charitable Status

As for Labour's hopes of removing charitable status from the schools which largely catered for the affluent this was found to be much more complex than had at first been supposed. Two bodies which grappled with this problem were the House of Commons Expenditure Committee and the Goodman Committee. Recommendations from the former supported an end to charitable status for most schools whilst the latter, which was not a Royal Commission but consisted mainly of charity officials, favoured the status quo, with the exception of Ben Whittaker who produced a minority report. Whilst the provision of education had been accepted as a public benefit since Elizabethan times, as far back as 1607 an eminent lawyer had argued it was charitable 'only or at least primarily if the benefit was for the poor ... "Poverty is the principle and essential circumstance ..."'. Today schools can be considered a charity providing they are non profit making institutions, even if the sons and daughters of the wealthy are foremost among their customers. Brighton College had won a lengthy ten-year legal battle beginning in 1915 to be granted charitable status even though it did not cater primarily for the poor and by doing so won the right for similar schools.[16] Today many fee-paying schools, from Eton to Gordonstoun, are able to claim charitable status and thereby pay reduced rates, and claim exemption from income tax and capital gains tax as well as VAT. Tax can also be recovered on deeds of covenant.

A few fee paying schools provide help to a number of children with various learning difficulties. How was it possible to make a distinction between these schools and the majority catering principally for parents on high incomes? The House of Commons Committee believed that one way was to accept that, '... purpose beneficial to the community (be adopted as) the overriding criterion'.[17] The Goodman Commission expressed concern at educational establishments which served only a fraction of the community but believed that it should be left to the charity commissioners and courts to decide upon the charitable status of public schools. Whittaker in his minority report stated, 'I fail to see why the community should be compelled to support financially exclusive schools which are restricted largely to those families who are already privileged'.[18] Given the scale of the problem in dealing with charities (which had by 1975 assets of nearly £3000 million with tax exemptions costing £100 million, and whose numbers were growing at the rate of 2500 per year, of which about 13 per cent were registered as educational) it is perhaps understandable to see why the Goodman Commission hesitated to make a clear distinction between those primarily helping the community and those which did not. With the lack of any clear cut decision the issue faded away although it has been raised once more in the 1980s by both the Labour and Alliance parties as an anomaly which should be ended.

Conservatives Return to Power—1979

A change in government in 1979 brought a change in attitude towards fee-paying schools. These schools might not wish to be so clearly linked with the Conservative Party but through a series of social networks and explicit political contacts they were, and this political liaison became apparent through the 1980s. There was at first the direct link in Parliament; of the 339 Tory MPs returned in May 1979, fifty-one had attended Eton and a further 152 had gone to other fee-paying schools. Among the Cabinet nineteen out of the twenty-one members had received a similar schooling and three of the four Education Ministers.[19] However, in the 1983 Parliament, although the Tory Cabinet contained a similar proportion from fee paying schools and whilst there were fifty ex-Etonians in the Parliamentary Party there were also a substantial number of ex-grammar school and provincial university MPs who had squeezed through often in marginal seats.[20] Although Conservatives might lament in public the decline in the numbers of grammar schools it was noticeable that in private they were less loyal in their affiliation. For example, where ex-grammar school Tory ministers had the opportunity to send their own children to such schools they opted instead for fee-paying education, such as Margaret Thatcher and Norman Tebbitt.[21]

Numerous studies throughout the period showed that there was little evidence of any substantial weakening of the established elite social networks.[22] Anthony Giddens writing in 1979 claimed that 'In whichever sector of British society we happen to look, we find the same phenomenon; our institutions are dominated by people educated in public schools.'[23] The examples he gave then were Anglican bishops 85 per cent, army officers of the rank of major general or above 86 per cent, principal judges 81 per cent, permanent secretaries 61 per cent, directors of industrial companies 73 per cent and directors of financial institutions 80 per cent. Similar patterns emerge when one looks through *The Stock Exchange Year Book*, the *Barr List of the UK* or *Who's Who*. Hence, all six chairmen of the major clearing banks in 1983/84 went to fee-paying schools, all but one of the chairmen of the leading merchant banks in 1984 received a similar schooling except two who were educated abroad, and eight of the nine law lords in the same year had been privately educated.[24] It does not follow that they are all therefore Conservative Party supporters, but circumstantial evidence suggests that this is where the sympathies of most of those in the top ranks of the establishment lie.

Such evidence is to be found in the general political views prevailing in the schools themselves. When a senior member of the Governing Bodies Association said, '... many governing bodies regard headmasters as dangerous left wing radicals' John Rae remarked, 'That headmasters who, by and large, were conservative both in instinct and political conviction should have been regarded as "dangerous left wing radicals" was an indication of how far to the right some members of the governing bodies were'.[25]

Irene Fox's study of parents who had sons at public schools during the academic year 1979/80 showed that approximately 75 per cent of husbands and wives voted Tory whilst only 2 per cent of husbands and just over 4 per cent of wives voted Labour.[26] This again is not surprising given the social class of the parents for one does not need to be a social scientist to know that voting loyalties show some correlation with income. At speech days or prize giving events attacks on the Labour Party by guest speakers or headmasters are common as a glance at any local newspaper will confirm.[27]

The Assisted Places Scheme

Both the manner of, and the reasoning behind, the establishment of the APS were destined to engender controversy within the educational world. The scheme resulted from talks between representatives of the fee-paying sector of schools and the Conservative Party. For the former, it was the Direct Grant Joint Committee followed by the Assisted Places Steering Committee; for the latter, Stuart Sexton, political adviser in turn to Norman St. John Stevas, Mark Carlisle and Sir Keith Joseph. The fee-paying sector was looking for some kind of compensation for the loss encountered by the end of the direct grant grammar schools, but naturally one on terms as favourable to themselves as possible. The Conservative Party wished to increase selection in secondary education and encourage the private sector of schooling. It may well be that there was also an intention to provide an 'escape route' for some of their middle class supporters to avoid under funded maintained schools.

The major educational rationale was that academically able pupils from low income families needed to attend fee paying schools if they were to gain suitable tuition. As Tapper and Salter have stated, 'The implication is self evident—independent schools are better equipped to cater to the needs of the intellectually able.'[28] To sell the scheme the Conservatives needed to stress the idea of extending parental choice and providing the opportunity for bright pupils from low income families to be given the opportunity to enter fee paying schools. Rhodes Boyson had declared, 'Able children from our poorest homes will once again have the opportunity of attending academically excellent schools.'[29]

Parental income would be considered according to five bands ranging from under £5000 through to over £11,000, and means tested assistance provided. These bands were raised over the years so that by 1985 families receiving less than £6376 paid no fees and some form of assistance was available up to £12,280. Sixty per cent of places were reserved for pupils who had spent at least one year in a maintained school, but the preparatory schools lobby did not want fee payers excluded for fear that parents might withdraw their children from prep schools in order to qualify for an APS when they reached secondary school age.[30] Because local authorities, parents' organizations, teachers' associations and other political parties had taken no part in the discussions concerning the APS the form it took fulfilled only the aims of the fee paying sector and the Conservative Party. Such close collaboration has made it difficult now for the former to plead political neutrality.

One question which has to be asked is how far the APS has been successful in terms of its stated intentions. It is also important to ask what effect it has had upon the schooling provided for the majority of the nation's children. In general the scheme has recruited better among younger pupils, less well among sixth formers; better for girls outside the London area than in the capital.[31] The majority of pupils have come from families in the lowest income band but this is not the same as saying they come from disadvantaged families living in depressed areas. For one thing the income bands are generous enough for a family with one parent receiving the annual average gross income to be eligible for some financial help with school fees. Douse has shown from his study that 41 per cent of pupils came from single parent families, 19 per cent from families where the main wage earner had recently been unemployed, about 20 per cent had a sibling at a fee paying school already whilst 32 per cent had at least one parent with a professional qualification.[32] Whitty and his colleagues who have been monitoring the APS almost from its inception, in a larger scale study, have shown that few of the pupils come from families traditionally considered to be socially disadvantaged: 33 per cent came from single parent families, only about 7 per cent of fathers and 2 per cent of mothers were registered as unemployed, about 50 per cent of fathers and over 20 per cent of mothers were in jobs classified as service class occupations, 58 per cent of mothers and 40 per cent of fathers had attended academically selective secondary schools whilst 10 per cent of mothers and fathers had been to fee paying schools. The majority of families may have modest incomes but the traditional blue collar working class parents or those from deprived inner city areas have not been helped by this scheme in the manner suggested by earlier supporters of the venture:

> While our evidence supports the claim made in defence of the scheme that the majority of assisted places are going to children from families with low or 'modest' incomes, they also point to low participation rates by manual working class families and especially those where the fathers are in semi-skilled or unskilled employment ... when taken together with more detailed case study evidence from particular families, these findings suggest that a considerable proportion of assisted place holders come from 'submerged middle-class' backgrounds already well endowed with cultural capital.[33]

The original assumption that it would primarily help bright children who would not otherwise have been able to receive an education suited to their ability, other than by attending a fee paying school must be declared 'not proven'. The current research of Whitty and his colleagues illustrates that most assisted place holders in their sample would not otherwise have attended state schools that were demonstrably unable to cater for them; most would either have attended private schools anyway or gone to maintained schools with well developed academic provision.[34]

The total number of pupils involved in the APS is negligible; about 1 per cent of pupils attending schools. Although recruitment at the younger age has enabled schools to fill their quotas, at sixth form level they have not attracted pupils so readily. Many have filled a portion of sixth form places by taking youngsters largely from their own or other fee paying schools and by trading off the agreed ratio of maintained to fee payer pupils with their younger entrants:

> London GPDST heads confirmed that a majority of assisted places at 16 + go to private sector applicants, mostly to their own trust school pupils.[35]

More alarming is the scale of subsidy some schools are, and will be, receiving from the Scheme. Clement Freud, Liberal MP, in 1984 asked for an estimate of the percentage of pupils in schools who would be paid for under the APS in 1988 and was told that there would be over 20 per cent of pupils in forty-seven schools, over 30 per cent in fifty schools and over 40 per cent in the remaining forty-four schools.[36] In the same month Gerald Kaufman, Labour MP, asked for the total sum of money paid to schools in the APS between 1981-1984; the sums ranged from several hundred pounds at some schools to £450,086 to Dulwich College, £455,753 to Emanuel School and £478,837 to Newcastle under Lyme School.[37] That such sums of money should have been provided for some fee paying schools during the very years maintained schools were being kept short of basic resources demonstrates clearly which section of schooling was most favoured by the Government.

The low take up at sixth form level is probably due to two main factors.

Where maintained schools get pupils successfully through 'O' levels they gain the confidence of both parents and pupils, hence neither are likely to look for a change of school. A further factor is the development of sixth form colleges which have produced a serious challenge to fee paying schools. As far back as 1981 they were producing 'A' level results as good as those obtained by grammar and independent schools.[38] Indeed the move of some pupils at sixth form level from fee paying schools to sixth form and tertiary colleges has received little publicity but the success of these colleges in academic terms partly explains why some fee paying schools have lobbied against their establishment in certain areas. It is not the scale of the APS, much reduced from Stuart Sexton's earlier design, which is of significance so much as its symbolic consequences; '... its capacity to reinforce belief in the inability of public sector schools to match the quality of private provision'.[40] It is for this reason that it can be judged as damaging to the maintained sector of education to which the majority of pupils belong.

Investment in Fee Paying Schools

From the 1970s to the 1980s fundamental changes have taken place within many of the schools; changes whose origins can often be traced back to earlier years. These changes have come about for a variety of reasons ranging from parental pressure and political ideology to plain pragmatism. There has been for example a large programme of investment in order to improve the resources of the schools, and much of this has taken place during the years that the maintained system has been deprived of such resources. The *Independent Schools Yearbook* publishes details about HMC, IAPS and SHMIS, and a second volume deals with girls' schools.[41]

The parkland settings, the sporting facilities, academic resources and individual study bedrooms of some make it clear that the school experience of pupils in well equipped fee paying schools is considerably different from that of pupils in many of the maintained schools, and almost a different world from that inhabited by many inner city school children. Lord Wandsworth College is, '... situated three miles south of Odiham, Hampshire, on its own estate of 2100 acres ...' whilst the main buildings of Stowe are surrounded by a park of 750 acres. There are about 400 boys in the former and just under 700 pupils in the latter. In each case there is more than one acre per pupil. Gordonstoun explains how 'Gordonstoun House, and its seventeenth century "Round Square" are near the centre of the 300 acre estate, which includes a mile of Moray Firth foreshore' whilst Workshop is situated 'on its own estate of 310 acres on high ground on the edge of Sherwood Forest ... overlooking the Clumber and Welbeck estates, to both of which the boys have free access'.

Good sports facilities have long been associated with public schools and whilst the playing fields of maintained schools have been threatened by the publication of Statutory Instrument 909, a document authorizing local authorities to put playing fields up for sale, many fee paying schools have continued to expand their sporting facilities. Heated swimming pools are common (Oundle has a fifty-yard pool), tennis courts (Radley has twelve plus a sixteen-hole golf course) and squash courts abound, Eton Fives is a popular option. Many sports halls have been built, thirty-six were mentioned by schools in 1984 and a number of all-weather pitches have been constructed. Then there are facilities which must be considered a luxury for any one school to own; Ellesmere has its own field study centre at Snowdonia; King Edward VII a residential centre in the Yorkshire Dales; and Highgate a cottage in North Wales. Cokethorpe, Emanuel and Radley have boat houses on the Thames; similar resources are owned by Ley School on the River Cam, Monmouth on the Rive Wye and Wycliffe on Berkeley Canal. Merchant Taylors has a lake available for its sailing club; Bradfield offers 'fishing in the Pang'; Kelly College has its own trout and salmon fishing. Radley is not alone in having a pack of beagles for hunting during the winter months thereby encouraging blood sports.

Upgrading what might be termed academic and cultural facilities really got under way in the 1950s with the establishment of the Industrial Fund for the Advancement of Science which supplied financial support for a large scale investment programme in the sciences, providing modern laboratories and equipment. Prior Park and Strathallan both acknowledge the aid they have received from this source. Kingswood with 520 pupils has eleven science laboratories, Blundells with 450 pupils has ten, Reeds with about 350 pupils has seven whilst Seaford College with 440 pupils manages with 'twelve fully equipped laboratories'. The language laboratories of the 1970s have been overtaken by a proliferation of computer centres in the 1980s. Stanford completed a new mathematics and computer studies centre in 1983, Cranleigh expanded and re-equipped its computing and electronics department in 1984.

The arts have also been well catered for: theatres and generous provision for music in terms of both practice facilities and staffing. Oakham has two theatres, Marlborough the use of 'thirty practice rooms, two music schools, a bandroom, a large hall for either of their two orchestras or the two brass bands, a large chapel and organ, twenty-one peripetetic staff and six permanent music staff'.[42]

Fee paying schools usually have the advantage of favourable staff:pupil ratios; about 1:10 in the HMC schools, although Cranleigh has 1:9. Whilst staff pupil ratios improved for all schools during the period considered, ratios in HMC schools always stayed well ahead of those in maintained secondary schools and so did related reductions in class size. Fee paying schools frequently stressed the small class sizes they were able to offer; Old Buckenham School quotes 'an average class size of thirteen' whilst Millfield Junior School states that the 'average number of pupils per class is nine'.

The superior resources available to many HMC pupils whether it be in sports, science, the arts, or more generous pupil/teacher ratios have been made possible by successful fund raising schemes. These schools are able to rely upon the support of wealthy patrons in the form of donations directly from affluent parents and old pupils as well as indirectly from organizations whose own ex-public school boy members are willing to vote generous funds to their old schools or those in a similar category, usually with some tax advantage in mind.

Eton enjoys an especially privileged situation. Even in the late 1970s it was enjoying an income annually of £1m not counting school fees,[43] although more recently questions have been raised about the source of some of that money in the form of indirect income from slum properties owned but not managed by the College.[44] At Taunton School with 690 pupils 'a successful appeal for £170,000 was launched in 1974 (and) the 1981 appeal has passed the target of £400,000'. St. Johns, a school founded in the nineteenth century for the education of sons of the clergy, describes how 'an appeal launched in 1968 raised over £100,000,... In 1975 a further sum of £60,000 was raised (and) ... from an appeal launched in September 1981, ... £375,000 ...' was received. Sherborne raised £400,000 in 1982.[45] Bangor explains that '£750,000 have been expended over the past thirteen years,' Durham tells how '£1m has been spent during the last fifteen years' and at Queen Elizabeth's 'a major building and improvement programme, started in 1975 ... cost ... over £1m'. Shrewsbury describes how 'in the course of the last ten years more than £1.5m has been spent on the school buildings', Cheltenham claims 'approximately £1,850,000 has been spent on the buildings since 1973' but Bromsgrove still leads the known big spenders informing parents that 'a further fifteen-year programme of modernization involving the expenditure of sums well in excess of £2m is now complete'. It is salutory to realize that much of this fund-raising has taken place when the country was living through a long and deep economic depression. Given the scale of the funding and resources enjoyed by some of the top HMC schools it is difficult to understand how Eric Anderson, Headmaster of Eton, could lecture maintained schools in 1981 as follows: '... the correct attitude for the state would be to say 'Thank you very much for showing us what standards are possible. That is what we must aim to achieve'.[46]

Moves Towards Co-education

One substantial change among many fee paying schools has been the move towards co-education in what were originally all boys' schools. There have always been co-educational schools in the private sector such as Bedales and Cheadle Hulme; indeed it was their co-educational status that may have denied them the title of public school in the past. A major reason for the move towards co-education in recent times has been economic. The number of pupils at school between 1975 and 1984 declined from about 11,222,000 to 9,876,000 due to the falling birth rate and even though the decline had been less among middle-class families who might favour fee paying education it was still sufficient for such schools to view the situation with alarm. This problem was aggravated for those direct grant schools which had chosen to go independent and thereby faced a fall in future numbers of pupils of some 25 per cent. Given the high fees the answer for the boys' schools was to go for the 50 per cent of the market they had previously ignored; the girls in the families of parents who could afford to pay such fees. The first HMC school to make the move was Marlborough back in 1969[47] but soon other schools were following this trend, usually making the first move by offering places for girls at sixth form level. This tactic not only brought extra finance in the form of fees but made possible further economies of scale in the sixth form. It was not just that sixth forms could be larger but a greater range of options could be offered by balancing subject groups; thus the different preferences of girls and boys, often due to a variety of social influences, could be used to make viable groups. Later an increasing number of boys' schools encouraged girls' entry for all years. The scale of the change is well illustrated by recent statistics from ISIS[48]:

HMC Schools

	Boys		Girls	
	Boarders	*Day*	*Boarders*	*Day*
1974	46,208	63,295	1195	2330
1986	40,577	86,242	5796	15,179

Taking girls also increased the 'pool of talent' from which boys' schools could draw which would lead to better examination results and hence further enhanced status.

Recruitment in the other direction from boys' to girls' schools has been negligible. By 1984 only twenty-nine boys aged eleven or more were to be found among all the GSA and GBGSA schools.[49] In taking some girls away from their traditional single sex schools boys' schools were safeguarding their own economic interests whilst undermining some of the girls' schools. Ironically whilst some girls' schools might complain at the poaching of some of their brightest pupils by the boys' schools they in turn continued to endeavour to poach some of the brightest pupils in the maintained sector through the APS.

During a time when some feminists were questioning the value of co-education for girls there were some parents anxious to get their daughters into boys' schools. Given the patriarchial nature of British society girls' fee paying schools have inevitably been of less influence than those boys' schools which could boast a long pedigree and generations of well established social networks. For some girls the move into HMC schools was an opportunity to make good use of the prestige and connections of these schools so that they might improve their own career prospects. Some girls believed the boys' schools had fewer petty restrictions. Rightly or wrongly many parents believed that the sixth form teaching in the HMC schools was superior to that found in many girls' schools. Less doubtful was the desire to get into schools which had good links with universities, especially the Oxbridge Colleges.[50] Not all the HMC schools have followed the co-educational path; none of the Clarendon schools are fully co-educational yet and only four of them admit girls at sixth form level on a regular basis.

Another market tapped has been that of foreign pupils and between 1974 and 1986 within HMC schools numbers in this category rose from 2591 to 4831. For all member schools of ISIS by 1986 there were 13,626 foreign pupils and the fees earned were according to ISIS an important contribution to the balance of payments. For those British pupils whose parents worked overseas, especially officers in the armed services and senior civil servants, the government made generous contributions to their school fees and travel expenses, and it was estimated that taxpayers were contributing to fee paying schools by such payments to the tune of £70 million in 1983.[51]

Growing Political Activities of Fee Paying School Lobby

There can be little doubt that the fee paying sector of schooling in the UK has enjoyed considerable success between 1973 and 1986. It has been aided in this indirectly by marked hostility towards the maintained sector by the Political Right often fostered by sections of the press. The quality papers have often contributed towards the public relations success of private schools by producing several articles on issues such as paying school fees or choosing a school, and at the same time attracting valuable revenue by filling a couple of pages of advertisements from the schools and insurance companies dealing with school fees.[52] Morale in the schools has been boosted by a Conservative administration which has heaped praise upon the private sector whilst denigrating the maintained system. In practical terms increased financial aid has been given indirectly by tax concessions to higher income groups who favour such schools and directly by the APS.

In the 1970s whatever the political views of the headmasters, parents and pupils of fee paying schools might be there was at least an attempt in public to be seen as politically neutral. The close links with the Tory Party in negotiations over the APS have made that approach less easy to defend. So too did the move by Tim Devlin in 1981 to encourage the private education lobby to raise £500,000 to fight Labour's plans as outlined in their booklet *Private Schools*[53] and the setting up by the private schools of an

'Action Committee' which helped to organize 150 groups in time for the 1983 General Election. Candidates considered to be hostile to private education, which clearly only included Labour and Alliance candidates, were opposed thereby exposing the politically partisan outlook of the private school lobby.

With growing confidence of the schools headmasters have been willing to adopt a higher profile, to use present jargon, and become more closely identified with those on the Radical Right who have been so critical of maintained schools. A recent publication from the Hillgate Group, most of whom have long been highly critical of local authority schools (such as Baroness Cox, John Marks and Roger Scruton) contains attacks on local education authorities, comprehensive schools and members of HMI. The headmasters of Eton and Radley, Eric Anderson and Denis Silk respectively, have given their support, alongside Stuart Sexton, in an attempt to persuade a future Conservative government to privatize schools throughout the country.[54]

Conclusion

The success of fee paying schools has been explained in various ways: the fall from grace of the maintained schools in the eyes of the media, the hopes of affluent parents to buy extra resources in terms of educational facilities for their children and the political ideology of the Radical Right. This latter force, although small in numbers, was able to capture key parts of both the Conservative Party and those newspapers politically sympathetic to that Party. The result was a 'turning back of the clock' in all areas of the economy in terms of privatization, including areas of education, centrally in the form of the APS, marginally in the case of school meals and cleaning services.[55] Yet for all that by 1986 the maintained sector of schooling still catered for the needs of approximately 94 per cent of school children and it could be argued that not only did many fee paying schools not deserve their success in terms of the quality of service they provided but that for many parents school fees were not money well spent. HMI reports were frequently critical of fee paying schools although such reports rarely seemed to attract the scale of publicity or reporting that accompanied any alleged problems found in maintained schools. Even reporters favourable to private schools and writing for their potential clientele have cast doubts on the existence of 'super teachers' in these schools accounting for the comparative success of the pupils:

> The shortage of real quality extends to the staff. One or two inspired teachers per school is a lot, and where they exist you can't miss them.[56]

> It is difficult to ascertain what many girls' schools are trying to achieve: great swathes, for example, claimed to be 'academic' and catering for 'high fliers' (by which they mean potential Oxbridge undergraduates) but are no such thing.[57]

In effect the good 'A' level results of the HMC schools have little to do with teaching techniques but more to do with fundamental differences between their clientele and those attending most local authority schools. A higher proportion of pupils in private schools stay on into the sixth form because for the majority of high income groups who send their children to such schools this is considered to be the norm for school careers. By contrast, the proportions, staying on into the sixth form in maintained schools, although they have risen over the past decade or so, are still below those in private schools. The pattern varies regionally but in general it would be fair to say that those in sixth forms following 'A' level courses are most likely to come from middle-class homes. Hence it is the sons and to a growing extent in recent years the daughters of 'top people' attending HMC schools, which provide the schools not just with the high income from fees and fund raising which in turn provide good resources, but also, committed customers who will study for traditional examinations because such an aim is the accepted goal for the families, schools and pupil peer groups generally to be found patronizing these schools. Given this general commitment and support the favoured financial circumstances and educational resources of the schools just make it that much easier for pupils to do well in these surroundings. In short there is a two-way path: the best of the fee paying schools provide access to areas of prestige and power in society and in turn they respond by showing favour to these schools. Who owes the greatest debt to who is not easy to tell but it is possible to suggest that among the really affluent their success is more likely to be due to their family circumstances than the school they attended. However for the aspiring upwardly mobile, in terms of economic and social life chances, the opportunity some of the schools might still provide to mix with the 'top people' of tomorrow would probably produce a good return on the investment made in the form of school fees. Throughout the period the fee paying schools reflected and reinforced in education the fundamental inequalities of British Society.

Between 1973 and 1986 the fee paying sector in general prospered. Total numbers in the schools increased, subsidies from local and national government together with financial support from private sources enabled the leading schools to invest heavily in resources. The move to co-education was substantial but bought at the expense of the girls' schools for although they retained their numbers they lost talented pupils to boys' schools. The struggle of some of the smallest poor quality schools lacking proper facilities or qualified staff largely went unnoticed, as did the move from private schools to local education authority sixth form and tertiary colleges of hundreds of pupils. Whilst the APS acted as a financial lifeline to many of the lesser known schools this support was bought at a price; the ever closer and publicly displayed link between the private sector lobby and the Conservative Party.[58] The future for many of these schools was therefore dependent more than ever upon the electoral fortunes of the Conservative Party.

Acknowledgement

I would like to thank Dr Ted Tapper of the University of Sussex for giving generously of his time to discuss material in this chapter.

Notes

1 In fact the Direct Grant Joint Committee (DGJC) had been formed in the 1960s to cope with the Labour government's *Circular 10/65* which was seen as likely to undermine direct grant grammar schools by allowing local authorities to stop purchasing places at these schools where it was considered that such schooling could be offered in the maintained sector. For the period prior to 1973 see SALTER, B. and TAPPER, T. (1985) *Power and Policy in Education: The Case of Independent Schooling*, chapter 6, Falmer Press.
2 Later much of the Black Paper material was discredited, such as the fraudulent work of Sir Cyril Burt, but the detailed studies contradicting these writings did not receive the publicity of the early Black Papers. For a critique of the first four Black Papers and the attack on education in maintained schools see WRIGHT, N. (1977) *Progress in Education*, London, Croom Helm; and BARON, S. *et al.* (1981) *Unpopular Education*, London, Hutchinson/CCCS.
3 RAE, J. (1981) *The Public School Revolution 1964-79*, London, Faber and Faber.
4 *Full time pupils:*

	1973	1985
Maintained Schools	8,648,276	7,067,847
Independent Schools	411,664	501,422
Pupil : Teacher Ratios:		
Secondary Maintained Schools	21.8	18.7
Independent	12.8	11.4

Source: DES (1973) *Statistics of Education*, Vol. 1, and DES (1985) *Statistics of Education.*
5 The exact number is unknown. There are in addition hundreds of language schools and numerous colleges of further education. In all of these areas the range goes from the good to the worthless. The more responsible colleges of FE have formed the Conference for Independent FE but since deregulations in this area scores of institutions have been set up, many of which take advantage of foreign students seeking British qualifications, see SELBY, D. (1983) 'Learning broken English', *The Guardian*, 9 August and AYERS, J. (1986) 'Welcome to the Arthur Daley college of non-accountability', *The Guardian*, 16 December.

6   In 1986 there were 266 HMC schools of which sixty-one were fully co-educational.

7   The Clarendon Report of 1864 covered the following schools: Eton, Winchester, Westminster, Charterhouse, St. Pauls, Merchant Taylor's, Harrow, Rugby and Shrewsbury.

8   BURNET, J. (Ed) (1981) *Public and Preparatory Schools Yearbook*, London, Adams and Charles Black, p. 327.

9   See SILVER, H. (Ed) (1973) *Equal Opportunities in Education*, London, Methuen, and HALSEY, A. H., HEATH, A. F. and RIDGE, J. M. (1980) *Origins and Destinations*, Oxford, Clarendon.

10 GRIGGS, C. (1981) 'Not so humble origins', *Times Educational Supplement*, 27 November.

11 RAE, J. (1981) *op cit.*, pp 15-16.

12 Report on Independent Day Schools and Direct Grant Grammar Schools. (Donnison Report) (1970) *The Public Schools Commission: Second Report* Vol. 1, London, HMSO p. 56.

13 *ibid.* p. 50.

14 *ibid.* p. 51.

15 GRIGGS, C. (1975) 'Save our schools', *Tribune*, 39, 27, 4 July.

16 JONES, M. D. W. (1983) 'Brighton College v Marriot Schools, Charity Law and Taxation', *History of Education*, 12, 2, pp. 121-32.

17 *Tenth Report from the Expenditure Committee Session 1974-75, Charity Commissioners and Their Accountability*, (1975) Vol. 1 Report, HMSO, 30 July.

18 *Charity Law and Voluntary Organisations: Report of the Goodman Committee* (1976) Bedford Square, Press of the National Council of Social Service.

19 WHEEN, F. (1979) 'Return of the jolly good chaps', *New Statesman*, 11 May.

20 BURCH, M. and MORAN, M. (1984) 'Who are the new Tories?', *New Society*, 11 October.

21 STRAW, J. (1986) 'Ministers boycott state schools', *New Statesman*, 12 September.

22 HEALD, T. (1983) *Networks: Who We Know and How We Use Them*, London, Hodder and Stoughton.

23 GIDDENS, A. (1979) 'An anatomy of the British ruling class', *New Society*, 4 October.

24 GRIGGS, C. (1985) *Private Education in Britain*, chapter 3, Lewes, Falmer Press.

25 RAE, J., (1981) *op cit.*, p. 66.

26 FOX, I. (1985) *Private Schools and Public Issues*, London, Macmillan, p. 119.

27 For example *Eastbourne Herald* 9 July 1983 and 19 July 1986.

28 TAPPER, T. and SALTER, B. (1986) 'The assisted places scheme: A policy evaluation', *Journal of Educational Policy*, 1, 4, p. 317.

29 *Daily Mail*, 25 June 1981 and quoted in FITZ, J., EDWARDS, A. and WHITTY, G. (1986) 'Beneficiaries, benefits and costs: An investigation of the assisted places scheme', *Research Papers in Education*, 1, 3, p. 171.

30 TAPPER, T. and SALTER, B. (1986) *op cit.*, p. 322.

31 WALL, D. (1986) 'The assisted places scheme at London GPDST schools', paper given at the British Education Research Association annual conference, 4 September.

32 DOUSE, M. (1985) 'The background of assisted places students', *Educational Studies*, 11, 3.

33 FITZ, J., EDWARDS, A. and WHITTY, G. *op cit.*, p. 185.

34 *ibid.*, p. 189. The full detailed study by WHITTY, G., FITZ, J. and EDWARDS, A., which has been funded by the Economic and Social Research Council will be published under the title of *Plucking Embers from the Ashes? The Origins, Implementation and Consequences of the Assisted Places Scheme*, Lewes, Falmer Press.

35 WALL, D., (1986) *op. cit.*

36 HANSARD, 14 February 1984, Cols. 145-147 W.

37 HANSARD, 29 February 1984, Cols. 206-212 W.

38 'Sixth form college success', *Times Educational Supplement*, 2 October 1981, p. 10.

39 There is no complete summary of total numbers and complete academic results of pupils in sixth form and tertiary colleges although their growth can be measured to some extent from material published in the *Compendium of Sixth From and Tertiary Colleges* (6th edn). The increase in the number of sixth form colleges is as follows:

1973-21	1978- 81	1983-106
1974-38	1979- 88	1984-106
1975-59	1980- 96	1985-106
1976-67	1981-100	1986-108
1977-74	1982-101	

Source: Question No 127, 4 March 1987, House of Commons, Giles Radice to Kenneth Baker.

There has been a steady intake of fee paying pupils into both sixth form and tertiary colleges in recent years. There are a variety of reasons for these moves but comparatively high fees of private schools are one factor considered by parents whilst the good academic record of these colleges has proved a positive attraction. This movement is more pronounced in the South and Midlands of the UK and has included pupils from HMC as well as smaller fee paying schools. Two examples of this trend are as follows:

Year 1 Yeovil Tertiary College

'A' level courses:	1978	1979	1980	1981	1982
From independent schools	57	64	63	88	85
From maintained schools	271	259	259	280	326
Others largely vocational courses:					
From independent schools	62	52	48	58	62
From maintained schools	327	350	312	404	376

Eastbourne Sixth Form College

No. of students emerging from independent schools:

	1982	1983	1984	1985	1986
	32	33	42	44	29

(I am grateful to Mr. F. Janes, ex-Principal of Yeovil College and Mr. J. Morris, Principal of Eastbourne Sixth Form College for this information.)

40 FITZ, J., EDWARDS, A., and WHITTY, G., (1986) *op. cit.*, p. 192.

41 BURNETT, J. (Ed) *The Independent Schools Yearbook* is published in two volumes by Adam and Charles annually: one deals with HMC, IAPS SHIS schools whilst the other covers girls' schools. Previously the first volume was entitled *Public and Preparatory Schools Yearbook*. It contains details of staff, fees, resources and many other features provided by the schools themselves. The facts concerning the schools are taken from this publication unless stated otherwise.

42 BIRLEY, R.H. to *The Listener*, 3 April 1980.

Clive Griggs

43 RAE, J. (1981) *op. cit.*, p. 173.
44 CRAIL, M. (1984) 'Slum tenants "subsidising" Eton', *Tribune*, 30 March; and ROSE, D. (1986) 'Tenants "harassed" in Eton Flats', *The Guardian*, 9 September.
45 HEALD, T. (1983) *op. cit.*, p. 60.
46 RUTHEUN, M. (1981) 'The wolf at Eton's back door', *The Guardian*, 17 July.
47 John Rae suggests that the motives of John Dancy in 1969 were primarily aimed at changing the ethos of the school and this was doubtless a contributory reason for many other schools which followed suit. RAE, J. (1981) *op. cit.*, pp 137-43.
48 *Annual Census 1986*, Statistical Survey of Independent Schools, ISIS.
49 WALFORD, G. (1986) *Life in Public Schools*, London, Methuen p. 156.
50 *ibid.*, chapter 6.
51 For an estimate of the scale of local and national government annual subsidy to fee paying schools see PRING, R., (1983) *Privatisation in Education* Right to Comprehensive Education, RICE, 7 February.
52 For example *The Times* 11 May 1985 and 6 October 1986; and *The Guardian* 27 May and 23 November 1986.
53 *Private Schools: A Labour Party Discussion Document* (1980) The Labour Party.
54 *Whose Schools? A Radical Manifesto* (1986) The Hillgate Group.
55 How far privatization has taken place during the Conservative administration of 1979 and 1983 compared with the demands of the Radical Right has been the subject of several articles: see PRING, R. (1986) 'Privatization of Education' in ROGERS, R. (Ed) *Education and Social Class*, Lewes, Falmer Press,
SIMON, B. (1986) 'The battle of the blackboard', *Marxism Today*, June;
MORRIS, M. (1985) 'Has Thatcherism so far revealed itself',
Education, 166, 4, 26 July, pp. 86-7.
56 ATHA, A., and DRUMMOND, S. (1986) extracts produced from their publication *The Good Schools Guide*, Harper and Queen, Ebury Press, published in *The Times* 6 October.
57 *ibid, The Times* 8 October 1986.
58 SALTER, B. and TAPPER, T. (1985) *Power and Policy in Education: The Case of Independent Schooling*, Lewes, Falmer Press, pp. 146-50.

Chapter 12: The Schools Council

Maurice Plaskow

Maurice Plaskow started his career in teaching, then spent seven years as a BBC Education Officer. He was seconded for three years to the Schools Council/Nuffield Humanities Curriculum Project, directed by Lawrence Stenhouse. In 1970 he took up a post at the headquarters of the Schools Council, where he was a curriculum officer until 1984. During his time at the Schools Council he was associated with a wide range of projects, mainly in the arts and humanities. He also attended most of the meetings of the major policy committees. He was particularly concerned with the Secondary Curriculum Committee, and its 14-18 working groups, and was responsible for putting together its document on one-year 16-17 courses. As one of the longest serving members of staff, he had an unrivalled view of the work of the Council over most of its life. He was editor of *Life and Death of the Schools Council* (1985).

★   ★   ★

In the Beginning

During the twenty years of its eventful life, issues within the Schools Council closely reflected those in the world outside. The changes in address gave an indication of status. It started life in an elegant house in Belgravia, but was dispossessed by Jennie Lee in favour of the Open University. Thirteen years were spent in Great Portland Street, perhaps appropriately in the centre of the rag trade. Just before its demise it moved westwards to Notting Hill Gate, in the offices now inhabited by its successor body, the School Curriculum Development Committee (SCDC) and the Secondary Examinations Council (SEC).

The 1960s were years of hope and expansion. There were rising numbers of pupils, and therefore teachers, in the schools, with financial investment in plant and resources. The slogans of *democratization* and *participation* were put firmly into the educational vocabulary: no taxation without representation.

There is an irony in the fact that three successive Conservative Ministers of Education initiated and supported the Schools Council: Sir David Eccles, Sir Edward (later Lord) Boyle and Quintin Hogg (now Lord Hailsham); a fourth, Margaret Thatcher, visited and spoke of its important contribution; yet a fifth, Sir Keith Joseph, with his Prime Minister's blessing (the same Margaret Thatcher) assassinated it.

There had been a Secondary Schools Examination Council (SSEC) since 1917, charged with coordinating secondary school examinations (in particular school and higher school certificate).

In 1962 a small Curriculum Study Group (CSG) was set up by the Ministry of Education, consisting of a few outside experts, with members of HMI and some administrators. Teachers, their representatives and local education authority people were understandably suspicious of these centralist initiatives.

In 1963 Sir Edward Boyle set up the Lockwood Working Party which, in March 1964, recommended the creation of a new body 'to provide cooperative machinery in the fields of school curricula and examinations'. This followed a suggestion by Derek Morrell, the civil service secretary to the CSG, that perhaps the SSEC and the CSG should be merged into one *representative* body outside the Ministry.

The Schools Council for the Curriculum and Examinations was born, almost full grown, in October 1964, with Sir John Maud, a former permanent secretary of the Ministry of Education, as its first Chairman and Derek Morrell as one of its first joint secretaries.

The speed from conception to realization—now associated only with the MSC—derived from the commitment of men of vision and energy (there were few women in positions of power and influence at that time). The momentum and excitement of a bold adventure were maintained for the first twelve years; that is, until 1976 when the Council began to be undermined.

The new body was to have a governing council of up to sixty-six members, with a Coordinating (later Programme) Committee which would take executive decisions. Curriculum committees corresponding to pupil age groups, examinations committees, a Welsh Committee and fifteen subject committees formed the substructure.

Although the Schools Council was to be funded jointly by the Ministry of Education and the local education authorities, on a basis agreed annually, there was to be a built-in majority of teachers (in the persons of teacher representatives) on all committees. This was one of Morrell's early proposals to guarantee that neither the Ministry nor the local authorities would be able to force a particular view of curriculum innovation on the teaching profession, thus also securing the principle of school autonomy in curriculum matters.

The other bold Morrell principle, enshrined in the combination of curriculum and examinations, was that the curriculum should have precedence, and examinations should serve it. This was one of the major unfulfilled hopes, finally confirmed by the creation of the Secondary Examinations Council (SEC) in 1983, and the adoption of the GCSE whose installation it was to oversee.

There was a constitutional review in 1968, just before the Council was registered as a charity in 1969, and achieved its independence in 1970. This was to have interesting significance when Sir Keith Joseph, in 1982, announced his intention 'to disband the Schools Council'. He and his advisers had ignored the fact that the Council wasn't his to disband.

In the years before the appointment of a permanent secretary to replace the troika of three very impermanent joint secretaries, senior staff had usually been on short-term secondment, from LEA, colleges, and, in the case of field officers, schools. In the early years half the staff were seconded civil servants from the DES. The constant turnover ensured that senior committee members, whose length of service was not determined, held control and maintained the continuity in policy and practice. This was particularly true after the departure of those first joint secretaries from the DES who dared to show involvement in the Council's proceedings. After 1970 the DES joint secretaries were much lower profile, with a brief of containment and management.

With the arrival of John Mann in 1978, as the first and only Executive Secretary, more staff were appointed on a permanent basis, and the number of DES personnel dwindled. Under the chairmanship of John Tomlinson the concept of partnership was extended not just within the Council membership, but between members and staff. By 1982, following the adventurous programmes of work which had emerged following the changed constitution, the partnership had become an exciting reality.

There is no doubt that the Council was a bureaucratic institution. It operated through an arcane network of committees, many of whom felt frustrated by the length and complexity of the decision-making process. To supplicants the procedures often seemed designed to test stamina and perseverance as a measure of quality and relevance of the proposals under scrutiny.

Changing the Curriculum

In the early years, although the Council promulgated broad priorities, it acted largely as a funding agency, responding to proposals mainly from university academics who saw in the Council a promising source of support for development projects.

In 1964 the decision had been taken to raise the school leaving age in 1970 from 15 to 16. Although this was later to be postponed for two years, the Council funded a strong programme to prepare for RoSLA.

The trauma which had rocked the USA when Russia launched Sputnik

Maurice Plaskow

into space at the end of the 1950s rippled across Europe in the sixties. The implication was that our education system had been shown up as inadequate, and the thrust was especially in the fields of mathematics, science and technology. During the 1960s the Nuffield Foundation had funded major projects in science and mathematics, which the Schools Council took over and extended. Project Technology was a large and prestigious venture, enjoying the patronage of the Duke of Edinburgh, which played a part in stoking the 'white-hot heat of technology' promised by Harold Wilson in 1964.

Most curriculum projects were located in subject disciplines, and investigated ways of bringing content more up to date, and improving teaching methods. The Council's structure of subject committees reinforced this model of a knowledge-based curriculum. It was difficult to launch projects which crossed subject boundaries, and even more difficult for them to gain access to schools whose hierarchies reflected subject departmental empires. The projects on integrated studies, environmental studies, humanities, technology, moral education tended to be relegated to less academic pupils, as though an attempt to relate and make patterns of knowledge was peculiarly appropriate to the less able.

Alongside this was a concern to extend the sixth form curriculum, in the context of expanded entry to higher education, and, under the influence of some of the new post-Second World War universities, to broaden the nature and content of first degree courses away from the narrow specialism which had been the distinctive tradition of the grammar school sixth forms.

Alas, one of the Council's most significant failures was in being unable to change the stranglehold of 'A' level, and the control this exerted not just within the sixth form, but the whole of the secondary curriculum.

The 'Q' and 'F' proposals of 1969, and then the 'N' and 'F' alternative painstakingly negotiated in 1977 were both blocked, mainly by the implacable opposition of the universities who had a controlling interest, after all, in seven of the eight GCE examining boards. With government encouragement it was argued that standards would be diluted if courses were broadened, and the quality of a three-year first degree would be inevitably impaired. Even an attempt to introduce a twenty-point grading scale was rejected, by Margaret Thatcher, although there was general agreement that the existing five-point scale produced unacceptable bunching, and made the reliance on 'A' level grades as the basis for selection more of a lottery than a science.

The influence of the public examination structure, with the power base of the universities as the legitimizing authority, was always a constraining influence on curriculum change. The curriculum reforms of the 1960s were essentially rooted in the notion of schools imparting knowledge to students.

The more innovative Schools Council projects were as much about pedagogy, attitudes and relationships as about content. And this complexity was one of the most difficult messages to communicate in the 'dissemination' process. The dilemma was neatly summarized by Professor Eric Hoyle: 'Innovation requires changes in the social system of the school. Change in the

206

social system of the school is a major innovation. This is the educational Catch-22.'

In one of his early articles about the Humanities Curriculum Project (1970) Lawrence Stenhouse set down the underlying principles:

> We need to establish a new climate of relationships with adolescents which takes account of their responsibility and is not authoritarian. Education must be founded on their cooperation, not on coercion. We must find a way of expressing our common humanity with our pupils, and we must be sensitive to the need to justify the decisions of authority to those affected by them. At the same time we need gradually to develop the capacity for independent study and enquiry with the flexibility of mind which this implies.
>
> In short, we need to transform our pupils into students.

This view of students as active participants in their learning imbued many other projects: Geography for the Young School Leaver (GYSL), History 13-16, Communication and Social Skills, Moral Education were all aimed at the adolescent group. The aspiration characterizes much good primary practice.

There were other studies sponsored by the Schools Council which helped our understanding of the nature of schools and the sensitive relationships of those within them, such as that carried out by Elizabeth Richardson in Nailsea School. And of the four programmes of work which emerged from the 1978 review which produced *Principles and Practice* the first was concerned with school organization and management, and the second with helping teachers to be more effective.

Assessment

If such radical changes are to be accepted then clearly the traditional forms of examinations are no longer appropriate. Testing cannot be just of information remembered over a period of two hours, but of general and specific abilities, skills and attitudes. A single system of examining at 16 + which would combine 'O' level and CSE was proposed by the Council in 1976. It took ten years for this to emerge as the General Certificate of Secondary Education (GCSE). The changes are deemed to be so radical that systematic inservice retraining for teachers on a 'cascade' model has had to be mounted.

In the first place the examination is attempting to shift from norm to criterion referencing. 'O' level was a not so Grand National to sort out the jumpers from the fallers. And to give a more reasonable and reasoned assessment of a student's performance and capacities far more of the judgment will be based on course work, assessed by teachers. The hope is that the system will provide a better diagnosis for the students of strengths and weaknesses, and a fuller and more useful account to users of what students know and can do.

There is of course an argument as to whether a formal examination procedure is needed at all: most other developed countries manage without one at school leaving age. Teachers appraise and assess all the time. Employers have been protesting even from the latter days of the Schools Council that they are more interested in a student's qualities and potential than in academic qualifications. It is interesting that industrial vocabulary has been entering the school, sharpened by interventions from the MSC like the Technical and Vocational Education Initiative (TVEI).

Schools now talk of a 'negotiated' curriculum, and even with drawing up 'contracts' which are regularly renewed and are appraised in the form of a profile, or record of achievement (ROA).

In this, too, Schools Council Programme 1 had been ahead, in developing Guidelines for Review and Institutional Development in Schools (GRIDS). The underlying principles were that: (i) the focus should be upon ways in which staff, with appropriate outside help, can collaborate in the process of reviewing and developing school policy and practice; and that (ii) staff of the school should be consulted and involved in the process as much as possible.

Programme 2, concerned with *Helping Teachers Become More Effective*, sponsored work on profiling, and indeed the Council coordinated a range of initiatives on this and records of achievement.

The style was collegial and cooperative, and the intention would be to extend these values to students. It is sadly at odds with a fiercely competitive society, intent on rewarding ruthless individualism.

Decline and Fall

In 1972 Margaret Thatcher, then Secretary of State at the DES, published *Education: A Framework for Expansion*, whose title summed up the continuing buoyant mood generated in the 1960s. It was to herald a great increase in nursery education, and a systematic programme of in-service opportunities for teachers, introducing INSET into our vocabulary.

Alas; 1974 deflated every balloon in sight, as the oil crisis created a new international currency of liquid gold and microchips. As with the technological shock of Sputnik, the economic trauma saw in education a kickable scapegoat. The schools must have been failing the nation, and had not delivered a curriculum relevant to the new post-industrial age.

In 1976, at Ruskin College, Oxford, the Prime Minister, James Callaghan, made a speech in which he strongly criticized the education system for not encouraging and preparing students to enter 'wealth-producing industry'. A 'Great Debate' was launched by Secretary of State Shirley Williams on a bewildered public who were scarcely more enlightened when it was over, but whose repercussions have been reverberating ever since. Debate, certainly;

educational, in part; great, it was not! The DES officials who had presumably briefed the Prime Minister were responsible for a document which was leaked at the same time, which became known as the *Yellow Book*, which contained damaging criticisms of the Schools Council, whose work was dismissed as being largely 'mediocre'. This from a partner in the enterprise; people who had a central role in the organization, were responsible for half the funding, and were members of all the policy committees which took funding decisions. The Council's policy committees had accepted in any case that there was a need to review the constitution and policy structure. There was agreement that the constituency should be widened, and procedures refined. After twelve years it was also felt that the early caution which had created an unwieldy, protective bureaucracy could with advantage be streamlined.

The results of the 1977 constitutional review were presented to the governing council by Sir Alex Smith in January 1978. The committee structure was to be altered, with Convocation to replace the governing council, a smaller Finance and Priorities Committee to represent the three partners—DES, LEA and teachers—to oversee policy, and a Professional Committee to supervise the educational decision-making. And only the latter would retain a teacher majority.

Convocation was Sir Alex Smith's vision of an education parliament, bringing together all those with a proper concern for education, including parents, CBI, TUC, the churches, ethnic groups and representatives from the larger community. It was an imaginative concept, and Sir Alex Smith would challenge other sectors of society by asking where else such a democratic forum existed, which brought together producers, consumers, politicians and administrators. The senior DES official, Deputy Secretary John Hudson, welcomed the proposals: 'The DES will support the proposals as they stand', he assured the Council.

I remember an exasperated comment after one of the early meetings of Convocation by another Deputy Secretary, Walter Ulrich: 'Of course, it doesn't work, does it?' I asked how he would recognize it if it did. The DES seems to find it difficult to live with democratic structures; they tend to be untidy and difficult to manage. They generate diverse, sometimes unorthodox and conflicting ideas, and are prone to take risks. They display feelings and admit to commitment—characteristics which are sedulously bred out of civil servants, as I was reminded on more than one occasion by a DES Joint Secretary.

An important administrative change was the appointment of a permanent secretary to the Council, John Mann. John Tomlinson succeeded Sir Alex Smith as Chairman. The Council developed a new stance towards its work, constructed at a residential conference, which emerged as 'Principles and Programmes'. This set out four programmes of work through which activity in future would be organized. In contemporary jargon the Council moved from being reactive, to being proactive. It had determined its priorities, in terms of helping schools to be more self-aware and efficient, helping teachers to be more effective, looking at special needs, and concentrating on those curriculum areas of high priority. Teacher groups, as well as R & D bodies were invited to work with the Council on identified tasks, which were to be more closely monitored and evaluated than in the past. There was a new impetus and sense of purpose in both staff and members, which produced greatly enhanced working relationships, within the monitoring groups for each programme, who met informally and regularly to keep their programme under close review.

With the return of the Conservative government in 1979 all previous bets were cancelled. A massive quango hunt was set in motion in the name of cost-efficiency, which provided a trap with which the Council was ensnared. Arising from *Principles and Programmes* the Council had set up a working party to look at the whole curriculum with a view to providing practical guidance for teachers, a planning instrument for building a curriculum. It was to be called the *Practical Curriculum*, and it was to present the curriculum as an activity, which considered each pupil's right of access to different areas of human knowledge and experience. 'The heart of the matter is what each child takes away from school...that is the effective curriculum.'

It was ready for publication early in 1981. The DES, having received a very unfavourable reaction to its document *Framework for the Curriculum* (1980) had been revising it with a view to republication. John Tomlinson was asked to delay publication of the *Practical Curriculum* so that the DES *School Curriculum* could appear first. They were both published in April 1981, with coincident-ally similarly-coloured covers. That was the only similarity between them.

In March 1981 Mrs Nancy Trenaman, Principal of St. Anne's College, Oxford, was invited to conduct a review of the Schools Council as part of the 'quango' investigation. In three months Mrs Trenaman moved from impartial ignorance to a strong defence of the Council, suggesting that it should 'continue, with its present functions.' Indeed, with a Voltairean flourish, she added that if it did not exist, it would need to be invented.

That was not the message which ministers or civil servants expected or wished to hear. There were six months of silence, then in April 1982 Sir Keith Joseph, who had succeeded Mark Carlisle as Secretary of State for Education, announced in the House of Commons his intention of 'disbanding the Schools Council' and replacing it with two bodies, one for examinations and the other for curriculum development.

No argument was produced, no reasons why the recommendations of the Trenaman Report were to be ignored. Nor did the Secretary of State seem to realize at that time that the Council was an independent charity which could only disband itself. The most he could do was withdraw funding. After some agonizing, the LEAs decided that it would not be possible for them to go it alone and provide all the funding for a totally independent Council, and they capitulated.

No reasons have ever been given as to the sequence which resulted in the decisions. The closure of the Council took two years—until March 1984. The whole time was punctuated by extended and convoluted discussions with the DES in which it was clear that rules were being invented as we went along, and changed regularly as they proved to be untenable. It was an unhappy and stressful time for staff, who were trying to complete valuable work while also attempting to protect their interests, look for other jobs, wonder whether they were to become redundant or might be employed in the new bodies, and if so, on what basis. The only people who prospered were lawyers.

The glaring paradox was that an exercise mounted in the name of cost efficiency wasted large sums of public money, had to pay considerable amounts of redundancy, mismanaged a move, and set up, still in the name of economy, two bodies which, although sharing premises and common services, were constituted on a quite different basis which inevitably must widen the gulf between curriculum and examinations.

It is tempting to speculate on why officials acted as they did, without making it read too closely like a script for *Yes, Minister!* There is an embarrassing gap between the rhetoric of 'power to the people' and 'democratic pluralism' and the reality of a need for governments to seek consensus so that they can claim support for ideologically-based decisions.

All governments seem to be responding to an increasingly complex and occasionally intransigent society by taking greater powers to the centre, while keeping the periphery busy with trivial pursuits.

Expanding school governing bodies, a three-tier health service, the threat of further reorganization of local government, all take more potential trouble-makers off the streets and into committee rooms. None of this *necessarily* leads to more effective decision-making or more sensible control procedures.

In 1978 the Schools Council really thought that it was in a position to control its destiny with confidence, and provide an arena for working out a rational, coherent practical future for the school system. It is not fanciful, I believe, to claim that teachers, their representatives, industry and the wider community were prepared to collaborate within the Council to provide a democratic leadership which had never previously existed in this form within education.

It has always been frustrating to the DES to accept the autonomy of local education authorities for the delivery of education and for handling resources. It was intolerable that control of the curriculum might be handed over *de facto* to an external, unaccountable body, particularly one dominated by teachers.

Shortly after his appointment as Permanent Secretary at the DES in 1977 Sir James Hamilton visited the Council. He made it clear that he found 'teacher control' (which he equated with NUT control) of the Council unacceptable, and he was resolved to 'cut the teachers down to size'.

He made no secret of his centralist views, to which he returned in a speech shortly after his retirement in 1984. 'In a country that has no tradition of national initiatives or curriculum policy, I am wholly prepared to use reforms of the exam system to bring about much needed changes in national attitudes towards curriculum'. Hence SEC and SCDC.

I was reminded of a comment of an exam board secretary many years earlier at a Council meeting, suggesting that if the money were given to the exam boards they would achieve curriculum change much faster than Schools Council through curriculum projects. And it has come to pass: GCSE rules, O.K.!

If civil servants could not be expected to master the complexities of curriculum matters, not least because they were moved about so frequently, then the position of HMI was more problematic and ambiguous. It was significant that HMI participated in all Schools Council committees and working parties, but this was never reciprocal.

I remember a meeting with Sheila Brown, Senior Chief Inspector, shortly after John Mann was appointed, when these matters were discussed. SCI agreed that she would suggest to her chief inspectors that there should be more liaison and interchange of information. It didn't happen. In fourteen years at the Council I was never invited to attend an HMI panel meeting, although I was involved in a number of HMI courses and other events as a result of personal contacts and friendships.

Curriculum development, like any R & D activity, is high risk and vulnerable. Governments prefer to avoid risk and limit vulnerability. Development projects admitted to learning from mistakes, and openly acknowledged to teachers the difficulties and demands of new ventures. Politics is the art of never having to say sorry!

Paradise Postponed

The Schools Council was replaced in 1984 by two bodies, the Secondary Examinations Council (SEC) and the School Development Curriculum Committee (SCDC). The differences in functions, importance and composition are immediately indicated in their titles, and reinforced by the fact that the SEC has powers over the examination system, whereas the SCDC is a puny, advisory body, enjoined to fill gaps and disseminate good practice: a kind of curriculum dentistry or pointing of the school brickwork.

The NUT refused to participate in both SEC and SCDC on the grounds that they are government appointed non-representative bodies. The LEAs, however, secured official representation on the SCDC.

The Schools Council's regularly repeated dictum was that 'examinations should serve the curriculum'. The reality, certainly in secondary education, was always the reverse, and this has now been institutionalized through the greater power and prestige given to the SEC.

The SEC has a major role in supervising the introduction of the GCSE. It has, through its advisory panels, set out general criteria, and scrutinized the subject-specific criteria and syllabi put forward by the GCSE consortia. The Schools Council never had this power in relation to GCE 'O' level, and it was not as strongly implemented with CSE. The close relationship with 'A' level has, one understands, been if anything intensified.

What is needed is some linkage in the examination structure to secure some coherence for 14-19 year-olds. With TVEI going national there is pressure for related accreditation; CPVE is a separate one-year course; there are other BTEC and CGLI courses available both in schools and FE; the proposed 'AS' will sit uneasily alongside 'A' level. It is not surprising that students, parents and even teachers are confused. The Schools Council, shortly before it closed, had produced in collaboration with the FEU an 'articulated map' of 16-19 courses, and a pamphlet on the development of one-year 16-17 programmes. There is now no representative mechanism for bringing together the disparate and often competing interests to help make some sense of what is available.

SCDC has funded curriculum development projects in maths, English (writing) and even the arts. It has set up a network of educational development centres in an attempt to create a resilient webbing to bounce the fall-out across the system. There is an oversubscribed small grant system to schools wishing to undertake interesting pieces of new work, and a growing databank which schools can tap into of interesting practice. But with inadequate funding and a fragile structure it is not possible to build a strong edifice which will provide systematic and independent guidance and support, as well as a forum for discussion and policy exhilaration.

At the time of the 1978 review the suggestion was made that what was needed was an Education Council which would bring together schools and further education in order to construct a coherent, linked system with interconnecting pathways right up to at least 19. One hopes that the twenty years of the Schools Council were not wasted. If it did little else, it contributed to raising the level of curriculum discourse. Teachers have a far greater awareness of the subtle and complex issues, and admit a recognition of the need for a prospectus which will engage the young, give them a sense of satisfaction and worthwhileness, with confidence to survive in an uncertain future.

For we must not lose sight of the fact that the whole educational enterprise is on behalf of the young, with the central aim eloquently set out in the Warnock Report (DES 1978):

> First to enlarge a child's knowledge, experience and imaginative understanding, and thus his (or her) awareness of moral values and capacity for enjoyment; and secondly, to enable him (or her) to enter the world after school after formal education is over as an active participant in society and a responsible contributor to it, capable of achieving as much independence as possible.

There's an agenda for the next millenium.

Maurice Plaskow

References

SCHOOLS COUNCIL (1981) *The Practical Curriculum*, London, Methuen.
STENHOUSE, L. A. (1970) 'Pupils into students', *Dialogue*, no. 5, Schools Council.
DEPARTMENT OF EDUCATION AND SCIENCE (1978) *Special Educational Needs* (The Warnock Report), London, HMSO.
PLASKOW, M. (1985) *Life and Death of the Schools Council*, Lewes, Falmer Press.

Chapter 13: The MSC: A Failure of Democracy

George Low

George Low is Editor of the weekly journal *Education*. Before joining Education as Deputy Editor fourteen years ago he was Senior Editor in the Faculty of Educational Studies at the Open University. He was a founder member of the Association of Recurrent Education and the Association's Chairman in 1982 – 83.

$\star$ $\star$ $\star$

The Manpower Services Commission (MSC) came into being on 1 January 1974 a few months after the oil crisis began to bite. The two events were not initially connected but rapidly became intertwined in their consequences.

One of the first consequences was the 10 per cent cutback in procurement expenditure in education. This was followed by a change of government but not of policy. Spending guidelines were issued by the new Labour government's Secretary of State for Education and Science, Reg Prentice, to maintain the core of the service—the statutory age range of 5 to the new school leaving age of 16. The youth service, further education and adult education were left to fend for themselves.

Ironically these were the very services which were needed to cope with the rapidly rising tide of unemployment, especially among the school leavers and young adults. Yet such was the instinctive reaction of the civil servants at the Department of Education and Science to the question of priorities that they cut back in the one area which left a yawning gap in which the MSC could grow—like a large fungus—between the sectors of the education system.

According to Bill Shelton, one of the most agreeable and often perceptive junior ministers at the DES, Mrs Margaret Thatcher put up quite a fight for the MSC to be located in her own department. That was one of the few battles she lost as Secretary of State or since. The MSC was (initially at least) about training and the Heath government decided that the logical place for it was in the bosom of the Department of Employment, though the DE did not then realize what a cuckoo it was harbouring. The first Chairman was Sir Denis Barnes, a civil servant who had made his name in the youth employment service.

The Employment and Training Act of 1973 was one of those broadly reformist measures, supported by MPs on both sides of the House, aimed at reducing shortages of skilled manpower and improving training. It was only incidentally concerned with the problems of the unemployed. Indeed, during the second reading the Labour shadow employment spokesman, Reg Prentice, berated the Minister Maurice Macmillan for 'making no mention of the fact that we still have 750,000 unemployed'. How could the House have an intelligent discussion on the Bill without asking whether it had anything useful to bring to bear in the fight against 'this appalling total'? he asked.

The MSC did indeed soon bring measures to bear on the increasingly alarming total. But one aspect of the Bill which the House of Commons never mentioned, let alone intelligently discussed, was the fact that the legislation was giving the Secretary of State for Employment powers of direct intervention in the education system of a kind that had never been enjoyed by the Secretary of State for Education.

And so it came to pass that the MSC waxed mightily in the house of Michael Foot, the Labour Minister for Employment. The trade unions felt at home there in a way they never had in the halls of the education service. It was the era of tripartitism—with the TUC, the CBI and the government running the country through such agencies as the National Economic Development Council (NEDC). The MSC was the servant of tripartitism and the most pressing problem to be solved was that of youth employment.

In July 1974 when the general level of unemployment was 2.5 per cent, those aged under 20 formed about 5 per cent of the total. Three years later, when the national percentage had increased to 5.5 per cent, those aged under 20 accounted for almost 30 per cent. That was the scale of the emergency and it was one which the MSC, with its go-getting style of management by objectives, was well placed to tackle.

Sir Richard O'Brien, who took over from Sir Denis as Chairman of the MSC, had been a staff officer under Montgomery in the eighth army. He had only to stand up before a Select Committee and assure the MPs 'We have got this problem in our gunsights' and they would entirely believe that the MSC would knock unemployment for six just as Monty had the Germans at El Alamein.

O'Brien was fortunate to have on his own staff a former tank commander Geoffrey Holland, who had the ability to deliver on the promises his Chairman made. Holland lacked the high mandarin style of the DES officials, he was a man of tongues who drank with the union bosses and hobnobbed with the CBI, fed the media with fine words while being fed by them at West End restaurants. He brought a new style to the civil service. He treated the education world with tact and charm and was soon able to win their cooperation. His earnest protestations about the young unemployed made him a favourite in Labour local government circles, where he was a frequent speaker.

One of the countries which the MSC officials visited soon after the Commission's establishment was Canada. Here they were attracted to the Local Initiative (LIP) and Youth Opportunity (YOP) programmes devised by the central government in Ottawa. These programmes aimed to deliver money over the heads of the provincial governments into local communities hit by seasonal or long-term unemployment. As one Ottawa official told them: 'The problem is to get the oats to the sparrows without going through the horse'.

The Ottawa solution was to put up some money, lay down some criteria and then ask for bids. Anybody was allowed to bid for the cash—youth groups, community associations, Red Indian tribes and even monks in enclosed orders—which was then parachuted in without interference from the provincial bureaucracies and their political patronage networks.

The Canadian experience really spoke unto the MSC condition. 'Payment by bid' was surely the way to bypass the tiresome local authorities with their bumbling bureaucracies. In October 1975 Sir Denis launched his own first Canadian-style experiment—the Job Creation Programme. It aimed to create 15,000 jobs within eighteen months, mainly for the young unemployed and a sum of £30m was put on offer for bids. 'Anybody who comes up with a bid within the criteria will get the money'; Sir Denis Barnes promised as he set up regional boards with academics, employers and trade unionists to vet the bids.

Within its first six weeks the Job Creation Programme had had so many applications that the Director was able to announce that the 15,000 jobs would be created within six, rather than eighteen, months and that the programme budget would be trebled to meet the demand. Significantly, the successful bidders included local authorities as well as voluntary agencies. Many educational institutions jumped onto the bandwagon.

The MSC's 'payment by bid' methods, borrowed from Canada, had paid off handsomely. It had showed that it could dent the numbers of young unemployed and offer an alternative to work and to unemployment for the age group. It took some time for stories of gangs of youngsters picking up driftwood on northern beaches to tarnish the image of the programme. And in the House of Commons they were marvelling at the speed at which the MSC could operate—'like a runaway train', as Bryan Davies, the MP for Enfield, put it.

But what meanwhile was happening in the world of education? In 1974 the Organization for Economic Cooperation and Development (OECD) carried out a study of national decision taking in the United Kingdom and criticized the DES for its passivity, inertia and obsessive secrecy. In the following year the House of Commons undertook an enquiry through its Select Committee on Education and largely substantiated the charges: the DES did too little planning, undertook too little research and conducted its affairs behind closed doors with a minimum of public engagement.

At the local authority level, the two LEA associations were engaged in a bitter battle with the Association of Education Committees (AEC) which was by 1976 in its death throes. In its place a largely paper body had been set up known rather grandly as the Council of Local Education Authorities (CLEA). But the new Council had very little executive power apart from the parent associations and its constitution and terms of reference were vague.

Down at education committee level chief education officers were already caught up in the toils of corporate management. Policy and personnel committees flexed their muscles at education's expense. In many LEAs there was a deliberate attempt by both Conservative and Labour politicians to 'cut education down to size'.

The teacher unions were still badly divided. Although the Houghton Report had brought a period of stability and calm, there was a growing battle looming over the teachers' contract, midday supervision and duties and responsibilities. There was still a simmering resentment and unease over the raising of the school leaving age in 1973.

Above all there was still a running battle between LEAs and central government over comprehensive reorganization and some LEAs such as Tameside and Calderdale swung to and fro like a windscreen wiper. As Lord Alexander often pointed out, rational planning at both national and local level had become exceedingly difficult, if not impossible.

Above all, the mechanism of rate support grant made it very hard for a Secretary of State to ensure that the oats got to the sparrows and did not disappear into the horse. Mrs Shirley Williams made the LEA associations promise that they would spend an extra £7m on in-service training which she had succeeded in winning from the Treasury, but at the end of the day only £4m of this could be accounted for.

At national level a new group of party politicians, from both the right and the left, had gained control of the Association of Metropolitan Authorities (AMA) and the Association of County Councils (ACC). In the case of the Conservatives they took their orders from Central Office, which even controlled the election of their leaders. On the Labour side, the arrival of Tom Caulcott as the Secretary of the AMA ensured that education was kept well and truly in its place. He had been the architect of the modern RSG and a long-time foe of Lord Alexander and the AEC. He arrived just in time to put the AEC to death with no quarter.

A subtle and ingenious man, Caulcott watched the growing might of the MSC with increasing envy and alarm. When the Conservatives took brief control of the AMA in 1979 Caulcott tried to play on the government's hatred of quangos by putting up a scheme for abolishing the MSC and distributing its functions to the LEAs. But the Thatcher administration hated local government more than quangos and the recent history of the education service at national and local level was far from presenting a reassuring alternative.

Although Mrs Thatcher had only ever had one ministry and that was the

DES, she owed it no loyalty. It was, she was heard to declare in her early days as Prime Minister, a 'disaster area'. She longed to do some of the things she had failed to do from 1970 to 1974 at education, like starting the assisted places scheme and reopening the direct grant list. Her advisers in the Centre for Policy Studies (among them David Young and Sir Keith Joseph) urged her to make the education system more responsive to industry's needs and susceptible to market forces. The chosen instrument for the former was the MSC, the preferred means of achieving the latter was parental choice and, if possible, the voucher.

Up until 1982 the MSC were scrupulous in not interfering in education. They saw training as essentially happening outside educational institutions and beyond the school leaving age. There was plenty of collaboration with education in drawing up the blueprint for the Youth Opportunities Programme (the Holland Report) and working together on the Special Programmes Board.

The Labour Party leaders of the AMA thought so highly of the MSC that they collaborated with it to produce a code of good practice for the YOP scheme. As their education officer Bob Morris put it, the LEAs' best interest lay in making themselves invaluable at local level and encouraging the MSC to make use of their expertise and keep their colleges filled. Even when the government's *New Training Initiative* White Paper appeared in December 1981, the AMA saw no undue threat. The MSC's stake, though growing with the YTS, was still marginal, Mr Morris wrote, and anyway the FE colleges would do better by collaborating than taking a stand-offish attitude.

Tessa Blackstone, another Fabian guru who studied the YOP on a Nuffield and MSC grant, also had high praise for the YOP, which she felt would teach the FE system to be more flexible and client-centred. She particularly admired the schemes run by the voluntary bodies, which could respond quickly and effectively to the needs of the disadvantaged. Her view was shared by Sir Peter Newsam of the Commission for Racial Equality (CRE), who told the North of England conference in Rotherham in January 1987 that the MSC were in many ways better than the LEAs in providing equal opportunities for ethnic minorities because they wrote it into their programme specifications and made sure that managing agents adhered to them.

The Rev. Canon Dr George Tolley was an early convert to the MSC and was soon headhunted for the Open Tech. project. He upbraided educationalists in 1981 for not taking advantage of the money and facilities offered by the MSC. Teachers and principals need have no fear of the MSC, they were there to help teachers with money to do what they wanted to do and were not out to control the system.

The YOP scheme was not short of critics, however, and they came from both Right and Left. Even the Employment Secretary, James Prior, and his junior Minister, the Earl of Gowrie, were known to be sceptical about the quality of 'Yoppery' and tried to set about improving the educational and training element in the two-year YTS. It was true that the off-the-job training element was weak and the low take-up by youngsters was laid at the door of the FE colleges by MSC Director Geoffrey Holland.

But, as had so often been the case with the MSC, the YTS was under way before the chickens of the YOP had come home to roost. One of these roosters was the low proportion of young people who were in work six months after leaving a YOP scheme. This was to leave a large pool of young adults unemployed which the adult training strategy, the least successful of the MSC programme areas, did not properly cater for.

Nevertheless, at the end of the five-year life of the YOP, Geoffrey Holland could claim with impunity: 'It was not just an alternative to employment, it was an educational and training innovation of the greatest possible signif-cance, economically and socially'. He then went on to announce the YTS as a 'permanent bridge between school and work'. But a few months before these brave words, something else occurred which irrevocably destroyed the cosy relationship between the MSC and the educational world. 'Now that Keith Joseph is at the DES and David Young is at the MSC I think you will soon find the Vandals stabling their horses in the temples', Employment Secretary Norman Tebbit told the education correspondent of the *Financial Times* one day in October 1982.

The Vandals arrived at 10.30 a.m. on Friday 12 November 1982, when the Prime Minister Mrs Margaret Thatcher announced a pilot scheme for establishing technical schools in ten areas of England and Wales for the 14-18-year-old age group. The news burst on an unsuspecting educational establishment like a thunderbolt. Nobody except the topmost officials in the DES and Department of Employment had had any inkling of what was afoot. The Director of the MSC, Geoffrey Holland, even claimed that he was first told about this invasion of sovereign educational territory at 4 p.m. on the Thursday afternoon (though not everybody believed this).

The local authority leaders, the teacher unions and the Inspectorate (whose leaders were bitterly hostile to the encroachment) were caught off balance. 'It was intended to be a *coup de foudre*', Walter Ulrich, the DES Deputy Secretary and probably the official closest to Sir Keith Joseph in his thinking, recalled later. To some local authority leaders like Alistair Lawton, Philip Merridale and Nicky Harrison it seemed like the educational equivalent of Pearl Harbour.

The ground had been quite well prepared at a political level between Young, Joseph and Mrs Thatcher. They had, for example, got the Depart-ment of Employment lawyers to check that the Employment and Training Act enabled the MSC to provide education for school age children. They were reassured to learn that there was no age limit to the training which the MSC could engage in and any 'education with a view to employment' could be subsumed under the broad term 'training'.

A few days later Young called in members of the educational press one by one for a drink and a chat and let drop a veiled threat that the local authorities had better play ball or else he would set up his own technical high schools in redundant premises and inner city warehouses. There was no problem about building regulations, teacher qualifications, or recognition which could not be got round, he purred.

Asked to explain the extraordinary intervention, Lord Young said it was a Prime Ministerial initiative. She had been dissatisfied with the progress report from the DES to the National Economic Development Council on education and training four days before. One of the participants at the fateful meeting recalls the strange events.

> The theme was education's contribution to economic regeneration and the DES had put up an incredibly feeble paper. Joseph wasn't there himself and one of the senior officials was wittering on. Suddenly the meeting turned into an education-bashing session. Norman Tebbit and Patrick Jenkin were leading the pack, but not far behind them was Len Murray of the TUC.
>
> 'The education system needs a short, sharp shock', said Tebbit. 'No, it needs a bloody great pneumatic drill', rejoined Murray. And so Young, Tebbit and Jenkin persuaded the Prime Minister and Sir Keith Joseph to administer the short sharp shock. And who better to administer the pneumatic drill than the MSC?

'You know as well as I do if we had gone through the usual educational machinery it would have been the end of the decade before anything happened', Lord Young said later. He had a point. It was easier for Young to slice off a tiny £7m fragment (increased to £40m the following year) from the unspent YOP budget than it would have been for Sir Keith Joseph to deliver through the RSG mechanism.

Sir Keith claimed that the ends justified the means. David Young had spotted, Sir Keith claimed, a definite and glaring weakness in the education system—in technical education—and wanted to put it right as quickly as possible. A former close associate of Sir Keith in the Centre for Policy Studies (which he had helped to finance and found) Young had followed Sir Keith to the Department of Trade and Industry and then to the DES as his political adviser. But the servant was becoming greater than his master and Young was nursing political ambitions of his own. These came to fruition when he became Chairman of the MSC in succession to the hapless Richard O'Brien, who made a critical speech on industry's commitment to training which Tebbit happened to hear about.

Where did Young get his educational ideas? He knew very little about further and higher education and not much about the training system. It is said that during all his time at the MSC he never once set foot inside an FE college. But as the Chairman of both British and World ORT (the Jewish training organization) he knew a lot about ORT schools in France, Israel, North Africa and the United States. He was an admirer of their vocational curriculum and the high job placement rate of the ORT schools. So was Sir Keith, who had just opened a special ORT unit at the Hasmonean Boys School, which was named after him (it is still probably the only school to have been called after the last Secretary of State).

Unbeknown to officials at the DES, the ORT organization had carried out several briefings of leading Conservative Ministers during the summer and autumn of 1982—among them Tebbit, Joseph, Jenkin and his Minister of State Kenneth Baker (the meetings are recorded in the international ORT magazine, Volume 3 No. 1, January 1983). Their object was to introduce a technical-vocational stream into the 14-18 curriculum with particular emphasis on computer technology. The DES remained blissfully unaware of all this. In fact, they often did not know what Sir Keith was talking about. Once when Sir Keith asked 'Have you asked what ORT think about this?' one DES official replied: 'I'm afraid ORT's abroad, Minister'.

With a ruthless mixture of bribes and threats, Young made mincemeat of the local authority associations. Their resistance crumbled within weeks. Even the stern warnings from Labour spokesmen Neil Kinnock and Phillip Whitehead failed to deter many Labour local education authorities from bidding for cash. The lure of the extra money was too great, prompting John Brace of the Welsh Joint Education Committee (WJEC) to observe that the MSC's initials should really stand for the 'Mad Scramble for Cash'. Altogether sixty-six LEAs put up bids for the money and fourteen were chosen for the first pilots while the rest were put on hold for the following year.

'Act first, consult afterwards' was Young's avowed motto which he compared unfavourably with the education service's traditional procedure of endless consultations. He set up a steering committee at national level and appointed a very able (and diplomatically very skillful) Director for the national TVEI unit. John Woolhouse's first aim was to win the cooperation of the educationists and this he succeeded in doing. One method was to hire up prominent and able figures from the education world—among them Jack Chambers, a past President of the NUT, Michael Harrison, CEO of Sheffield and a leading figure in school technology, and Richard Knight, Director of Education, Bradford (one of the first pilot areas for the TVEI). Knight was later to become one of Young's main advisers at the Downing Street Enterprise Unit and was one of the main architects of the TVEI in-service programme, which gave the MSC a powerful foothold in in-service teacher training.

Rationalizing their capitulation afterwards, the LEA leaders claimed their opposition, though brief, had forced the MSC to give them a large say in how the scheme was run, while their willingness to take part had headed off Young from setting up his own technology schools. There was an element of truth in this claim, though the technology colleges were to resurface again in a new guise four years later. The national steering group managed to set up national TVEI criteria which were benign towards a comprehensive system and did not force early specialization or narrow vocational training on the schools.

The teacher unions were badly divided over the new initiative. They saw the MSC's appearance as a Trojan horse. On the other hand it brought badly needed money and jobs to many schools in a time of severe cuts. It also gave a welcome opportunity for creative curriculum development. In July 1985—in the middle of the teachers' pay campaign—the NUT actually sent out instructions to their branch secretaries telling them not to disrupt the TVEI programme. NUT General Secretary Fred Jarvis (a member of the national TVEI Steering Group) justified the decision by claiming that the TVEI was an exemplary case of curriculum development being properly funded and teachers being given extra money through scale posts and promotion and smaller class sizes and teaching groups.

So it was that Young's foray into the education system paid off. The next sector to find the vandals in the stables was adult education. In April 1983 the MSC made a bid to become the national coordinating body to run the proposed 'adult training strategy'. The aims of this initiative were not just to offer labour market advice and provide some training and retraining courses, but to act as a broker to the world of industry and commerce for continuing education and training courses. The MSC was to have a leadership role in the whole field of vocational education and training. 'We wish to work with and through others, and to act as a catalyst to secure necessary changes at both national and local levels', the discussion paper said.

There were many adult educationists who welcomed the tenor of the document, partly because the DES had neglected and mistreated adult education over the past few years. Most of the recommendations of the Advisory Council for Adult and Continuing Education (ACACE) had been ignored and Sir Keith Joseph had made it clear he was not going to set up a national development body or spend any more money. So far as he was concerned, adult education was ripe for do-it-yourself and privatization—until he suddenly had a last-minute conversion in 1985, but by then it was too late for him and for adult education.

The local authority associations demanded to know more about their own responsibilities before they agreed to join in as partners—they had already been bounced into the TVEI and were still feeling sore and suspicious. The DES too disputed the MSC's leadership role and demanded an equal partnership. The DES was already responsible for £750m spending in adult and continuing education and did not need the MSC to tell it what to do, it retorted.

Fortunately the relevant branch at the DES at the time was commanded by a civil servant of unusual vigour and energy, whose brisk and business-like style of management had already earned respect in the continuing education field. He had carried out a full-scale review of the adult and continuing education field and had developed a far-sighted and coherent view of its future (even if it was in some ways rather idiosyncratic). By pushing ahead with the PICKUP programme of short courses and updating material and launching the REPLAN programme for the unemployed, Noel Thompson was able to steal a march on the MSC and was well placed to hold his own from a position of strength.

Even at the outset it was apparent that the MSC could not provide the market intelligence on which the adult training strategy was supposed to be based. The MSC's own Director of Manpower Planning and Intelligence, Graham Reid, admitted to a conference of educationists: 'It's the blind leading the blind, I'm afraid'.

The MSC also received a sharp rebuff from the employers at the CBI who did not like some of the aspersions being cast by the MSC consultative paper on their own training and retraining efforts. In September 1983 MSC Director Geoffrey Holland wrote: 'We must not aspire to usurp the role of others for continuing and adult education. Overarching ambition will offend the Commission's friends and partners and not aid the more collaborative approach we must seek'.

The MSC was nevertheless given the lead role in the adult training strategy as the officially designated 'national training authority'. But despite Holland's uplifting rhetoric the adult training strategy has probably been the MSC's least successful programme. Too diffuse and ill-targeted, it also suffered from changes in funding criteria from the European Social Fund in Brussels. The MSC was created at least partly in order to act as a conduit for Euro-money for unemployment programmes. Quite how much of the £2 billion budget is being laundered for Brussels is a closely guarded secret. The figures officially released in parliamentary questions have been so fanciful as to be quite unbelievable. This means that if the European Parliament or the Council of Ministers decide to cut back on Social Fund money and alter the criteria the Commission is bound to reflect this.

The MSC has now been found wanting in its most crucial role—that of market intelligence. The MSC has moved with such rapidity from one programme to the next, from one three-letter initiative to another that the full weakness of its research and information base was not fully realized until February 1987. However, the National Audit Office has now revealed that the MSC has no idea of the skill base of the adult population and only a rough hunch about the extent to which the training courses it is funding are actually meeting individual or industry's needs.

The almost child-like ignorance of the MSC was nowhere better demonstrated than in its adult literacy programme. In November 1986 MSC Chairman Bryan Nicholson made a major speech complaining about the 'thousands and thousands' of youngsters who were leaving the schools and entering the Youth Training Scheme without the ability to read or write. He therefore announced a joint venture with the Dyslexia Institute to provide training modules in every approved training centre so that YTS entrants would be screened and given basic literacy training if needed.

But when Nicholson was asked how many 'thousands' he was talking about, he had not the faintest idea. Nor did he have the remotest idea what sort of literacy criterion should be applied. He seemed totally unaware that the adult literacy service had tackled the problem with increasing success over twelve years and had built up a considerable research base. Indeed many LEA literacy organizers have been collaborating with MSC regional offices for some years.

A similar lack of research has now been found to underlie the Job Training Scheme for adults aged 18-24. According to the National Audit Office, the MSC has almost no knowledge of what skills this age group has or what they need or what industry needs. This was a criticism of the Training Opportunities Scheme (TOPS), where the rate of job placement was found to be low. But it now appears that the MSC having scrapped TOPS is about to make the same mistake again.

It is little wonder then that the MSC is said to be undertaking an urgent review of literacy in the 18-24 age group. But it is typical of the MSC that it does the research after it has announced the programme. As Geoffrey Holland once said: 'We learn as we go along'.

This piece of instant 'research', based on the evidence of RESTART interviews with the long-term unemployed and the long-standing evidence of the Adult Literacy and Basic Skills Unit (ALBSU), is known to have 'discovered' that 20 per cent of the long-term unemployed in the 18-24-year-old bracket have literacy and numeracy problems.

This evidence has been seized on by Lord Young as proof of the 'deficit' theory of unemployment—that if adults are unemployed there must be something wrong with them or the school system. It is thus a useful statistic which can be used to justify a further incursion by the MSC into the school system and a switch of funds from adult training to the 'young adults' aged under 25.

Unfortunately, the figures prove that the YOP and YTS schemes have had very little effect in helping those with reading and writing problems. The switch of funds from mid-career adult training to remedial help for the young unemployed is also already having a severe and damaging effect on the nation's retraining and updating programme. In the tension between the MSC's role as the national training agency and its short-term function of making work or simulated work for the young unemployed, the latter has won the day overwhelmingly—especially in the context of 1987, when there was a clear political imperative to massage the unemployment figures down below three million.

But the MSC's biggest incursion into the education field came on 31 January 1984, when the White Paper *Training for Jobs* proposed that £200m of spending on 'work-related non-advanced further education' should be transferred from the local education authorities through RSG and disbursed through the MSC by bids from the LEAs. The MSC would thus 'purchase' courses as and when it wanted them from colleges. The idea was to make the FE colleges more 'responsive' to market demands as determined by the MSC with its superior market intelligence and links with industry.

The local authorities were even more incensed than they had been in November 1982. This time there was not even the sweetener of new money, the LEAs were losing a large slice—25 per cent—of the total FE budget and being forced to bid for their own money. There were even rumours that Lord Young had originally sought a 60 per cent 'share'.

The original justification for the move was that the colleges were not meeting the demands of industry in new technology and robotics. It was claimed through a planted story by Biddy Passmore in the *Times Educational Supplement* that a forthcoming HMI report would show this. In fact, the HMI report showed nothing of the kind. In a small-scale study of short courses for employers it showed that some 20 per cent of the courses were rated by the employers as not meeting their needs. The two members of HMI—Terry Melia and Ned Norris—were furious that their work had been misinterpreted by the official government information machine and by the Secretary of State Sir Keith Joseph.

The battle with the local authorities was long and bitter. The Conservative controlled ACC finally caved in under pressure from Central Office (the Vice-chairman of the Education Committee actually went off to work there). But the Labour-controlled AMA Education Committee held out and commissioned their own study to disprove, if they could, the assertion that the FE system was unresponsive and inflexible.

A study of more than 100 colleges by a group chaired by Sunderland CEO Jackson Hall looked at three sectors—construction, catering and information technology—as 'tracers across the system'. It found that despite hard times in financial terms an increase of 300 per cent in the five years from 1980-81 to 1985-86 had been achieved in computer studies courses and the penetration of information technology into business studies, design and engineering presented an encouraging record of achievement. There had been a 30 per cent increase in the range of courses in construction and catering—a testimony to the freedom and discretion colleges enjoyed under LEA 'control'.

But at the same time the study found that the MSC had been unable to provide any worthwhile market information to the colleges. 'The need to undertake an enquiry at all is highly significant; the ignorance beyond the level of the LEA about what has been happening is indefensible—a dimension of management has been absent which is patently an essential prerequisite for a healthy future', Jackson Hall wrote.

The study pointed up the problem of the volatility of funding and income over the period and the negligible contribution from industry of about 2 per cent. It showed the wide discrepancies in needs and demand between areas, proving the case for local flexibility and discretion rather than central direction by a musclebound bureaucracy based in Sheffield.

What was missing was an agreed national framework for priorities and resource allocation, flexible enough to meet local need. The DES could long ago have provided this by calling for development plans, but never did so.

In the end a truce was called and the new Chairman of the MSC, Bryan Nicholson, reached agreement with the local authority associations and set up a joint policy group with Sir Roy Harding as its Chairman. But not before two years had been largely wasted.

It is even now recognized that joint control of NAFE is only a temporary solution. Lord Young is known to be poised for a future grab at the FE colleges and is laying plans for a future Department of Enterprise extending from 14 upwards, cutting the secondary school in half and probably involving a lowering of the statutory school leaving age. 'The problem of youth unemployment is not so much the economy', he told the Society of Education Officers, 'as the attitude of mind of youngsters leaving school at 16'. Thinking along those lines has inevitably led Lord Young to demand a larger and larger say over the secondary curriculum. His transfer to the Department of Trade and Industry is not likely to change much, except perhaps to create another MSC-type agency at the DTI education unit.

The MSC is therefore now a familiar succubus on the education system. It is a substitute for strategic planning which should have been done in the DES. It is able to move quickly and deliver programmes direct to certain defined target areas. It is in no sense a democratic body; it does what it is told by the Secretary of State for Employment (as it did in the last resort over the control of non-advanced FE).

But does it know what it is doing? The evidence is growing that, in the words of its own Director of Manpower Planning and Intelligence, it is 'the blind leading the blind'.

References

ADVISORY COUNCIL FOR ADULT AND CONTINUING EDUCATION (1982) *From Policies to Practice*, Leicester, ACACE.

ALEXANDER, Sir W. P. (1975) 'Week by week', *Education* 17 October, p. 405.

ASSOCIATION OF METROPOLITAN AUTHORITIES (1981) *The Youth Opportunities Programme and the LEA*, MSC Special Programmes Division, May.

ASSOCIATION OF METROPOLITAN AUTHORITIES (1986) *Survey of Aspects of Non-advanced FE*, March, (The Jackson Hall report).

BARNES, Sir D. (1975) 'The job creation programme', *Education*, 17 October, p. 403.

BLACKSTONE, T. (1983) Gulland Memorial Lecture, Goldsmiths' College, 22 March.

DEPARTMENT OF EDUCATION AND SCIENCE (1987) *NAFE in Practice: An HMI Survey*, London, HMSO.

GOVERNMENT WHITE PAPER (1981) *A New Training Initiative: A Programme for Action*, Cmnd 8455, December, London, HMSO.

GOVERNMENT WHITE PAPER (1984) *Training for Jobs*, Cmnd 9135, January, London, HMSO.

HOLLAND REPORT (1977) *Young People and Work*, London MSC.

HOLLAND, G. (1983) Nineteenth Tayney Lecture, University of Nottingham Department of Adult Education, Matlock, 21 September.

JOSEPH, Sir K. (1982–85) Speech to CLEA conference, *Education* 23 July 1982; speech to NIAE conference, *Education* 30 April 1982; speech to NIACE conference, *Education* 26 April 1985.

MANPOWER SERVICES COMMISSION (1981) *A New Training Initiative: An Agenda for Action*, MSC, December.

MSC (1982) *Youth Task Group report*, April.

MSC (1982) 'Review of special programmes', *Special Programme News*, October.

MSC (1983) *Towards an Adult Training Strategy*, April.

MSC (1984) *Focus on Adult Training*, 20 November.

MORRIS, R. G. (1982) 'Time for action: A critical look at the Government White Paper', *Guardian* 19 January.

NEWSAM, Sir P. (1987) Speech to the North of England education conference, *Education*, 9 January.

YOUNG, D. (1982) Interview in *Education*, 19 November, pp. 385–6.

Chapter 14: Books and Libraries: The Devaluation of the Printed Word

John Davies

John Davies was born in 1941 and educated at Magdalen College School, Oxford, Christ Church, Oxford and the University of Sheffield. Prior to joining the Publishers Association, he worked for the Bodleian Library and for the Education Committee of Montgomeryshire and as a Librarian and Education Officer in Newcastle-upon-Tyne. He has been Director of the Educational Publishers Council, and University, College and Professional Publishers Council for ten years. He is a councillor of the London Borough of Barnet and has been a Parliamentary candidate.

★   ★   ★

Introduction

In 1973, the public provision of books was still undergoing expansion. People who worked in libraries and education over that period will still remember extra funding for the raising of the school leaving age, and additional resources for local government reorganization. Mrs Margaret Thatcher was Secretary of State for Education and Science and was actively encouraging this development. Mr Anthony Crosland had not yet made the statement, more melancholy and telling than he knew, that 'The party's over now'.

There are three main sources from which books may be obtained for public education: (i) the school; (ii) the public library services; and (iii) the libraries of universities and colleges. The state, under the principles of the 1944 Education Act[1] and the 1944 Public Libraries and Museums Act,[2] provide books at no charge through these outlets for the betterment of learning, information and research and as basic tools for the best education of the people. Funds made available for items such as books were always likely to be vulnerable at times when government expenditure was being restrained as a result of national and international policy dictates, at times when pupil rolls were falling. As there are legal and contractual obligations governing the employment of staff, the maintenance of buildings and the operation of many other services, cutting the book fund was always likely to be the softest option when invidious choices had to be made. Few would have foreseen, however, that this course would have been resorted to with such regularity and to such drastic effect. For books and libraries, these have indeed been 'the locust years'.

School Book Provision

Figure 1 and table 1 show the pattern of expenditure on school text and library books between 1976/77 and 1984/85. The figures have been deflated against the General Retail Price Index rather than the Book Price Index. In the early years of the 1970s, book prices kept below the general increase in prices, but, latterly, declining sales and print runs forced the price above that level. The decline in real expenditure related here, therefore conceals a worse drop in terms of actual book provision. In 1984/85, expenditure fell in cash per pupil at both primary and secondary level.

The only countervailing movement against this sad pattern of decline occurs, oddly enough, in the period leading up to the two General Elections. This suggests that the condition of books, a very visible indicator of the

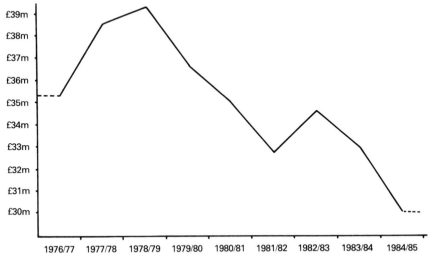

Source: ROI Forms/CIPFA
Deflater: RPI

Figure 1 *Real Expenditure on School Text and Library Books 1976/77–1984/85 (Primary and Secondary)*

Table 1: Expenditure on School Text and Library Books 1976/77−1984/85 (Primary and Secondary)

	Current	Constant	
1976/77	35,363,595	35,363,595	
1977/78	43,681,930	38,647,086	(+9.3%)
1978/79	48,080,437	39,366,600	(+11.3%)
1979/80	52,574,431	36,671,606	(+3.7%)
1980/81	58,064,134	35,122,340	(−0.7%)
1981/82	60,765,343	32,827,937	(−7.2%)
1982/83	68,299,862	34,725,903	(−1.8%)
1983/84	68,263,682	33,103,593	(−6.4%)
1984/85	66,248,880	30,613,334	(−13.4%)

standard of provision being made for pupils, does impinge upon the consciousness of central and local government authorities at such a time. Recent surveys of costs in independent schools[3] show that, in the private sector, two or three times as much is spent on school books and equipment as is the case in the public sector. The Educational Publishers Council has produced, since 1980, a series of detailed pamphlets[4] on the regions of the United Kingdom. These catalogue a sharp overall decline, compounded by the fact that local authorities have been stretching capitation allowances, out of which books are bought, to cover an increasing range of items which are not of direct use in a child's immediate education.

Central government has made repeated statements, through successive Secretaries of State, that book expenditure should not be cut, and blames local authorities for not heeding that advice. Local authorities complain that the actions of the central government leave them no other option. An office desk on which the buck stops has yet to be found.

In many areas, parental funding has provided some measure of salvation. Parallel surveys by the Educational Publishers Council and the National Confederation of Parent Teachers Associations[5] suggested that over £20m might be being supplied from this source to cover shortfalls in school books. There is heavy debate as to whether such a method of raising funds is equitable, and there are also growing signs of irritation from parents who do not believe that it is their duty to sponsor the provision of the basic essentials of education, like books, and consider that this should be met from the budget collected from their rates, rents and taxes.

Examples of the results of book shortages in schools abounded throughout the period. Books were tatty and out-of-date. Books were shared. There were no books to take from school for homework. A survey of books in West Midlands schools in 1979 found children still using books about Africa published in 1946, so-called modern chemistry courses published in the early 1960s, books about money which preceded decimalization.

The depression of the school book market stymied the progress of publishing. Imprints gradually disappeared. Print runs decreased. Prices began to rise above inflation. The combination of a shrinking home market and a volatile export market hampered innovation. Progressive educational publishing was a particular casualty. The Educational Publishers Council, in cooperation with the Equal Opportunities Commission (EOC) and the Commission for Racial Equality (CRE) produced advisory documents on sex stereotyping[6] and multicultural education,[9] but, because funding was not available to purchase new products, books with old, less enlightened messages remained on school shelves.

The malaise spread to school book supply. Local authorities, desperate to obtain as many books as possible, pressed for higher and higher discounts on the supply of non-net text books. Selling books to schools became less profitable and several notable school book suppliers either pulled out of the market or disappeared. These included E J Arnold, for long the country's leading school book supplier. Direct purchasing organizations, run by local authorities, increased their influence from one-tenth to one-fifth of the total trade. This competition further depressed school bookselling. A joint committee of local authorities, publishers, booksellers, librarians and teachers, chaired by Baroness David, warned at length in 1981[8] of the dangers of placing financial considerations above levels of service, but its advice went largely unheeded. The difficulties remain, as of this date, unresolved.

Plans to introduce new technology were similarly still-born. Educational publishers responded vigorously to calls to produce software for microcomputers. The Department of Trade and Industry tried to motivate this development with special allocations of fundings. However, sales of software stubbornly stagnated at £1.5m, a tiny fragment of the total market.

These dismal realities flew in the face of all that was said by informed opinion. The seminal Bullock Report[9] on language teaching was published in 1975. This strongly criticized current levels of book provision in schools, and urged the formation of a working party to consider standards of book provision. Such a working party was formed by the National Book League and reported in 1979.[10] It recommended that expenditure on books should be at approximately twice the then average level. Repeated reports from Her Majesty's Inspectorate drew attention to a significant percentage of primary and secondary schools being under-provided with books. In 1986, the Select Committee of the House of Commons[11] put forward the proposal that there be a minimum requirement for provision of books and equipment in primary schools. Two comprehensive surveys by HMI on primary education[12] and aspects of secondary education[13] found disparities in the availability of textbooks in schools.

Other impeccable educational sources can be quoted in defence of the book. Two important Schools Council projects, on *Extending Beginning Reading* by Southgate, Arnold and Johnson[14] and on *The Effective Use of Reading* by Lunzer and Gardner[15] both emphasized at primary and secondary level the importance of a wide range of quality books. The same necessity underpinned the report in Schools Council Working Paper 52 by Whitehead, Capey and Maddren on *Children's Reading Interests*.[16]

In 1986, the Educational Publishers Council sponsored the publication of a massive, independent research study on *Books and the School Curriculum*.[17] In over 400 pages, almost every educational opinion of the past fifteen years on the value, role and use of books in school was included. The hefty conclusion of the research was inescapable. Books are of paramount importance. Books are the prime teaching aids for teachers in schools. Alongside this, a survey[18] of teachers' actual use of books in the classroom throughout the school day was conducted in five distinct local authorities. Books were in constant use for almost the entire school time.

It is surprising, not to say amazing, that in the period from Mr Callaghan's Ruskin speech to Mr Baker's pronouncements on the curriculum, when so much introspection has been turned upon the education system and its output, that so little high political attention has been given to the correlation between the achievement of literacy and the presence of books. Evidence can be produced ad nauseum to confirm one simple fact: children cannot be expected to become literate if there is nothing for them to read.

In the wider context of literacy, the effect of the shortages on library provision, the base for children's voluntary reading, is even more worrying. The stark statistics show that, when money is short, text books are bought, library books are not. Library books have fallen from one-third to one-fifth of all purchases. The levels of school library provision envisaged in the Library Association's guidelines of 1977[19] are now in the realms of fantasy.

The overall situation has not been helped by the manner in which the content of books has been dragged into the political arena and the unbending attitudes of protagonists of the right and left attempting to force moral content in sex education or social change in the community through the selection of books. Such activities verge dangerously on a return to censorship, whereas true education depends on a diversity of books.

This treatment of school book provision may read very much like a catalogue of gloom, and, in many ways, that would not be an unfair description. Book provision in British schools has suffered catastrophically over the past thirteen years, and there will be few able to rebut that statement. It must be said, however, that, as of the present moment, the omens for the future are brighter than they have been for some time. Primary school rolls are at last beginning to rise and that development should lead to increased provision in that sector. The Secretary of State has been persuaded to release some £40m for additional books and equipment to support the introduction of the GCSE examinations. This will go some way both towards meeting the demands of the new examination and towards bolstering total secondary book expenditure which might otherwise have been expected to plunge. The long night is not yet over. The damage which has been inflicted will take time and commitment to remedy, but there are some rays of sunshine.

Book Provision in Universities, Polytechnics and Colleges

School book publishing basically depends on state provision. If adequate funding has not been provided, as has been the case for the last thirteen years, both children's education and the publishing industry suffer. Academic and scholarly publishing, in contrast, sells its product more widely and through a larger variety of outlets. If students cannot afford to buy books and academic libraries also cannot afford to purchase them, there is likely to be a severe effect on higher education and research. The extent to which students will buy books is, however, a less predictable equation than that which may be calculated from a set amount of capitation allowance given to a school or teacher. In addition to this, the fruits of academic and scholarly research are not confined to educational digestion as are the produce of education projects.

There is a considerable sale for scholarly publications to individuals whose professions or interest converge upon the subject at this level. Industry and academe are closely interrelated in their information needs. A survey conducted by the University, College and Professional Publishers Council[20] indicated that purchase of books and journals by the libraries and information services of commercial and industrial companies indicated that the total expenditure there might exceed £90m per year. This type of spending is not affected by government policy on restraint of education finance. It is more closely, very closely, affected by the performance of the economy as a whole. If the economy is prospering, companies will be able to expand on information services. If the economy is languishing, information provision will be one of the first areas of activity to be cut. It is therefore possible for academic publishers, on certain occasions, to compensate on the roundabouts of industry for what they lose on the swings of higher education. A heavy export market for British publications of a scholarly nature is the other significant segment of the total market.

Concentrating solely on the educational aspect of book provision, the story is not a happy one. Figure 2 and table 2 show the pattern of university library book expenditure since 1978/79. Ceaseless pressure has brought about an improvement of late, but expenditure in 1984/85 is still, in terms of the general Retail Price Index, well below the level of 1978/79. The point of departure in itself represents a decline on previous levels of spending in the 1970s. Research by the National Book League[20] published in 1979 indicated that expenditure on books and periodicals per university student had already fallen by over 12 per cent since 1973/74. Our base year for study was, apparently, the high water mark of university book provision.

The use of the general Retail Price Index conceals a very much heavier decline in library stocks, which have dwindled by over one third since 1978/79. The bulk of university library purchases are of monographs and journals, themselves high cost, short-run productions. An exceptionally vicious circle of price rise and intellectual deprivation commences when funds are cut off at the central, if not sole, point of purchase.

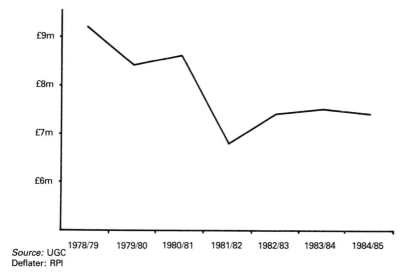

Source: UGC
Deflater: RPI

Figure 2   Real Expenditure on Books in University Libraries 1978/79—1984/85

Table 2: Expenditure on Books in University Libraries 1978/79—1984/85

	Current £m	Constant £m	
1978/79	9.2	9.2	
1979/80	9.6	8.4	(−8.7%)
1980/81	11.5	8.6	(−6.5%)
1981/82	10.1	6.8	(−26.1%)
1982/83	11.7	7.4	(−19.6%)
1983/84	12.5	7.5	(−18.5%)
1984/85	13.0	7.4	(−19.6%)

Book expenditure in university libraries has suffered inordinately over the period in question. The National Book League's latest analysis of university library book and periodical spending[22] shows a huge drop in the provision of books as opposed to periodicals. When the invidious decision has to be made as to whether to buy fewer books or cease a run of periodicals, the periodicals have, in many cases, been retained. But the cancellation of periodicals is now also a common feature of university library life. According to a survey by the Association of University Teachers, sixty-one universities have lost 6600 periodical titles and 165,000 books since 1980/81.

The University Grants Committee (UGC) has made repeated represent-ation against the decline in library spending. The Standing Conference of National and University Libraries has pointed out in a statement[23] that 'Cuts in funding in real terms cannot but harm the development of a library service and reduce the support given to teaching and research'. The European Working Party of Publishers and Librarians has approached the Commission of the European Communities in similar vein. There is little indication that these warnings have been treated with much seriousness.

The emphasis of recent government policy has been on training specialists in science and technology and on vocational education. Figure 3 and table 3 illustrate the pattern of expenditure on books in polytechnics and colleges of further education since 1978/79. A small recovery since 1981/82 has been dashed. Book spending is back to its lowest level. As far as specific expenditure on books and periodicals in polytechnic libraries is concerned, figures produced by the Council of Polytechnic Librarians indicate a real decline of over 33 per cent in book purchases and an overall decline of nearly 20 per cent in book and periodical acquisitions in one year between 1982/83 and 1983/84. Some polytechnic libraries spend as little as £2.66 per student on books. The situation in colleges of further education is even worse, where expenditure per student per year can sink as low as 43p. Overall, in colleges of further education, there is a shortfall of 50 per cent between the allocations reported by the Group of Libraries in Colleges of Further and Higher Education and the guidelines laid down by the Library Association and the National Association of Teachers in Further and Higher Education (NATFHE).

The dwindling book provision in academic and college libraries might be excused were there any signs that students were themselves able to spend more on books. The recent report from the Education, Science and Arts Committee of the House of Commons on Student Awards[24] has these comments to make: 'Book prices have also risen more steeply than prices generally, and this, together with the demands of other expenditure, has

Deflater: RPI

Figure 3 *Real Expenditure on Books in Polytechnics and Further Education 1978/79 – 1984/85*

Table 3: Expenditure on Books in Polytechnics and Further Education 1978/79–1984/85

	Current £m	Constant £m	
1978/79	15.2	15.2	
1979/80	16.0	14.0	(–7.9%)
1980/81	16.5	12.4	(–18.4%)
1981/82	18.3	12.4	(–18.4%)
1982/83	21.6	13.6	(–10.5%)
1983/84	22.0	13.2	(–13.2%)
1984/85	21.4	12.2	(–19.7%)

meant that students now tend to buy fewer books'. A survey published in 1983 indicated that students were spending on books 'less than one-third of the notional sum provided in the grant for book purchase'. The survey in question,[25] from the University, College and Professional Publishers Council, in fact showed an expenditure per student on books of just over £50 per year against a notional allocation from grant of over £180. Later research by the National Union of Students (NUS) presented very similar results.

Lecturers' opinions have also been canvassed by the University, College and Professional Publishers Council in two surveys[26] about attitudes to the use of books. Lecturers in colleges of further education, universities and polytechnics were asked across a range of disciplines in humanities, social sciences and sciences to identify the elements which they considered most important in teaching, education and study. The provision of books easily topped the table of importance, being mentioned by between 92 and 96 per cent of lecturers. In contrast, direct teaching was only rated important by just over 60 per cent of respondents. It is interesting to set this research alongside the findings of the World Bank overseas that 'the provision of textbooks is the most solid determinant of academic achievement' and its consequent switching of funding to textbook provision.

The conclusion is a straightforward one and the argument unacademic. The direct availability of books to students and their access to them through libraries have been severely curtailed in recent years. In that sense, there has been a wastage of potential both in courses and research because of insufficient support materials.

Public Library Book Provision

The public library service stands outside the formal education system, but is very much its partner and supporter. In essence, its objectives are generally educative. Figure 4 and table 4 record the level of public library book funding since 1978/79. A brief respite to the general pattern of decline occurs again in the period around the 1983 General Election, but thereafter provision drops once more. The overall fall in the spending of public libraries on books has had serious implications for print runs and prices in those areas of publishing

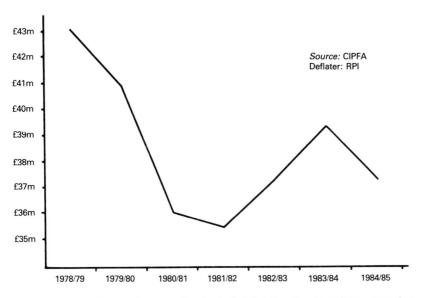

Figure 4 *Real Expenditure on Books in Public Libraries 1978/79—1984/85*

which are heavily dependent on sales to public libraries, most notably hardback fiction. The decline in terms of books actually bought across the nation as a whole is consequently over 33 per cent. Faced with this situation, public libraries have moved increasingly towards the acquisition of paperback to the detriment of the publication prospects of first novels, so essential to the continuing life of literature.

The role that public libraries play in the popular dissemination of important and worthwhile literature is often overlooked. They provide its first platform and market place. They bring it immediately to the attention of a huge public audience. Although events like the Booker Prize promote literature through the press and the media, it is the public library service which actually places it in the hands of the people. These statistics show a great social and cultural function in diminution.

A report by Christine Lambert of the School of Advanced Urban Studies for the Library Campaign[27] provides the story behind the statistics, with detailed studies of the situation in nine local authorities: three county councils, three London boroughs, two Metropolitan districts, one Scottish district. It is clear from these that the decline began before 1978/79. In Somerset and Northumberland, the first year of difficulty is specified as 1976/77. In such times of constraint, the book fund is described as an 'easy target' and a 'vulnerable item'. Somerset cut its book fund in 1979. In 1981/82, 23,000 fewer books were bought than in the previous year. In 1985/86 there was a suggestion that no new adult fiction could be purchased. Surrey reports a 45 per cent reduction in its book fund since 1978/79 and the sad abandonment of all direct work with schools. Tower Hamlets made a massive reduction in the

Table 4: Expenditure on Books in Public Libraries 1978/79—1984/85

	Current £m	Constant £m	
1978/79	43.1	43.1	
1979/80	46.9	40.9	(−5.1%)
1980/81	48.1	36.1	(−16.2%)
1981/82	52.6	35.5	(−17.6%)
1982/83	59.3	37.3	(−13.5%)
1983/84	65.6	39.4	(−8.6%)
1984/85	65.3	37.3	(−13.5%)

book fund in 1981, from £248,000 to £58,000, and never recovered. Despite a devastating fire at the Central Library in 1982, Waltham Forest still found itself short of £72,000 for its book fund in 1983/84. Manchester added 37 per cent fewer books to stock in 1984/85 as against 1979/80. In Wigan, the purchase of new books fell by 50 per cent through the 1970s. Edinburgh experienced similar problems over this period. The results of these setbacks are reflected in much the same language from varied sources: 'more selective acquisitions' in Northumberland, the loss of reference books in Wigan, book issues affected in Edinburgh, a 'dramatic impact on issues' in Tower Hamlets.

Much the same sorry tale is related in a survey by the Association of Metropolitan Authorities (AMA):[28] the number of volumes purchased sinking from 91,000 to 27,000, books remaining on shelves for ten years, books being selected solely on the basis of price, whole subject areas being abandoned, 50 per cent failure rates in searching for books, one title purchased where four are needed. A pamphlet from the National Book Committee[29] lists twenty-four local authorities where the book fund has effectively been halved since 1978/79.

The implications of these developments for education must be heavily underlined. Public libraries have a vital support function for both formal and informal education. At present, there is high unemployment in this country and a continually restated need for retraining. There is a steady increase in the number of retired people. More children are coming into primary schools. Secondary schools need extra support material for new examinations. All these groups should see the public library as a centre which will cater for their aspirations. Statistics reveal that it is not doing so. While visits to libraries have increased, issues, according to an analysis from the Public Lending Right Office,[30] have heavily declined. The books just are not there. The Minister of Arts and Libraries is correct to ask himself the question 'Should we give more priority to books?' but a satisfactory answer has yet to be found.

Copyright

The mention of Public Lending Right prompts further discussion on the remuneration of those who produce books for education and libraries. In the

United Kingdom, 50 per cent of books are borrowed rather than bought. The matter as to whether this situation was just to authors received long consideration and debate in the 1970s and was resolved on the side of the authors. There are, however, other ways in which intellectual work and property can be misused.

The preceding sections of this chapter have restated at length evidence that public book provision has been seriously eroded over the past thirteen years. This contention has been put forward on many occasions and now receives only the most half-hearted rebuttal, since instances of this are continually before people's eyes. The absence of the books which would formerly have been the stock in trade of teachers and librarians does, however, present them with a less obvious problem and difficulty, which is how to provide materials for pupils, students and readers when money is not available for books. The most immediate and tempting solution is recourse to the photocopying machine.

Copyright law is a cornerstone of authorship and publishing in this country, and the right of authors and publishers to exploit their work has been defended by statute since the reign of Queen Anne. Without it, the whole edifice of the dissemination of learning and knowledge would crumble. Piracy of whole works overseas is a major threat to British publishing, involving the purloining of entire texts and selling them at prices which undercut those of the original creations. Larceny of this dimension does not occur in the more orderly atmosphere of the British educational and literary world, but there is widespread use of photocopies as a means of replacing works or parts of works which cannot be bought.

Teachers copy classroom sets of materials for pupils. Study packs are made up and sold to students. Duplicate copies of works appear on library shelves. Research articles are circulated by industrial companies. The British Library, itself increasingly short of funds for acquisitions, operates, by photocopying, a national document delivery service. It has always been recognized that a certain amount of legitimate 'fair dealing' to enable notes to be retained should be allowed to a student or researcher strictly for her or his own private study, but this exception was never meant to replace the purchase of instructional texts or direct payment by a community of people for those works which they, in common, wish to use and exploit. The distinction between these two types of use has long been apparent in sections 6, 7 and 41 of the Copyright Act.[31]

A government-initiated committee under the chairmanship of Mr Justice Whitford[32] reported on this problem in 1977. It urged copyright owners to prepare a solution to the problem by setting up licensing schemes through which individuals in the various organizations would be allowed to undertake such copying but through which they would also be required to make a reasonable payment to the originators of the work and publication, the authors and publishers. The Whitford Report also recommended the removal of 'fair dealing' exceptions.

A committee of authors and publishers, chaired by Lord Wolfenden, was formed to pursue these objectives. Long negotiations ensued, extended to a certain extent by periodic waiting for Government pronouncements on the subject, a *Green Paper*,[33] a *White Paper*,[34] and the Copyright Bill about to be published.[35] The statements which slowly arrived from the government varied, but did not drastically change, the copyright situation. Cases of serious infringement continued to come to notice and culminated in the Manchester Local Education Authority being taken to court, yielding up around half a million illegal photocopies and paying substantial damages.

A solution clearly had to be found. The local authority associations cooperated in commonsense and goodwill with the authors' and publishers' organization, now called the Copyright Licensing Agency. An experimental 'pilot' scheme led to a three-year agreement. Schools received licence and sanction to copy. In return, a number of them kept full records and a small sum was paid by each authority per copy towards their share of the gross total. This scheme will remain in operation until 1989 and will probably continue beyond that date, after review.

Progress was slower in higher education owing to the very much higher incidence of single copying by individuals and its close relationship to the discussions with the government prior to the introduction of the Copyright Bill. With the arrival of the Copyright-Bill at the end of 1987, agreement was reached on an experimental scheme to cover systematic and multiple copying in universities.

The impact of the new technology impinged upon these considerations, posing a new range of copyright questions. An elementary Computer Software Amendment Act was passed in 1985. The publishing and library world searched assiduously for a mechanism through which copyright could be protected and the benefits of electronic publishing, information databases and document delivery services could be developed, and a joint project has been set in motion with the Department of Trade and Industry towards the establishment of an electronic Knowledge Warehouse and Archive Trust.

Conclusion

A contrast may be drawn between the section of this essay which concerns copyright and the preceding sections which are concerned with public expenditure on books. On copyright, there has been cooperation and progress over what seems, at first sight, a very difficult, if not intractable, problem. On public expenditure on books, where the argument for proper provision is so self-evident that it barely appears to require advocacy, there has been vacillation, evasion of the issue, regression. Time has been well-spent on the resolution of copyright problems and opportunities have been seized. On public book expenditure time has been wasted, book stocks have deteriorated, opportunities to redress the situation have been ignored. On this latter matter, in a very real sense, the years since 1973 have been 'wasted years' and years of waste.

In the study by the Schools Council of children's reading habits, to which reference was made earlier and which was published in 1975, there was talk of the 'devaluation of the printed word'. The authors were then thinking of the influence of television and other media upon the reading of books, but their phrase can be used in a very changed context today. Infringement of copyright devalued the printed word, by devaluing its creators, by ignoring their right to remuneration. This devaluation was accepted as being inequitable and harmful and solutions were found. Equally serious, however, was the devaluation of the printed word through its complete relegation within the priorities of public educational and library provision. This devaluation has been very harmful and unjust to the educationalists, teachers, librarians, students and pupils who wish to use the books that they see everywhere upon exhibition. Britain's reputation as a nation that cares for literature, education and libraries has been sullied by this dismal attitude to a great potential national resource over the past thirteen years.

Notes

1 *Education Act 1944*, section 8, London, HMSO.
2 *Public Libraries and Museums Act 1964*, section 7, London, HMSO.
3 *Independent Schools Costs Survey 1986*, London, Institute of Chartered Accountants.
4 *School Book Spending Series 1 and 2*, London, Educational Publishers Council, 1976-1985
5 NATIONAL CONFEDERATION OF PARENT TEACHERS ASSOCIATION (1985) *The State of Schools in England and Wales*, London, NCPTA.
6 EDUCATIONAL PUBLISHERS COUNCIL (1981) *Sex-Stereotyping in School and Children's Books*, London, Educational Publishers Council.
7 EDUCATIONAL PUBLISHERS COUNCIL (1983) *Publishing for a Multicultural Society*, London, Educational Publishers Council.
8 *Supply of Books to Schools and Colleges* (Lady David Report) 1981.
9 DEPARTMENT OF EDUCATION AND SCIENCE (1985) *A Language for Life.* (The Bullock Report), London, HMSO.
10 NATIONAL BOOK LEAGUE (1979) *Books for Schools*, report of a working party, London, National Book League.
11 SELECT COMMITTEE OF HOUSE OF COMMONS (1986) *Achievement in Primary Schools*, London, HMSO.
12 DEPARTMENT OF EDUCATION AND SCIENCE (1975a) *Primary Education in England: A Survey by HM Inspectors of Schools*, London, HMSO.
13 DEPARTMENT OF EDUCATION AND SCIENCE (1975b) *Aspects of Secondary Education in England. A Survey by HM Inspectors of Schools*, London, HMSO.
14 SOUTHGATE, V., ARNOLD, H. and JOHNSON, S. (1981) *Extending Beginning Reading*. London, Heinemann Educational Books for the Schools Council.

15 LUNZER, E. and GARDNER, K. (1979) *The Effective Use of Reading*, London, Heinemann Educational Books for the Schools Council.
16 WHITEHEAD, F., CAPEY, A. and MADDREN, W. (1975) *Children's Reading Interests*, London, Evans' Methuen Educational for the Schools Council.
17 DAVIES, F. (1986) *Books in the School Curriculum*, Report for the National Book League, London, Educational Publishers Council.
18 INGHAM, J. with BROWN, V. (1986) *The State of Reading*, Report for the National Book League, London, Educational Publishers Council.
19 LIBRARY ASSOCIATION (1977) *Library Resource Provision in Schools: Guidelines and Recommendations*, London, Library Association.
20 UNIVERSITY COLLEGE AND PROFESSIONAL COUNCIL (1985) *Book Buying by Commercial and Industrial Libraries*, Postal Survey.
21 NATIONAL BOOK LEAGUE (1979) *University Library Expenditure 1971-1977: Six-year Survey*, London, National Book League.
22 NATIONAL BOOK LEAGUE (1986) *Library Book and Periodical Spending in Universities, Polytechnics and Colleges 1981-1984*, London, National Book League.
23 STANDING CONFERENCE OF NATIONAL AND UNIVERSITY LIBRARIES (1985) *University Library Expenditure Statistics 1984-85*, London, SCNUL.
24 EDUCATION, SCIENCE AND ARTS COMMITTEE, HOUSE OF COMMONS (1986) *Student Awards*, London, HMSO.
25 UNIVERSITY COLLEGE AND PROFESSIONAL PUBLISHERS COUNCIL (1983) *Student Book Buying*, London, UCPPC.
26 UNIVERSITY COLLEGE AND PROFESSIONAL PUBLISHERS COUNCIL (1982) *Use of Books by University and College Lecturers: Two Postal Surveys, February 1981 and June 1982*, London, UCPPC.
27 LAMBERT, C. (1985) *Expenditure Cuts in Public Libraries and their Effects on Services*, London, Library Campaign.
28 ASSOCIATION OF METROPOLITAN AUTHORITIES (1986) *Library Survey*, Bradford, AMA.
29 NATIONAL BOOK COMMITTEE (1986) *Public Library Spending in the United Kingdom*, London, Book Trust.
30 PUBLIC LENDING RIGHT OFFICE (1987) *Annual Report*, London, PLRO.
31 *Copyright Act 1956*, London, HMSO.
32 DEPARTMENT OF TRADE (1977) *Copyright and Designs Law* (The Whitford Report), London, HMSO.
33 DEPARTMENT OF TRADE (1981) *Reform of the Law relating to Copyright, Designs and Performers' Protection: A Consultative Document*, London, HMSO.
34 DEPARTMENT OF TRADE AND INDUSTRY (1986) *Intellectual Property and Innovation*, London, HMSO.
35 COPYRIGHT BILL 1987, London, HMSO.

Appendix

Year	Prime Minister	Secretary of State For Education and Science	Major Reports, Papers, Acts of Parliament Concerning Education*
1970	Edward Heath	Margaret Thatcher (20 June 1970— 4 March 1974)	*Report of a Committee of Enquiry into Teacher Education and Training* (The James Report) (1972) White Paper: *A Framework for Expansion* (1972) Report of a Committee of Enquiry entitled *Adult Education: A Plan for Development* (The Russell Report) (1973) Industrial Training Act 1973
1974	Harold Wilson	Reginald Prentice (5 March 1974— 10 June 1975)	Houghton Committee on Teachers' Salaries (1974)
1976	James Callaghan	Fred Mulley (11 June 1975— 10 September 1976)	*Education Act* (1976)
		Shirley Williams (11 September 1976— 3 May 1979)	Report of a Committee of Enquiry entitled *A New Partnership for Our Schools* (The Taylor Report) (1977) Green Paper *Education in Schools: A Consultative Document* (1977) *Report of the Committee of Enquiry into the Education of Handicapped Children and Young People* (The Warnock Report 1978)
1979	Margaret Thatcher (1979-83)	Mark Carlisle (5 May 1979— 14 September 1981)	Education Act (1980) *School Government and APS* Education Act (1981) *Children with Special Educational Needs* White Paper on *New Training Initiative* (1981)

244

Year	Prime Minister	Secretary of State For Education and Science	Major Reports, Papers, Acts of Parliament Concerning Education[*]
		Sir Keith Joseph (14 September 1981— 21 May 1986)	Report of the Review Group on the Youth Service in England and entitled *Experience and Participation* (The Thompson Report) (1982) White Paper: *Teaching Quality* (1983) White Paper: *Training for Jobs* (1984) *Better Schools* (1985)
1983	Margaret Thatcher (1983–87)	Kenneth Baker (22 May 1986-)	Education Act (1986) *Governing Bodies, etc.* Education Act (1987) *Teachers' Pay and Conditions*

[*] Extracts from many of these documents are to be found in MACLURE, J. S. (1986) *Educational Documents England and Wales 1816 to the Present Day*, London, Methuen.

Name Index